KT-178-646

GREENWICH LIBRARIES

3 8028 01962903 6

FORGOTTEN VOICES

Also available in the Forgotten Voices series:

Forgotten Voices of the Great War
Forgotten Voices of the Great War (illustrated)
Forgotten Voices of the Somme

Lest We Forget: Forgotten Voices from 1914–1945

Forgotten Voices of the Second World War
Forgotten Voices of the Second World War (illustrated)
Forgotten Voices of the Blitz and the Battle for Britain
Forgotten Voices of the Holocaust
Forgotten Voices of the Secret War
Forgotten Voices of D-Day
Forgotten Voices of Burma
Forgotten Voices of Dunkirk

Forgotten Voices of the Falklands

FORGOTTEN VOICES
OF THE
VICTORIA CROSS

IN ASSOCIATION WITH THE
IMPERIAL WAR MUSEUM

RODERICK BAILEY

EBURY
PRESS

1 3 5 7 9 10 8 6 4 2

First published in 2010 by Ebury Press, an imprint of Ebury Publishing
A Random House Group company

Introduction © General Sir Richard Dannatt 2010
Text © Roderick Bailey and Imperial War Museum 2010

Photographs © Imperial War Museum 2010

Roderick Bailey has asserted his right to be identified as the author of this
work in accordance with the Copyright, Designs and Patents Act 1988

All rights reserved. No part of this book may be reproduced, stored in a retrieval
system, or transmitted in any form or by any means, electronic, mechanical, photocopying,
recording or otherwise, without the prior permission of the copyright owner

The Random House Group Limited Reg. No. 954009

Addresses for companies within the Random House Group can be found at
www.randomhouse.co.uk

GREENWICH LIBRARIES		
3802 801962903		
Askews		12-Jan-2011
355.1342		£16.99
3054065		Wo BL BE

A CIP catalogue record for this book is available from the British Library

The Random House Group Limited supports The Forest Stewardship Council (FSC),
the leading international forest certification organisation. All our titles that are
printed on Greenpeace approved FSC certified paper carry the FSC logo.
Our paper procurement policy can be found at www.rbooks.co.uk/environment

Mixed Sources
Product group from well-managed
forests and other controlled sources
www.fsc.org Cert no. TT-COC-2139
© 1996 Forest Stewardship Council
FSC

Printed and bound in Great Britain by Clays Ltd, St Ives PLC

ISBN 9780091938161

To buy books by your favourite authors and register for offers visit www.rbooks.co.uk

Contents

Author's Preface

For almost four decades, the Sound Archive of the Imperial War Museum has been recording and preserving the recollections of men and women with experience of recent war and conflict. It is a vast resource, running to almost 60,000 hours of eyewitness testimonies. This book is a collection of unique personal accounts, transcribed from recordings held in the archive, shedding light on the character and exploits of a selection of men who, during the last century, were awarded the Victoria Cross.

Introduced by Royal Warrant in 1856, the Victoria Cross was created as the highest award in the British armed forces for gallantry in the face of the enemy. It is a simple bronze medal of a basic design: a cross pattée, bearing a crown, a lion, a scroll and the inscription 'For Valour', beneath a bar decorated with laurel leaves and a crimson ribbon.* It takes precedence over all other orders and medals and, at the time of writing, has been awarded only 1,358 times.

The first VC was earned in 1854 by a Royal Navy midshipman, Charles Lucas, for picking up and hurling overboard a live enemy shell, its fuse still burning, that had landed on the deck of his ship during an action in the Baltic against Russian shore positions. More than one hundred VCs were awarded for the Crimean War of 1854–56, nearly two

---

* When the ribbon alone is worn, it bears in its centre a small bronze representation of the cross. Until 1918, naval recipients of the VC were awarded a medal with a blue ribbon.

hundred for the Indian Mutiny of 1857–58 and eighty-one for the Anglo–Boer War of 1899–1902. Further VCs were earned in smaller colonial wars and campaigns, including eleven, the most for a single action, for the famous defence of Rorke's Drift during the Anglo–Zulu War of 1879.

The First World War saw more than six hundred awards, almost half the total ever made: a stark illustration of that struggle's vast and terrible scale. In the Second World War, 182 VCs were won. Ten men received the medal in the period between those two great conflicts. To date, fifteen have been earned since: four in Korea; one in Borneo; four by Australians in Vietnam; two in the Falklands; one in Iraq; and three, including one award each of the new Victoria Cross of New Zealand and the Victoria Cross of Australia, in Afghanistan. Since the end of the nineteenth century, when eligibility was extended – informally, at first – to men who had died as a result of their actions, 299 awards have been posthumous. Although women are eligible, none have yet received a VC.

The accounts that follow range from the testimonies of soldiers, sailors and airmen who have themselves been given the medal to the recollections of civilians and other servicemen, including close comrades and friends, who saw VCs being won. Many add graphic detail, much of it unpublished until now, to the official citations issued with the announcement of each award and convey a sense of emotion and wonder that the citations, which tend to be formal in tone and guarded in detail, often lack. 'I was lying about ten yards behind Wakenshaw at the time,' remembers one soldier who watched this anti-tank gunner earn a VC in the Second World War. 'He had the top of his head off, his arm was away and he was blind and that, and his two mates was dead, and he was just shouting, "Left a bit! Right a bit! Up a bit!" and he was firing…'

Most accounts here relate to VCs won in the Second World War. Since embarking upon its task of collection and conservation, the Sound Archive has inevitably found veterans of that conflict more numerous than those of others. Nevertheless, several rare interviews exist that describe or touch upon VCs awarded on the Western Front and in the air in the First World War, including the memories of a regular soldier, a scarce survivor of the British Army of 1914, about the earliest VC action of the war. Here also is the first-hand account of a Royal Navy officer who received his Victoria Cross for his exploits in 1919 during Britain's little-known intervention in the Russian civil war.

Many of these stories serve as subtle reminders of the fact, sometimes obscured by the awe with which VC-recipients are rightly viewed, that those who are awarded the medal are ordinary men, albeit capable of the most extraordinary feats. 'I said, "Cheer up, old boy. What's wrong?" remembers a Royal Flying Corps engineer of his final words with Albert Ball, moments before the famous First World War fighter ace, who would be awarded a posthumous VC, took off on his final flight and was killed.

He said, 'Oh, I've got a hunch I don't think I am going to last very long.'
I said, 'That's absurd, that's absurd, you'll be here for a long time yet. Don't you worry.'
He said, 'I don't think so, I don't think so.'
Well, we got his machine repaired and he got into it and that was the last that was seen of him.

Especially poignant are memories like those of a First World War stretcher-bearer who spotted a VC ribbon on the tunic of a soldier lying dead in a field ambulance post, as are the testimonies recorded for broadcast by Bomber Command aircrew who were subsequently killed in action.

Also striking is the modesty, understatement and self-deprecation that runs through the accounts of those awarded the Victoria Cross. The words of Patrick Porteous, for example, a commando officer who earned the medal in the 1942 raid on the French port of Dieppe, are made no less revealing by the fact that it is left to other soldiers to draw attention to his courage. Indeed, appreciating men like Ball and Porteous as distinct individuals with personalities, hopes and fears can show their actions to be still more impressive and, perhaps, go some way to understanding what it takes to earn a VC.

While personal recollections can add significantly to our understanding of the past, oral history has its limits. The scope and structure of this book is defined by the interviews in the Sound Archive, which, of course, are themselves dependent on the willingness and ability of veterans to share their stories and the museum's capacity to record and preserve them. Moreover, since memories can be distorted by time, hindsight and a host of other factors, care has been taken to select accounts whose likely accuracy is borne out by other sources.

Yet care has also been taken not to defer blindly to written records. The eyewitness accounts required to support recommendations for a VC are themselves subjective and can be coloured or clouded by the confusion of battle. One remarkable testimony printed here is that of Edward Chapman, an infantryman who received the Victoria Cross in 1945 and whose careful dissection of his VC citation is a lesson in why even official documents may not always be infallible sources of fact.

Chapman's account is especially detailed. Others in this book are simple and short. Yet sometimes a few words are enough to throw light on the character of a man who has received a Victoria Cross. 'From time to time we'd say to him, "So how did you get your VC?"' recalls the daughter of Gabriel Coury who was awarded the medal for his actions as a twenty-year-old second lieutenant on the Somme in 1916. 'He just said, "For being a bloody fool". It was never made much of. He never mentioned the war.'

Roderick Bailey, June 2010

Acknowledgements

My first acknowledgement is to the men and women who have shared their stories with the Imperial War Museum's Sound Archive and to those others whose testimonies, recorded in different places and at different times, have also come to be preserved there.

For their assistance and advice, I am grateful to Margaret Brooks, Richard McDonough, Richard Hughes, James Atkinson and Peter Hart of the museum's Sound Archive. Thank you, too, to Roderick Suddaby and Sabrina Rowlatt of the Department of Documents, Abigail Ratcliffe and Liz Bowers of the museum's Publishing Office, Alan Wakefield of the Photo Archive, and the staff of the museum's Reading Room. Thanks also to Liz Marvin and Charlotte Cole at Ebury, and to Bernice Davison and Caitlyn Schwartz. I am grateful to Alan Pollock for making available to me the recordings of his conversations with Edward Chapman VC, Tommy Gould VC and Ernest Seaman. For clarifying details about Captain Ian Liddell VC I would like to thank RHQ Coldstream Guards. For information about Private Robert Dunsire VC I would like to thank Graham Ritchie of Fife Council Methil Heritage Centre. For double-checking my German I am grateful to Judith Moellers. Finally, thank you to my father, Chris Bailey, for his keen interest in this topic and for his valuable thoughts on structure and selection of material.

Every effort has been made to find copyright holders and I apologise to those whom I was unable to locate.

Roderick Bailey, June 2010

Introduction
by General Sir Richard Dannatt

Since shortly after its inception in 1856, the Victoria Cross has established itself as the supreme symbol of courage, bravery and selfless commitment. Quite properly the simple inscription upon the plain bronze medal – *For Valour* – is itself a masterpiece of understatement. This important new book by Dr Roderick Bailey seeks to get inside the mind and character of some of the 1,358 men, to date, who have been decorated with this medal. Almost without exception those that survived the action for which they were honoured emerge as men of modesty and humility, speaking of just doing their duty for Sovereign, country and their mates, or not even speaking at all. Indeed, if anything has to be said, that simple cross and crimson ribbon says it all.

In the century and a half of the Victoria Cross's existence, the criteria that qualify a soldier, sailor or airman to be awarded the medal have been jealously guarded to preserve the stature of the award. In the conflicts since 9/11 only one VC has been given in Iraq, to a British soldier, and three in Afghanistan, one posthumously to a British soldier, one to a New Zealander and the latest to an Australian. The degree of scrutiny of contending citations is immense, along with the George Cross – for equivalent actions, but not in the face of the enemy – the final recommendations being made at the level of the Chiefs of Staff. I participated in one such deliberation; no stone was left unturned to ensure that the recipient was indeed worthy of the highest recognition.

And it is in the spirit of this rigour that Roderick Bailey's book makes such an important contribution. The voices heard here underline, in terms of great awe and respect, the integrity of the awards made to remarkable, but often ordinary, people.

As a young Green Howards officer, I grew up on the proud regimental stories of Henry Tandy VC, the most decorated private soldier in the First World War, Stan Hollis VC, who won the only VC on D-Day and the Seagrim brothers, Derek and Bunny, the only siblings to have been awarded a VC and a GC respectively. But this book digs deeper beyond the well-known stories and, through the medium of first-hand accounts drawn exclusively from interviews recorded with veterans and preserved in the sound archive of London's Imperial War Museum, provides some unique insights. The accounts provide snapshots of the deeds and characters of a selection of men who have been awarded the VC in a broad range of conflicts and campaigns of the last century. Some come from men who have received the VC; some from men who have seen VCs earned, or who knew or met men – or were friends with men – who were awarded the medal. The vast majority of these accounts are previously unpublished and provide personal perspectives and detail that cannot be found in other books.

Given Roderick Bailey's use of interviews in the Imperial War Museum's sound archives it is not surprising that the book focuses predominantly on twentieth century VCs from the Second World War onwards. However, the rarity of such oral history reflecting the Great War makes the insights from that earlier and terrible war even more special. Throughout, a wide variety of deeds are described, from saving the lives of wounded men while under fire, to storming enemy machine-gun nests, to nursing crippled aircraft to the target and back, to manhandling unexploded bombs out of a damaged submarine. Airmen (both pilots and other aircrew), sailors (including submariners and a Royal Marine) and soldiers (all of diverse ranks and backgrounds), are represented. Furthermore the book features VC recipients of many nationalities: British (English, Scotsmen, Ulstermen and Welsh), New Zealanders (including Charles Upham VC, one of only three men to be awarded the VC twice), an Australian (Rawdon Middleton VC), Indians (Nand Singh VC, Umrao Singh VC), a Canadian ('Hammy' Gray VC), a Gurkha (Thaman Gurung VC), a white Kenyan (Nigel Leakey VC) and a British-born Lebanese–Frenchman (Gabriel Coury VC).

Many of the accounts provide graphic and vivid detail that goes far beyond the formal language of a VC citation, which itself must dwell on fact, letting those facts illuminate the wider drama for evaluation by the scrutiny committee before an award is made. However some of the accounts here are very detailed: for example, the memories of men who watched Tommy Durrant VC and John Cruickshank VC earn their medals. Not all accounts in the book deal with VC deeds: some serve to illuminate the personalities of men who have been awarded the Victoria Cross. Corran Purdon's memories of Charles Upham VC are a good example; so, too are memories of John Harman VC. As I suggested at the start of this introduction, the modesty present in the personal accounts given by VC recipients speaks volumes in the revealing of a man's character. It is the people behind the deeds that make this book so compelling.

It is sad reality of the world in which previous, present and future generations live or will live that conflict and violence characterise our human existence. Yet it is how we respond in these extreme circumstances that marks out one man from another, or one woman from another. This profound study by Roderick Bailey goes a long way to identifying the common characteristics of the bravest of the brave. The word 'hero' has become massively over-used in recent times, but these men were truly heroes, yet they would not recognise that accolade for themselves. They were soldiers, sailors and airmen simply doing their job in the best way they knew how. However, their stories provide great inspiration to all who read or hear them – Roderick Bailey knew that these stories must not become forgotten voices, and he has ensured that this will not happen. Here is a testament to what is good about humankind against the backdrop of what can be the worst. The abiding thought with which the reader is left is one of hope; that adversity can indeed bring out the best in us. These 'forgotten voices' are eloquent in proclaiming this enduring truth.

Richard Dannatt, July 2010

The First World War

THE WESTERN FRONT, 1914–16

For Britain and its Empire, the First World War began in August 1914 when German troops marched into Belgium. The British and Belgian governments had previously accorded a treaty of mutual assistance to acts of aggression and, within days, an advance force of British troops – the British Expeditionary Force – was dispatched to the Continent in support. Very soon the BEF was engaged in heavy fighting.

For several weeks the German army pressed steadily through Belgium and into northern France. By the end of 1914, however, movement by either side was grinding to a halt. Trenches stretched from the Channel to the Swiss border. For more than three years, both sides were to search repeatedly for a decisive breakthrough. Artillery, machine guns and protective belts of barbed wire ensured that the front remained largely static with the defender invariably having the advantage. Casualties reached staggering proportions.

For acts of gallantry in British offensive and defensive actions from the great battles at Mons and Ypres to those at Loos and the Somme, and in the day-to-day grind of trench warfare, forty-three Victoria

Crosses were awarded to soldiers fighting on the Western Front in 1914 and more than one hundred in 1915–16.

Private Sidney Godley
4th Battalion, Royal Fusiliers

Sidney Frank Godley received the first Victoria Cross of the First World War to be awarded to a private soldier. Born in East Grinstead on 14 August 1889 and brought up in Willesden, London, he had left school at fourteen and worked for a time in a Kilburn ironmongers before joining the Royal Fusiliers in 1909. When the war broke out his battalion was sent immediately to France as part of the BEF. Within days, at Mons, Belgium, it was in the thick of the fighting against the advancing German army; and it was there, on 23 August 1914, that Godley earned his VC.

Godley's battalion was ordered to hold two bridges over the Mons-Condé canal to allow other units to retreat. It was for his actions in keeping the enemy at bay for two hours despite heavy enemy fire and his own wounds, which included a bullet lodged in his skull, that he was awarded the Victoria Cross. For his own actions on one of the bridges, the battalion's machine-gun officer, twenty-four-year-old Lieutenant Maurice Dease, received a posthumous VC. 'It was a suicide job,' Godley recalled twenty-five years later. 'The Germans were advancing on the French frontier and greatly outnumbered our "contemptible little army" as the Kaiser called it. Lieutenant Maurice J. Dease and I were detailed to defend the Nimy bridge with our lives. All we had was a single machine gun.'*

Godley saw out the war as a prisoner in Germany and returned to Britain after the armistice. Later he worked for thirty years in London as a school caretaker and, dressed as Bruce Bairnsfather's character

---

* *Daily Herald*, 22 February 1939

Private Sidney Godley VC, the first soldier to earn the Victoria Cross in the First World War.

Q 80449

'Old Bill', to whom the walrus-moustached Godley bore a strong resemblance, raised money for service charities. He died in 1957.

Private William Holbrook
4th Battalion, Royal Fusiliers

Godley, I was in his barrack room at Aldershot. He was quite a sportsman; he played football. Oh yes, I knew him quite well, we were very friendly. He could be a little bit quarrelsome at times; he was a very nice fellow, mind you, but if there was any trouble going on Godley would be in it.

War broke out on 4 August and we left for France after we'd got the reserves on 14 August. From Cowes we went across to Southampton by boat and from Southampton we got a troopship to Le Havre. We camped there for about three or four days, then we entrained at Le Havre and went up to the front – we didn't know where we were going – and the whole brigade came together. Then we got to Mons and we lined a canal bank. The ground was rather rough. It was hilly; there was quite a few rises in the ground. Machine guns were on the bridge on our left, that's where Godley and Dease were. Bit of cover. Nothing much. No trenches or anything like that.

I could see the Germans coming, they were getting close to the canal bank, they were in waves coming over. As far as I could see there was quite a number, more than what we'd got. There was shelling – shrapnel shells – and rifle fire across the canal and we had a few casualties where I was; but the machine-gun party on the bridge, they had the worst part of it and quite a number of those got killed and wounded. That left Lieutenant Dease, the officer in charge of the machine-gun party, and Godley.

Dease wasn't with the machine-gun party at first, he was away from it as far as I can remember. But when things got a bit closer and he was wounded about three times, he still went to the gun and he got killed there, Dease did, leaving Godley in charge of it. There were some villagers, some kids, up there, I remember, quite near the riverbank, and I remember Godley shouting at them, 'Get away!' during the attack; these kids were within about fifty yards. And when the Germans started crossing the bridge Godley got sense enough to take the breech-block out of the gun and tipped the gun over the bridge into the water so that they couldn't use it on us, see, as we were retreating. Course, he got captured there.

Able Seaman Alf Bastin
Royal Naval Division, imprisoned in Doberitz prisoner-of-war camp, Germany, 1915–18

One Sunday the whole camp, the whole British section, was turned out and we were told it was to hear some news from the American Ambassador. We thought, 'Well, what the hell is this going to be?' Of course, America wasn't in the war at this stage.

It transpired that the American Ambassador had been requested to inform Private Godley of the Royal Fusiliers that he had been awarded the Victoria Cross for his courageous efforts in the early weeks of the war when the 'Contemptibles', as they were called, were being hounded out by the Germans. Apparently what had happened, this Private Godley was a machine-gunner and he had got on to a certain position on a bridge and kept firing, stopped the Germans from advancing by shooting them down as they tried to get to the bridge. That went on for quite some time and eventually he got captured and joined in with the others.

He was quite an unassuming sort of chap. He was congratulated by all the British, of course, and they cheered when the announcement was made. The German commandant of the camp shook Godley's hand.

Lieutenant Philip Neame
15th Field Company, Royal Engineers

Philip Neame was awarded the Victoria Cross for his actions at Neuve Chapelle, northern France, on 19 December 1914. An engineer officer who specialised in trench construction and defence, Neame earned his medal when he single-handedly checked an enemy counter-attack, killing and wounding several by throwing bombs, and oversaw the safe evacuation of British wounded from his own position.

Born in Faversham, Kent, on 12 December 1888 into the Shepherd Neame brewing dynasty, Neame had been educated at Cheltenham College and joined the Royal Engineers in 1908. He survived the war and in 1924 became the only man to receive both a Victoria Cross and an Olympic gold medal when, at the Paris Olympics, he was part of the winning four-man rifle team in the running-deer competition. A career soldier, he rose to the rank of lieutenant general and served again during the Second World War, being captured in North Africa in 1942 (though he subsequently escaped). Later he served for eight years as Lieutenant Governor of Guernsey. Interviewed by the Imperial War Museum in 1974, he died in 1978.

Lieutenant Philip Neame
15th Field Company, Royal Engineers
I was stationed at Gibraltar when war broke out and we didn't get to France until the beginning of October 1914. By that time trench warfare had really started and it had become fairly clear that there was not going to be a rapid war of movement ending in a quick, decisive campaign.

By the time of the First Battle of Ypres the trenches were very elaborate and, where the ground was not waterlogged and so on, the front-line trenches were six foot deep with a firing step on the side of it which you stood on, standing up, to fire. Every ten yards there was a traverse, so that if a shell dropped into one length of trench its effect was limited to

IWM SR 68

Philip Neame VC, who was awarded his Victoria Cross for his actions at Neuve Chapelle, France, in 1914.

that particular short length of trench. Trenches were also designed with traverses between each fire bay, as it was called, with the purpose of preventing the enemy, if they captured a length of trench, from enfilading the whole length of trench. And because you can't shoot the enemy in the next fire bay, the only way of getting at him is by lobbing a hand grenade over the traverse into the next bay of the trench. Then the hand grenade goes off with a terrific explosion and will probably kill or wound all the soldiers in that length of trench: that's the use of the hand grenade in trench warfare.

The Germans were very well supplied with very well-made hand grenades and they started using them in trench warfare and we had no proper reply. Although there was an official British hand grenade, it had never been used, hardly at all in peacetime training, and there was a very, very limited supply. Therefore, the Royal Engineers in France started devising home-made hand grenades, which were called bombs, made out of empty used jam tins which were filled with rivets, hobnails, any small bits of metal. The explosive was usually two small bits of gun-cotton with a detonator and the necessary bit of fuse projecting from the end of the jam tin. The only snag about this was the difficulty of igniting the fuse and the easiest way of doing this was with a fusée. This was easily struck on a matchbox and then the glowing head of the fusée held against the end of the fuse which leads into the jam tin. They were made locally in each division in a little home-made factory purely for producing jam tin bombs, the sappers manufactured them, and in the winter of 1914 they were kept busy manufacturing as many as were needed.

The 8th Division carried out an attack on 18 December near Neuve Chapelle, and during the early hours of the nineteenth, in fact in the middle of the night, I was ordered to go up to the area of the attack with my Royal Engineers section to help consolidate the captured area. When I got up to the front I was told that the Germans were counter-attacking and the CO of the infantry battalion concerned asked me to go up into the line and see what I could do in making our defences strong. I took my sapper section forward, got up into the front and heard noise of fighting and bombs – they were called bombs then, they were hand grenades – heard the noise of these exploding. I thought it best to go forward myself and I left my section of sappers – about thirty-six men – under a sergeant in our old front line while I crawled forward up a ditch and got into the German trenches, where our leading infantry were, to see what was happening. When I got there I saw the infantry officer in command who said the Germans were counter-attacking with bombs and that his own bombers had all been wounded and that the bombs that were left would not go off. So I went up to talk to one of the few remaining unwounded bombers whom I found up in the front and discovered that he couldn't light our own bombs because there were no fusées left and he didn't know how to light the safety fuse without a fusée. Well, I did know how, because you can do it by holding a match-head on the end of the fuse and striking the matchbox across it, so I got up to the front and started throwing bombs back at the Germans and that's how the whole affair started.

There were crowds of our infantry all crowded up into the remaining bit of trench we'd captured from the Germans and the Germans were throwing their bombs at us from two different directions, so I had rather a business being the only person there who knew how to light our bombs. I quickly shouted for all our available bombs to be sent up to me and told two or three of the infantry – the West Yorks – to stay by me in a bit of trench in case the Germans tried to rush us. I then started lighting and throwing bombs in the two different directions from which the Germans were throwing bombs at us. I very quickly stopped the Germans bombing from a trench away on the right, which didn't run into ours, it was some branch trench, and any further trouble from that stopped. Then I had a good deal of bombing coming from straight in front of me, from Germans throwing from about twenty or thirty yards away, and so I quickly threw several bombs as quick as I could and with as good an aim as I could. To do this, I had to stand up on the fire-step and expose myself so that I could see where I was throwing with some

11

accuracy. Every time I stood up a German machine gun fired at me, but luckily he was a bit slow and I always managed to pop down again having thrown my bomb before the stream of machine-gun bullets came over more or less where I'd been standing.

Anyway, after some little time and at all events the German bombing eased off very much. I might say that after I'd thrown one or two bombs I heard what sounded like shouts and screams from the Germans in the trench where I'd been throwing my bombs, so evidently they had been effective. And after about a quarter of an hour or so the German bombing almost stopped – only one came over at longish intervals – and after a bit it stopped altogether. So I was able to hang on to the trench we'd captured, having only had to withdraw by one bay, that's to say some eight or ten yards. And then, with two or three West Yorks infantrymen whom I'd hung on to in case the Germans tried to rush along the trench, we stayed there.

The West Yorks officer in command, Captain Inkpen, came along to see how things were going on and he offered to send more infantry up. I said, 'No, I don't want any more. These three fellows are quite enough to hold this bit of trench. It's only a case of a few Germans trying to run along the trench bottom, so if you'll leave two or three of your best men here that's all that's necessary.' He also told me that he had had orders to evacuate the German trench and take all his men back to the British line from where we'd started the attack, so I stayed there for the next half an hour, or three-quarters of an hour, holding that bit of line.

Then I got a message to say that all the British troops had got back safely. Mind you, a great many had been killed and wounded by the German bombs and by machine-gun fire before I'd got up there and when I'd gone up, and also still more when I was going back. In the bottom of the trench were numbers of dead British soldiers lying there and a certain number of wounded who hadn't been got back, so we managed to help some of the wounded to get back to our own line. And when we finally had a message to say we were to come back, I finally gave a quick two or three bombs as a final goodbye to the Germans, really to keep them quiet while we moved back down the trench.

I went back and reported to our own battalion headquarters thinking I'd done my day's work. My task had been to go and prepare the captured German trenches for defence and, as there were no longer any captured German trenches, I presumed I could go back to our billets behind the line. However, the two infantry colonels, from the West Yorks and the Devons, asked me to take my section of sappers back to the front line again and make sure that our own original line was in a good state for defence, because they were afraid the Germans might now set-to and counter-attack. So, after this very exhausting morning's work I'd already had, not so much work as an hour and a half's fighting, I had to take my section back again to the front line and set my men to patching up broken breastworks and trench defences and so on for the rest of the day.

All I knew was that the CO of the Devons, Colonel Travers, whom I knew very well from working in the trenches, in fact he was quite a great friend of mine, said, 'I will see that the brigadier knows what you've done today.' I just thanked him and didn't think any more about it. Then, when I got back to my field company headquarters that evening and told my OC what had happened during the day, he said, 'If you're not careful, Neame, you'll be getting the VC.' Well, I never thought anything about it. I thought he was just joking in a sort of way.

Then, one or two days after, the chief engineer of the corps, a brigadier, came up, which he did from time to time to visit the field companies of the division. And having been told about this by the CRE and the field company commander, he said to me, 'I'll see that my corps commander hears about this, Neame.' I thanked him and didn't think anything special about it until on Christmas Day, that's six days after, our divisional commander, Major General Davis, came to our billets just to wish the people who weren't out working – and I wasn't that morning – a Happy Christmas. And he said to me, 'A Happy Christmas to you, Neame. I've recommended you for the Victoria Cross.' And that was the first time I really knew about it seriously. I just said, 'Well, thank you very much, sir,' and his ADC came up to me afterwards and said, 'Well, that's a nice Christmas present, Neame, isn't it?'

Well, I still didn't write home and tell my parents. I'd written in my letters and told them about the exciting battle I'd had, but I still didn't tell them about being recommended for the VC because I'd still no conviction that I would get it and I didn't want them to be disappointed. However, they heard in a roundabout way from an officer in our division whose parents lived near us at home – he'd heard all about it and wrote to his parents – and it got through that way.

Private John Lynn DCM
2nd Battalion, Lancashire Fusiliers

Private John Lynn was awarded the Victoria Cross for his actions on 2 May 1915, near Ypres, Belgium, when German infantry assaulted the British lines behind thick clouds of asphyxiating chlorine gas: one of the first gas attacks of the war.

Born in Catford, South London, on 21 April 1888, Lynn had joined the Lancashire Fusiliers as a band boy in 1901 and served until 1913. As a reservist, he had been recalled at the outbreak of war and was soon sent out to France. In December 1914 he was awarded the Distinguished Conduct Medal for taking charge of a Vickers machine gun after his sergeant was killed. He died from gas poisoning the day after the act that earned him his VC.

Lieutenant Victor Hawkins
2nd Battalion, Lancashire Fusiliers

Sunday 2 May dawned the most lovely day; but it was the only lovely thing about it, as it turned out. The Hun strafed us in the morning with some big stuff but didn't do much damage. Actually we weren't in trenches, we were behind a bank with a hedge on top and a ditch which we'd wired a bit, and our left was resting on the moat of rather a famous farm called Shell Trap Farm, up in the [Ypres] Salient. We had a pretty quiet day after the preliminary strafing and at about a quarter to five I went along to my company headquarters to have a cup of tea. I'd only just poured out my tea when the sentry in front called out, 'Will you come and look, sir?' So I got up to look. And out of the German trenches – I suppose about six hundred to eight hundred yards away – great jets of yellow cloud were shooting up in the air like water out of a hose. We had come up and seen the effect of the first gassing on our way so we knew what it was; and I didn't get my cup of tea, we had to get busy.

The first thing I saw was a man called Jackie Lynn, who was a Vickers machine-gunner with us, getting his gun out of its proper position and putting it up on top of the parapet and getting up behind it without putting his so-called gas mask on. We had been given bits of flannelette to tie round our faces – I'd got back to my platoon as quick as I could, warning all the men on the way – and the only thing to do was to try to get these flannelette things over our mouths and shoot. We had to wet them and there wasn't very much to wet them with on the spur of the moment. I know some chaps dipped them in their tea, some of them had a bit of water in their water bottles and poured that on, but a lot of us dipped them straight into the latrines. It was the only thing to do, it wasn't very pleasant, and even then, wet, they weren't much good.

As the gas went up into the air out of these jets it formed together into a cloud and dropped on to the ground and started rolling towards us with a slight breeze behind it, and we were very soon enveloped in this thick, yellow and filthy cloud and could see nothing. We didn't really know whether the Germans were coming up behind it or not, so we just let fly with everything we had and went on shooting.

Private Alfred James Bromfield
2nd Battalion, Lancashire Fusiliers

We all opened up as fast as we could go – it was a real mad minute, I'll tell you – blazing away, continually firing into the gas, although we didn't know whether we was hitting anybody. As we were doing this, the rifles were getting hotter and hotter with the continual fire, fat was pouring out the woodwork of the rifles, the muzzles were beginning to extend. We had a medical officer, name of Captain Tyrrell, Irish chap he was, rugby player; well, he realised we'd want some help and he was running along the back of the trench with a can of rifle oil in his hand and pouring it on our rifles as he went by. We stopped firing long enough for him to splash on a drop of oil on to the bolt – that's all we wanted, for the bolts to work properly. And that's how it went on while the gas was still pouring over the top of the trench and coming down into the trench.

Anyway, we stopped Jerry. He must have been coming over because when we looked over the open ground again there was quite a number of them laying out there, some of them wriggling about that had been wounded and quite a number of course dead. But I thought the greatest havoc was caused by one of our machine-gunners, Jackie Lynn. He was out to the right of our lines, in advance of our lines, in a position where he could enfilade the whole ground in front of the German trenches, and he'd worked his machine gun the whole time on his own because his numbers two and three [the members of a Vickers machine-gun team who controlled and supplied the belts of ammunition] had already conked out with the gas. They had to drag him away from that gun, pull him away from it. He died of poison gas but he got the VC for what he did.

Lieutenant Victor Hawkins
2nd Battalion, Lancashire Fusiliers

I suppose we were in that gas cloud about fifteen minutes altogether and then, quite suddenly, one got a breath of fresh air and it was the most marvellous feeling and one fairly sucked it in. And it was just at that moment that I turned round and I saw Jackie Lynn. He'd kept his gun going right the way through and he was carried past in the ditch behind me on a stretcher, blue in the face, dying. I'd never seen a chap blue like that. All these men who'd died of this gas, they were all blue in the face and it was the most beastly thing to see.

Private Robert Dunsire
13th Battalion, The Royal Scots (The Lothian Regiment)

Born in Buckhaven, Fife, on 24 November 1891, Robert Anderson Dunsire had been working in a coal mine in Kirkcaldy when war broke out. He enlisted, with many of his fellow miners, in January 1915, joining over a million men who had volunteered in response to Parliament's call for new recruits. His battalion went to France in July 1915 and Dunsire earned the Victoria Cross that September at Hill 70, at Loos, France, for saving the lives of wounded men left in no-man's-land after an attack on the enemy front line. As he explained in a letter home:

I was sitting on the parapet of the trench looking over the battle-field of Hill 70 when I noticed a man crawling over the parapet of the ridge which separated our parapet from theirs. With the glasses [binoculars] I made out he was one of our lads so I made a dive out of our trench. Got him on my back, and brought him in. I had not been back a quarter of an hour when I noticed another lad. This time it was worse than the first, as the shells were bursting all around, and when the snipers saw me they kept up a continuous fire. I can't tell you how I escaped being hit, as I was a good target, running about 100 yards with a man on my back. I was still in the firing line when the colonel of an East Yorkshire regiment shook hands with me and told me I was a brave lad. I told him anybody would have done the same.

HU 63277B

In a remarkable snapshot taken by a soldier from the trench they have just left, British troops advance through a cloud of poison gas on the opening day of the Battle of Loos, 25 September 1915. Private Robert Dunsire earned his Victoria Cross in this battle the following day.

Dunsire believed that he had been recommended for a Distinguished Conduct Medal. On 20 November he heard that he had been awarded the VC.

After being told of his award, Dunsire was immediately sent on ten days' leave and was met by a cheering crowd at Kirkcaldy railway station. Functions and formal dinners followed before he travelled to Buckingham Palace to receive his medal from King George V. 'I congratulate you on your brave action,' the King was recorded as saying to him, 'and I trust you will live long to wear your decoration.' Dunsire returned to the trenches but was mortally wounded on 30 January 1916 in the explosion of an enemy trench mortar bomb.

Sergeant William Collins
No 1 Cavalry Field Ambulance, Royal Army Medical Corps
We went up to a place called Noeux-les-Mines – that's on the Loos front – and we went into the line at a place called Vermelles. I took up twelve stretcher-bearers and we had a cellar under the ruins of the brewery. The brewery was flattened to the boards and there was a hole in the ground, and down it, down some steps, was a big, largish space where we'd got a crate so the medical officers could examine the patient. We'd lift him up on to the crate and after the examination he would be lifted down and taken out and the next one brought in. It wasn't a big cellar; it was only big enough to take one casualty with a couple of officers bending over him.

We had a variety of medical officers there. There was Captain T. O. Graham, who was an ear, nose and throat specialist and afterwards became president of the Irish Medical Association; he was a Dublin man. I had Captain Ambrose Heath, who was a leading dietician with a famous laboratory in London. There was Captain Blood, who was a tropical diseases specialist. I tell you, we had some very celebrated men in that little combined field ambulance.

On 30 January 1916 came a day which I shall remember as long as I'm alive; to my last breath I shall remember this brave fellow, this unfortunate fellow. I was walking up Hulluch Alley and I came across a stretcher party of the 9th Division – Scottish regiments – and I saw them carrying a man on a stretcher; there were four of them carrying him low. I stopped them and said, 'Is there anything I can do?' and they looked at me and said, 'Have a look at him.'

I looked at him and he was very badly wounded. I just turned him a bit and looked at his chest. I said, 'Well, come down to our aid post because we're the nearest point here'. It was not far off the bottom of the communication trench and I took them down to our hole in the ground at Vermelles and we put him on the crate and I think it was Captain Graham who leaned over him and looked at him. He took his jacket off and stripped him down and he'd got multiple wounds, he was literally like a pepper pot, and he gave a little sigh and died. And then Captain Graham said, 'Well, there's nothing we can do,' and he said to me, 'You go through his pockets,' and he told the chaps from this regiment, it was the Royal Scots, 'Anything he has, we'll send them through to his next of kin. There's sure to be a letter in his pockets. Tell your officer that we're going to send these little things home to his next of kin.'

And I looked at his chest and I saw the ribbon there. I said, 'That's the Victoria Cross, sir,' and Captain Graham looked and said, 'Yes, so it is. This is a VC.' I took his documents out and he was Private Robert Dunsire VC, Royal Scots. There was a letter from home, so I got his address, and an envelope with a document telling him he'd been promoted to lance corporal and in the envelope was his lance corporal's stripes: he'd never had time to put them on his sleeve. It was the most tragic thing to me.

Private Arthur Proctor
1st/5th Battalion, The King's (Liverpool) Regiment

Private Arthur Proctor earned the Victoria Cross on 4 June 1916 after a raid on the enemy trenches near Ficheux, France, and was presented with his VC in the field by King George V. Two wounded British soldiers had been left lying in view of the enemy about seventy-five yards from the British lines, and Proctor, on his own initiative and under heavy fire, ran and crawled out to them, got them under cover and dressed their wounds. Later that day they were brought in alive.

Born in Bootle, Lancashire, on 11 August 1890, Arthur Herbert Proctor survived the war, was ordained in 1927 and served during the Second World War as a chaplain in the Royal Air Force. He died in 1973.

Second Lieutenant Ernest Haire
14th Battalion, Cheshire Regiment

Arthur Proctor was an orphan. He was in my father's Bible class, he was a religiously inclined boy, and father got him a job in the Liverpool Provision Exchange Market and at one time took him on holiday to the farm in Ireland and Arthur frequently stayed with us. In May 1914 he had pneumonia; he was always a delicate-looking lad. He tried to enlist in August and they wouldn't take him but they took him in November, and he went in '15 to France with the King's Liverpools and became a stretcher-bearer.

Well, in 1916, just before I got five days' leave to go home, the *Daily Mail* said that the King, in France, had awarded the Victoria Cross to a Private Arthur Proctor. I got back at three o'clock that afternoon and Arthur had arrived at our house the day before and had spent the night, so I saw his Victoria Cross.

He said they'd had a very nasty attack repulsed. He said, 'Ernest, I walked up and down the trench and I heard the groans of the wounded from the shell holes and it was dreadful. I couldn't stand it any longer, I either had to hop it or go after them' – and if he'd hopped it he'd have been court-martialled. So he climbed on the firestep and he went through the wire and those that were alive he bound their wounds as best he could – and the Germans were firing at him – and at dusk he took another party and brought them in.

About a fortnight later the colonel sent for him. He went to the colonel's headquarters and there was a staff officer there and the colonel said, 'Proctor, get your buttons cleaned, you're going on a little journey with Captain Williams.' So he did, in a car. They drove about twenty-five miles to a village. Well, outside he saw a parade and the car stopped and he got out with the captain and he saw General Haig.

He said, 'I walked in and Haig came towards me and I stiffly saluted him – and he shook hands! He said, "His Majesty's here, Proctor. He would like to see you." I went there and I recognised the King and he looked at me and put his hand out. "I'm glad to meet you, my boy, I've got something for you" – and he pinned the Victoria Cross on my breast! Then Haig said, "Well, my boy, you've had a rather terrible experience, but what I want you to do is to take this Victoria Cross back to your unit and show it to your commanding officer and your friends. Then the captain will take you to Boulogne because you're going home for a month."'

Next morning, he and I went to Liverpool – he was with me, though he was not supposed to travel with an officer – and I took him to the Provision Exchange and he was mobbed. They gave him a cheque for six hundred pounds.

Second Lieutenant Gabriel Coury
3rd Battalion, The South Lancashire Regiment

Gabriel Coury was a twenty-year-old subaltern when he was awarded the Victoria Cross for his actions on 8 August 1916, near Arrow Head Copse, close to Guillemont, during the Battle of the Somme. His citation reads:

During an advance he was in command of two platoons ordered to dig a communication trench from the firing line to the position won. By his fine example and utter contempt of danger he kept up the spirits of his men and completed his task under intense fire. Later, after his battalion had suffered severe casualties and the Commanding Officer had been wounded, he went out in front of the advanced position in broad daylight and in full view of the enemy found his Commanding Officer, and brought him back to the new advanced trench over ground swept by machine-gun fire. He not only carried out his original tasks and saved his Commanding Officer, but also assisted in rallying the attacking troops when they were shaken and in leading them forward.

Born at Sefton Park, Liverpool on 13 June 1896, Gabriel George Coury had been educated at Stonyhurst College and gone to work as an apprentice in a cotton brokers before enlisting on the outbreak of war. Returning to his old firm after the war, he served again in the army in the Second World War and died in 1956.

Joan Marie Louise Bird (née Coury)
Daughter of Gabriel Coury

My father was not English at all, there was no English blood in him; his mother was French and his father came from Lebanon. His name was Coury, which is a Middle Eastern name.

Well, we were three girls in our family and growing up with the fact that your father was a VC didn't seem to have a great importance to us, I suppose, as girls. But people were always asking us, 'Well, how did he get his VC?' so from time to time we'd say to him, 'So how did you get your VC?' He just said, 'For being a bloody fool.' It was never made much of. He never mentioned the war. Never, ever mentioned the war.

Second Lieutenant Tom Adlam
7th Battalion, Bedfordshire Regiment

Tom Adlam won the Victoria Cross during the Battle of the Somme, in September 1916, for his actions during an attack on the enemy front line. His citation reads:

> A portion of a village which had defied capture on the previous day had to be captured at all costs to permit subsequent operations to develop. This minor operation came under very heavy machine gun and rifle fire. Second Lieutenant Adlam, realising that time was all important, rushed from shell hole to shell hole under heavy fire collecting men for a sudden rush, and for this purpose also collected many enemy grenades. At this stage he was wounded in the leg, but nevertheless he was able to out-throw the enemy and then seizing his opportunity, and in spite of his wound, he led a rush, captured the position and killed the occupants. Throughout the day he continued to lead his men in bombing attacks. On the following day he again displayed courage of the highest order, and though again wounded and unable to throw bombs, he continued to lead his men. His magnificent example and valour, coupled with the skilful handling of the situation, produced far-reaching results.

Born in October 1893 and brought up near Salisbury, Tom Edwin Adlam had just qualified as a teacher when the First World War began. He survived the war and returned to teaching, becoming headmaster of Blackmoor School, Liss, and saw service again during the Second World War as an embarkation officer at Glasgow and Tilbury overseeing the loading of ships at the docks. He was interviewed by the Imperial War Museum in 1974 and died in 1975.

© F. A. Swine Q 69155

Second Lieutenant Tom Adlam VC, awarded the medal for his actions at the Battle of the Somme.

Second Lieutenant Tom Adlam
7th Battalion, Bedfordshire Regiment

I'd just finished my training as a teacher, I was in the Hants Territorials, and I went to do my summer camp on the Saturday before war broke out and I was mobilised straightaway. When I got to my regiment, down at Sittingbourne in Kent, I was put on as a bombing officer. I was just throwing bombs and things like that; training was to see how far I could throw a bomb. I found that I could occasionally take a Mills bomb [the standard hand grenade adopted by the British Army in 1915] and throw it with a bent arm like a cricket ball, but you couldn't throw too many. The weight of the thing, being a five-ounce bomb, jerks your arm tremendously; if you did it without proper training, I think you'd jerk your arm out. But with an ordinary throw I have thrown a Mills bomb about forty yards and that was considered pretty good. I also practised with both arms; I don't know why I did it, I just thought I'd try left-handed throwing. It stood me in rather good stead in the end.

We were down at Thiepval and it was after the Somme battle had started and things had been held up especially on one flank and our battalion was put in: we'd been in the reserve and we were put in to try and straighten out the line. I was lucky, because the part that my platoon was opposite was only about a hundred yards away and then the trench swung back about forty-five degrees, you see, so that the platoon on the left, they had a long trek, three or four hundred yards. We only had about a hundred yards. But then the machine guns started and we all went in the shell holes.

So I thought, 'Well, we've got to get in this trench somehow or other. What are we going to do about it?' I went crawling along from shell hole to shell hole till I came to the officer in charge of the next platoon and I said, 'What do you think about it?' He said, 'I'm going to wait here till it gets dark then crawl back. We can't go forward.' I said, 'Well, I think we can. Where I am, I'm not more than fifty yards from the trench, and I think I can get in.' I remember he shook hands with me solemnly. He said, 'Goodbye, old man.' I said, 'Don't be such a damned fool. I'll get back all right. I'm quite sure I can get back.' It didn't worry me. Of course, I was abnormal at the time: I didn't feel that there was any danger at all at that moment.

I got back to my platoon. I went across to them and I said, 'You all got a bomb?' – we always took two bombs with us – and I said, 'Well, get one in your hand. Pull out the pin. Now hold it [the lever, to prevent it from exploding] tight. As soon as I yell "Charge!" stand up, run two or three yards, throw your bomb and I think we'll get into that trench, there's practically no wire in front of it.' And they did, they all upped and ran, and we got into our little bit of trench.

By this time we had no more bombs but there were bags of German bombs in the trench like a condensed-milk can on the top of a stick. On them was written '5 secs' and you had to unscrew the bottom and a little toggle ran out – you pulled that and you threw it. I'd noticed that the Germans were throwing them at us and I'd seen them coming over, wobbling about as they did, pitching a bit short of me luckily, and I could count up to three nearly before the 'bang!' came, so I experimented with one. I took a chance and I said, 'I'm going to count three before I throw it,' I pulled the string – 'One, two, three' – and threw it. My servant was beside me and he was looking over the top of the trench and he said, 'Bloody good shot, sir. Hit him in the chest. You hit the bugger.'

I think that when the Germans found their own bombs coming back at them it rather put the wind up them. I don't know whether they thought I was picking them up and throwing them back, the ones they'd thrown, but there were bags of them in the trench. So with my few men behind me I got them all to pick up bombs – the men all brought these bombs along, an armful of them – and I just went gaily along throwing bombs. As I say, I just counted every time I threw it – 'One, two, three' – and the bomb went, you see, and it was most effective.

Then we got up close to where a machine gun was and that was zipping about – we daren't look up above. But I got a whole lot of bombs ready and I started throwing as fast as I could and my servant, who was popping up every now and again, said, 'They're going, sir! They're going!' So I yelled, 'Run in chaps, come on!' and we just charged up the trench like a load of mad things. Luckily they were running. Never caught them but we drove them out. Then we came to another machine-gun post; I don't know whether it was another one or whether they'd stopped again to have another go at us. By the time we got him out of the way the rest of the battalion followed in behind us and they did the cleaning-up of the dugouts. Well, they took nearly a hundred prisoners, I think, out of the dugouts.

So then we got to a certain point and the CO saw two trenches leading up towards Schwaben Redoubt and he said, 'It would be a good idea to get an advance post up there, about a hundred yards between the two,' and they started off and a man got killed straightaway. I said, 'Oh, damn it, let me go. I can do it; I've done the rest of it, I can do this bit.' So I went on; I bombed up the trench, put some men to look after that, bombed along this other one, got to the other corner, bombed them out of the corner there and then bombed back down the way. We took more prisoners down there in dugouts and things of that kind and we had our advance point, our two points, out towards the enemy, and then we went home for the night. Another company came up, took over from us, and we went back a bit, a quarter of a mile back, I think, and we rested, had a meal, and then we lined up the next morning.

The attack on Schwaben Redoubt was going to be, I believe, at one o'clock. As our company had done most of the fighting the day before, they put us in the last line of the attack. The other people were in front, three other companies, and we sat down, as I say, waiting till one o'clock. What we did then was to sort of chatter away to keep the spirits up. You see, waiting for an hour for an attack is not a very pleasant thing. We told dirty stories and made crude remarks. I remember quite well there was a nasty smell about there and of course we all suggested somebody had had an accident; but it wasn't, it was a dead body, I think. And then the shells started. You'd never think anything could have lived at all in the bombing that went on at Schwaben Redoubt. And the old earth piled up and we went forward.

We got quite close to this Schwaben Redoubt and there was a huge shell crater there, I remember. Well, it was a mine crater, I think, because it was about fifty feet across, and this was all lined with Germans popping away at us, you see. So I got hold of the old bombs again and started trying to bomb them out. After a bit we got them out of there and we started charging up the trench, all my men coming on behind very gallantly. We got right to within striking distance of Schwaben Redoubt itself and just at that minute I got a bang in the arm and found I was bleeding. Having been a bombing officer who could throw with both arms, I used my left arm for a time and I found I could bomb pretty well as well with it as I could with my right, and we went on for some time holding on to this position and working our way up the trenches as far as we could. And then my CO came up and he said, 'You're hurt, Tom.' I said, 'Only a snick in the arm.' He said, 'Let's have a look at it,' and he put a field dressing on it. He said, 'You go on back. You've done enough.'

It was very funny how I heard about the VC. I was at Colchester, I'd been in the town for an evening out, I think, and when I got back to the mess at night the orderly room porter said, 'There's a lot of telegrams for you, sir, up in the mess. I was told to tell you.' So I went up to the mess and there were about a dozen telegrams. 'Congratulations!' 'Heartiest Congratulations!' 'Congratulations from all at home!' 'Congratulations from the regiment!' I said, 'Can you get a wire off for me to my father?' And they said, 'Yes, if you like.' I said, 'Why "Congratulations"? I know nothing,' and I sent that off to my father and he wired back: 'Have heard papers are asking for a photograph of you as you've been awarded the VC.' That's how I heard. And, of course, on Monday there were photographs of me all over the papers.

When I was a schoolmaster I don't think it made a bit of difference at all. The schoolchildren might swank a bit about it outside; in fact I heard afterwards that they did. But to me it made no difference at all. I was just 'Boss'. The man before me was known as 'Boss' and I was known as 'Boss'. But I had a grand lot of children in those days. They weren't little saints, I don't think that for a minute, but I think they were quite different from the children of today. I enjoyed being a schoolmaster in Blackmoor.

During the Second World War I was on 'Embarkation' once, it was a foggy night I remember, and the people on board one of the ships complained they were too crowded; all the colonels and what-have-you were saying they couldn't go on ships like that, you see. So my CO said to me, 'Tom, you go down and tell them, no matter what they say, that the accommodation stands as it is. We can't alter it.' I remember I lost my way to the docks twice on the way down but we got there eventually and I came in with my overcoat on and said, 'Sorry I'm late, gentlemen, but the fog's very thick outside and we got held up.' They said, 'What about this?' and I said, 'Well, I'm sorry, gentlemen, but there's no other accommodation. Nothing can be done.' They all looked at me down their noses and they started arguing, of course. I was a bit bald-headed then, you see, an old doddery thing; I could see it written all over their faces, 'Oh, he's some Home Service man, he doesn't know what he's talking about.' So I said, 'Excuse me, gentlemen, I'll take my coat off,' and they saw the VC ribbon and their eyes opened. Do you know, I got everything I wanted! They realised they were talking to a man who had been a soldier.

Lieutenant Colonel Roland Bradford MC
9th Battalion, Durham Light Infantry

One of the only pair of brothers to receive the Victoria Cross during the First World War, Lieutenant Colonel Roland Bradford was awarded his VC for his actions in securing the flank of his division during an attack on the Somme on 1 October 1916 at Eaucourt l'Abbaye, France. As his citation explains:

Lieutenant Colonel Roland Bradford VC MC.

Q 114620

A leading Battalion having suffered very severe casualties, and the Commander wounded, its flank became dangerously exposed at close quarters to the enemy. Raked by machine-gun fire, the situation of the Battalion was critical. At the request of the wounded Commander, Lieutenant Colonel Bradford asked permission to command the exposed Battalion in addition to his own. Permission granted, he at once proceeded to the foremost lines. By his fearless energy under fire of all description, and his skilful leadership of the two Battalions, regardless of all danger, he succeeded in rallying the attack, captured and defended the objective, and so secured the flank.

Recognised as an outstanding commander, Bradford was promoted to the rank of brigadier in November 1917 when he was still only twenty-five, making him the youngest general officer in the British Army. He was killed ten days later, on 30 November, at Cambrai, France.

Born in February 1892 and educated at Epsom College, Roland Bradford had joined the Durham Light Infantry (DLI) in 1912 and gone to France with the 2nd Battalion in 1914. He received a Military Cross for leading an attack later that year at Armentières. His brother, Lieutenant Commander George Nicholson Bradford, was posthumously awarded a Victoria Cross for his actions during the British naval raid on Zeebrugge in April 1918.

Charles Gee, whose memories of serving under Roland Bradford after he had earned his VC were recorded in 1994, fought with the Durham Light Infantry on the Western Front in 1917–18. After the war he taught at Clifton College before rejoining the DLI in 1939, being captured in France in 1940 and seeing out the war in a series of prison camps. He then returned to teaching. The last surviving DLI officer of the First World War, he died in April 1998 at the age of 100.

Lieutenant Charles Gee
Adjutant, Headquarters Company, 9th Battalion, Durham Light Infantry

I had to go alone up in a train to a detail camp of the 9th Battalion, which was up at Arras. And on the way up in the train some officers were returning from leave and asked where I was going and one of them said, 'Oh, when I was going on leave, I shared a carriage with two officers who'd been dismissed after a few days by Bradford for being incompetent or unfit to be officers.' And they told me a bit about him. I'd never heard of him before. My hair was very long, and they said, 'You'll have to have your hair clipped all over,' and I did before I saw Bradford. I was very anxious about it. There would have been blue murder if any officer had arrived with the long hair that I'd had.

I'd never seen a colonel except old ones. I'd gathered from people that it was unusual having a colonel that age with a VC and MC and everybody said he ought to have had lots more decorations. He did become a brevet. He told me later that if the war ended now he would go back to being a full lieutenant who would be a brevet major when he was promoted to captain, but he couldn't be promoted to captain because all the captains were in safe employment so he'd go back to being a full lieutenant after being a colonel and eventually brigadier. Also he got the idea that because there was nothing in civil life for him it would be better for him to die in action. He said that to me. He was devoted to the battalion and he did make them enormously efficient and I think he inspired me with the impression that we were as good as the Guards.

I got an order one day to go up to headquarters to be adjutant, sometime in May 1917. I was very junior and knew nothing about it and I spent hours standing to attention watching him dealing with this, that and the other. Very often he'd say, 'There's an order. Lose it.' He did it an awful lot: anything futile from a higher command, he'd just ignore it, and he was strong enough with the VC and MC to get away with a lot. He had his own standing orders, all sorts of things, like, 'Every man must go out on patrol. Every man has got to be used to no-man's-land.' And, 'If possible, don't use communication trenches. If you know your way and it's safe, use the top': we always walked out on the top if we could. And all sorts of things about training and, as I've afterwards learned or he told me, he wrote various sort of pamphlet things that used to come round the army. He was always trying to design some method of getting infantry across wire or across the few hundred yards to the German trenches so they wouldn't get shot by the machine guns, like a sort of cover you could carry with you. All sorts of designs he'd got; he was always working on things of that nature. I remember him drawing pictures and so on and talking to me about it. He did an enormous amount himself.

He could tick people off. He ticked me off enough. I can't remember making any serious mistakes but I got ticked off an awful lot. He was jolly rude. Very rude, often. I think if he was cross about something he probably took it out on me – I can't remember any mistakes. He'd say, 'I don't know what your mother would think of you,' and so on.

A new man came in while Bradford was there and Bradford said, 'You're a fine chap and you're coming into this marvellous battalion,' and so on, gave him enormous praise, and then looked at him for a long time and said, 'You deserted from the second battalion two years ago.' He'd recognised him. And then he gave him such a ticking off. I told Bradford later that he'd deserted again and he said, 'I'd wanted him to.' He ticked me off once or twice pretty savagely but with this deserter he was really frightening: 'I'll shoot you with my own hand!' that sort of thing. Very aggressive, very frightening, he could be. Wasn't normally. I think it came out of his zest for perfection: he wanted to *frighten* the person.

He was tall and good-looking and very fit and assured. He wore a different uniform from anybody. He never wore a Sam Browne that I saw; he wore a specially designed leather belt with two straps down the front. He got arrested for it once in London, on leave, but on the way to the War Office he found fault with the man taking him and said he'd arrest him so he got away with it. He wanted to be different, I think. And I think, really, looking back on it, he wanted to be a corps commander; I think he realised that he had the ability, that he was conscious of that. He told me that if he was a corps commander he'd carry an umbrella. It was rather essential to be important and different. Montgomery found the same: he wore two cap badges.

Very, very fussy about everything. A button undone: when he appeared you checked your buttons and so on. People would be marching past and he'd say, 'Write to B Company and tell them to explain in writing for the information of the Commanding Officer why Private so-and-so had his left button undone.' I was supposed to fire off rude remarks like that every day. The men had to be shaved always in the line, even if it was a big sweat getting water, and the trenches had to be kept absolutely spotless. No cigarette ends on the ground or anything. It was efficiency, efficiency for the war, to beat the enemy. They had to be occupied in the trenches; they'd get a little sleep at night, they'd get sleep in the day, but they mustn't get idle. They had to do musketry practice as far as they could and keep it absolutely spotless and have a proper place for the lavatory. Efficiency: it's part of discipline having your buttons done up and so on. Being disciplined to beat the enemy: everything was on that.

When I got there he was trying to organise a strike against whisky – so many officers were drinking so much whisky, really living on it. He didn't take it and I didn't like it personally but a lot of people were drinking too much. He was trying to ban it and to get other units to ban it. I think he may have banned it in the headquarters mess. People were taking too much, I think.

He tried to make the men's leave better. The men had been out two years without leave; officers got leave every six months. It went on for a long time, hundreds of men had been two or three years without leave. When he was sent on leave to get his medal he tried to get the men more leave. He failed. And he put in a complaint to the staff every day and they'd got into the habit of stopping it in the division but it somehow got through to the corps commander and some big noise came down, absolutely furious, and I heard a lot of the row. He made me find the letter he'd sent in, a copy of it, and it was a bit stark in its criticism. The men's leave was scandalous, it said, and the men were getting into a state and it was unfair and officers should have less leave. But the main accusation was that the staff, the people who were quite safe, got too much leave. I heard the man speaking to him very rudely, Bradford went on arguing and arguing, but nothing happened about it. He even tried to refuse his own leave, he did refuse leave, but they ordered him to go to get his medal.

He was enormously careful with his men's lives. He wasn't careful when we were out of the line, training; he wanted everybody playing about with rifles and real ammunition, not sham, so it would come easy and it didn't worry him at all if the occasional bullet hit somebody. I remember somebody saying – not quite true – that we had more casualties in training than we had in the line, but it was very nearly true.

He knew what fear was. He taught us all to get down even if a shell landed a hundred yards away. It wasn't bravado; it was teaching the men to save their lives, to live to fight. But if it were necessary to, when people were frightened, he would stand, take risks, to get the situation right.

He would be unpopular, but in the line he ceased to be. He would go up to the line and he frequently didn't come back till suppertime: he sort of lived with the men. One particular time he came back and said that such-and-such a portion of the line was having trouble because the Germans were putting one or two shells over. He said, 'I've told the men exactly what to do, because I think there's going to be a raid.' Well, there was a raid, exactly as he prophesied, and he sent me round the next day and the men were absolutely astonished by what the colonel had said. 'He knew exactly what the Germans would do,' they said. 'He always knows what's happening and he's always right.'

I remember, early on, getting a wire that the enemy was massing for an attack opposite, and I said, 'Should I send that around to the companies?' He thought a bit and he said, 'No, I've been round there and I'm quite happy. The sentries are there; everything's all right. No panic at all.' And of course we weren't attacked.

Some men would talk well and so they became sort of favourites and they knew the colonel's mind more than the officers did, so we sometimes got information from them about what the colonel was planning or doing. Bradford and the men were in very close touch and the officers were bullied along to be adequate.

I think I had a bad company commander when I was in the company because I don't remember him taking me round the men or introducing me or anything: I don't think he worried. But Bradford knew all the men as far as was possible. Literally, he'd know them by name and they would know him.

The night the colonel was wounded, I went in and found him mopping his face: a wound. He'd been talking to a company commander up in the front and the company commander had got up and a bullet hit his helmet and a piece of the helmet got chipped off and hit the colonel somewhere in the side of the face. And I think it was the same day this message came that he was to be sent away to command a brigade, and I took the message into him. He said, 'I don't want to go.' I said, 'Read it again. It's an order, not "Do you want to…?"' He was very sad. I suppose half of him must have been delighted to have been promoted because he obviously was fit for it and trained for it and he'd commanded the brigade several times: he'd got his VC when he was commanding two battalions at least.

We were moved to that division the next year and my impression is that various senior officers, such as brigadiers in charge of gunnery, were so impressed by his knowledge of gunnery that they wanted to resign their jobs and serve under him in any capacity he'd have them. That's the story I was told.

He was killed by a casual shell somewhere. They must have retired a good bit by then, I think, and he went out after dark to somewhere not far away and he was found dead. And I think his watch and things had been stolen; somebody had stolen them.

A tragedy, an awful pity. I think I was one of the people who sort of worshipped him. My wife was going to call our son Roland, if we'd had one.

THE WAR IN THE AIR

In 1914, Britain had two air services: the Royal Flying Corps (RFC), and the Royal Naval Air Service (RNAS). Both were fledgling bodies, tiny in strength, and their purpose was expected largely to be one of reconnaissance and observation.

In time, the demands of the war saw both services increase dramatically in size. The RFC in France, for example, grew from four squadrons in 1914 to twenty-seven at the time of the Battle of the Somme. The RNAS, while envisaged as a force for coastal and carrier duty, also sent squadrons to the Western Front. The role of both services expanded too: on the Western Front, for example, it soon came to include the tasks of bombing enemy positions and intercepting and shooting down enemy aircraft and observation balloons. Home defence was another role and, based in Britain, squadrons of both services were used in attempts to counter raids by German airships and Gotha bombers.

In April 1918, the RFC and the RNAS were combined to become the Royal Air Force. New RAF decorations were introduced, although all air force personnel continued to be eligible for the VC.

Second Lieutenant Gilbert Insall
11 Squadron, Royal Flying Corps

Born in Paris on 14 May 1894, Gilbert Stuart Martin Insall was training to be a dentist when the First World War began. He joined the Royal Fusiliers in September 1914 and transferred to the Royal Flying Corps in 1915, being posted that summer to the Western Front where he earned the Victoria Cross on 7 November 1915 near Achiet-le-Grand, France.

A month later, Insall was shot down and captured after chasing an enemy aircraft deep behind the German lines. While a prisoner in Germany he made several daring escape attempts, which included the use of elaborate disguises, and finally succeeded in August 1917. Nine days after tunnelling out from Ströhen camp, near Hanover, and after walking 150 miles, he reached neutral Holland. For that achievement he was awarded the Military Cross.

Still in the RAF, Insall was instrumental after the war in the identification of the Bronze Age archaeological site now known as Woodhenge, near Stonehenge, which he spotted and photographed from the air in 1925. He served again in the Second World War and died in 1972.

Lieutenant Robert Hughes-Chamberlain
Pilot, 11 Squadron, Royal Flying Corps

Major Dawes was the squadron commander. Dawes simply didn't like Insall, I can't think of any particular reason but they didn't get on, until he did this job and then he was racing about the place to get Insall this VC: to the French, to get reports from them; reports from all over the place. It made a very good story.

I was in the office, the squadron office, and Dawes was cursing Insall up hill and down dale because he hadn't arrived back in the squadron. 'What the hell's the fellow doing now?' – that sort of stuff. Then the telephone rang and he picked it up and he started to blaspheme until Insall

Q 114633

Second Lieutenant Gilbert Insall VC receiving his medal from King George V.

got it into his head to tell him, 'We've shot down a German aircraft over the French lines.'

Then he proceeded to describe how they'd followed him down to the ground, the two men had got out and run and then Insall started to shoot them up. The men disappeared into the hedge at the back of a field or something so Insall's observer dropped a small bomb, about as big as your fist, and it fell on the German machine and set it alight. Smoke and so on came up. Then Insall discovered that he was practically on the floor, it was getting dark and he hadn't any petrol left to speak of and he couldn't get upstairs once more, so he'd shouted to Donald [First Class Air Mechanic T. H. Donald, Insall's observer] and said, 'Look, we'll hedge-hop over the trenches and trust to luck.' Their luck didn't hold because a bullet came from a trench on the German side and went through the petrol tank. Well, when that happens, it's goodbye. He could just land in a field on the other side, whereupon the Germans started chucking shells across. Insall and Donald went and bunked for the hedges and watched the bombardment but it didn't hit the machine at all and darkness supervened.

Insall, who was educated in Paris, his father was something or other there, he spoke French like a native and went down and saw the colonel commanding that part of the French line and explained what he wanted. He said, 'I'm the aeroplane pilot, I want to let my squadron know that the tank's busted,' and the French colonel gave him every assistance and that's how Dawes heard Insall's voice coming through, telling him all about it.

So Dawes was highly excited and he yelled for Rees, the chief flight commander of 11 Squadron, who came along and he said, 'Take a tender, a new tank and all the appliances and petrol and everything else that you want and some mechanics to run the show. He's on the French line, fifteen miles away.' Rees, who was very good indeed at anything of that kind, a first-class man, he went and took all the apparatus necessary and under masked lights they took out the old tank, put in the new one, filled it up and got it generally ready to start and then Insall got in and flew it away at dawn. That's how the citation ended.

Well, they made a good thing out of it but it wasn't a VC job in my opinion, it was very ordinary, shooting down a machine and escaping over the trenches. I should have reversed it. What he did in escaping from Germany was a VC job in my opinion; he told me the whole story one day at Dover when I was in command there and I always thought that was an extraordinary job, the other one was an MC job. He got them both but the wrong way round.

Major Frederick Powell
Pilot, 5, 40 and 41 Squadrons, Royal Flying Corps

Insall, who earned his VC in No 11 squadron in a Vickers fighter, he went out and he shot down a German aeroplane which landed the German side of the lines. Being so terribly aggressive, Insall followed him down, right down to the ground, and then, as the pilot and observer ran out, he came after them and shot them up as they ran away. It depends how brave you were. If you were like myself, you sat up there and watched in the hope that he'd crash.

Lieutenant William Leefe Robinson
39 Squadron, Royal Flying Corps

The first man to be awarded the Victoria Cross for actions on, or above, British soil, William Leefe Robinson was a fighter pilot with a night-flying squadron based near Hornchurch, Essex, when he was awarded the medal for his actions over Cuffley, Hertfordshire, on the night of 2/3 September 1916 during the time of Germany's airship bombing raids on Britain. Flying a BE2c fighter, he intercepted an enemy Schütte-Lanz – not, as has often been assumed, a Zeppelin, which was a different type of airship – and shot it down in flames. For all their size, airships posed a formidable target, being hard to find at night, difficult to reach owing to their altitude, armed with machine guns and, to a small attacking fighter, dangerously combustible.

Born in India on 14 July 1895 and educated at the Dragon School, Oxford, and St Bees School in Cumberland, Robinson had previously seen action on the Western Front as an observer in the Royal Flying Corps. Wounded in action over Lille, he had then retrained as a pilot. Sent back to France in 1917, Robinson was shot down and captured on his first patrol over the lines. While in prison he made several foiled attempts to escape and was held in solitary confinement as a punishment, which saw his health deteriorate badly. Though repatriated when the war was over, he remained very weak and eventually succumbed to the Spanish Influenza pandemic, dying at his sister's home in Middlesex on New Year's Eve, 1918.

Robert James Thelwell-Smith
Schoolboy in Hackney, east London

The war was rather remote from us until the Zeppelins came. The first air raid, everybody was out in the street looking because they focused all the searchlights on this white cigar-like object up in the sky and that turned out to be a Zeppelin. After that we became conscious of the fact that it was silly to go out into the streets and we gathered in the inner room where we had a big round table we could get under if it were necessary. Some friends of ours across the way, they had an off-licence; well, they couldn't stop in there with all the bottles so their family used to come over and we had card parties and played the gramophone and we kids thought it was marvellous. But it got tedious after a time. Too frequently we were losing our sleep.

We used to hear the noise and everything and suddenly one night there was a lull in the firing. This went on for some time so we realised something was on, and for some reason everybody in our area seemed to be out in the street trying to find out what was on. Suddenly we saw, right

Q 66934

Lieutenant William Leefe Robinson VC, the first man to be awarded the medal for actions on or over British soil.

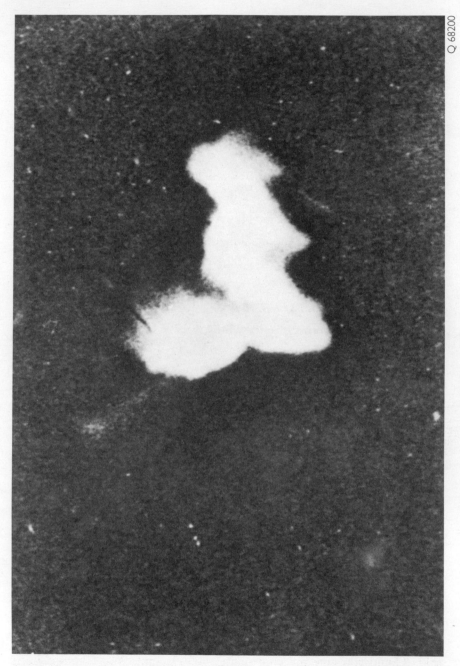

Q 68200

A rare photograph of the final moments of SL 11, the German Schütte-Lanz airship shot down in flames by Lieutenant William Leefe Robinson on the night of 2/3 September 1916. The airship crashed finally at Cuffley, Hertfordshire.

up to the north-east, this bright Zeppelin with its nose on fire and as it dipped so the flames went right up and the Zeppelin plunged to earth. Everybody cheered, everybody thought it was marvellous. Actually, not everybody acted that way. Other people were thinking how terrible it was for the Germans in there, people who were less sort of carried away with patriotism, I suppose, more human. But we, as kids, thought it was marvellous.

Lieutenant Robinson it was that carried out the attack. Course, they didn't know what would happen if he did set the gas on fire, they thought it might explode and he'd be blown out of the sky. Luckily it didn't happen that way, it was a more gradual thing, and he was able to get away and land safely.

Private Vernon Coombs
Artist's Rifles, stationed at Gidea Park, north-east London
I was on fire duty – if there was a fire I'd help put it out – and that same night was the night when Leefe Robinson brought down that Zeppelin. I saw this Zeppelin in the sky all in flames and after it came down I could hear his plane droning about and I heard him land. He was at Hornchurch, which wasn't far from Gidea Park, and he landed in the dark and I could hear the cheers from that aerodrome when he landed. I shall never forget that.

Grace Hallam (née Bateson)
Telephone switchboard operator, Women's Royal Air Force, Bicester, 1918
Demobbing of prisoners of war went on from Bicester. The girl that was in charge of demob, one day she wasn't feeling too well and I was off duty so I went in and helped her and a tall good-looking captain walked in. I said, 'Could you give me your name, sir?' He said, 'Yes. Captain Leefe Robinson.' And I just looked at him and I said, 'Oh! The Cuffley VC!' and he said, 'Yes.'

He was very, very ill at that particular time. I got him an aspirin and a drink of whisky, both together, which I shouldn't have done. We pleaded with him to stay and not to go on but he wanted to get home, he'd been two years in a prison camp. And then, within a few weeks, he was dead with this flu that was going about.

Captain Albert Ball DSO MC
56 Squadron, Royal Flying Corps

Of all the First World War's fighter pilots, none caught the British public's imagination as much as Albert Ball and today he remains the best known. He was awarded the Victoria Cross, so his citation states, for 'most conspicuous and consistent bravery' between 25 April and 6 May 1917. During that time he took part in air combat on twenty-six separate occasions, destroying eleven enemy aircraft, driving down two out of control and forcing several more to land.

In these combats Capt. Ball, flying alone, on one occasion fought six hostile machines, twice he fought five and once four. When leading two other British aeroplanes he attacked an enemy formation of eight. On each of these occasions he brought down at least one enemy.

Several times his aeroplane was badly damaged, once so seriously that but for the most delicate handling his machine would have collapsed, as nearly all the control wires had been shot away. On returning with a damaged machine he had always to be restrained from immediately going out on another.

In all, Capt. Ball has destroyed forty-three German aeroplanes and one balloon, and has always displayed most exceptional courage, determination and skill.

Q 56140

Captain Albert Ball VC DSO MC sitting in the cockpit of his SE5 aircraft.
This photograph was taken in April 1917, days before his death.

Born in Nottingham on 14 August 1896, Ball had been an engineering student when the First World War began, whereupon he enlisted in the army. In 1915, after brief service in the Sherwood Foresters, he had transferred to the Royal Flying Corps and in 1916, flying a Nieuport 17 biplane fighter, was credited with thirty victories during a three-month period in support of the Somme offensive. By the end of that year he had been awarded three DSOs and a Military Cross. He returned to action in 1917 and flew an SE5 biplane as a flight commander with 56 Squadron until he was killed on 7 May. At the time of his death he was not yet twenty-one.

Captain H. N. Charles
Engineer officer, 56 Squadron, Royal Flying Corps

The first SE5 came over from Farnborough and we commenced to get a hand-picked collection of fighter pilots. All the pilots were specially selected for their ability to handle small fast aeroplanes and it was felt that after a period of intensive training the squadron might be, with the new fighter, a really crack squadron. The most celebrated pilot who came to us was Captain Albert Ball from 60 Squadron who at that time had a very great reputation indeed, and he played a very great part in bringing about the proper training and morale of the squadron.

Albert Ball was of medium height with dark eyes and a mass of dark hair. He was a very cheerful and happy person. He loved flowers and he loved music. As a matter of fact we built a sort of little greenhouse on the end of his Nissen hut and he and I sat in this thing for many hours at night trying to work out how to make the SE5 work. He had decided that the SE5, as it then was, was such a bad aeroplane that it would be quite unsafe to fly it over the lines.

Albert Ball was the very unusual combination of the fighter pilot with a real interest in aeroplanes. The majority of them didn't have much aeroplane knowledge but he definitely had and between the two of us we finally cooked up the SE5 so that it really worked. General Trenchard came down to see us on this matter, approved, and finally all our other aeroplanes were altered to the same design that we'd evolved and improved on Albert Ball's machine. The SE5 owes a lot to Albert Ball, not only for his example as a great pilot, but also for what he did in helping to actually get a reasonable standard of performance out of it.

Second Lieutenant Charles Alfred Ernest Beard
Pilot, 19 Squadron, Royal Flying Corps

Captain Ball never wore a helmet; he had a mop of hair. He was the youngest VC in the Royal Flying Corps and I'll tell you a true story about him. We were giving a concert – we ran a concert party in the squadron – and they were invited down and he was sitting with all the officers in the squadron in the front and his batman came running down and said, 'Captain, your hut's on fire.' They were Nissen huts, canvas and wood. And he said, 'Bugger the hut, I'm enjoying the concert.' That's Captain Ball.

Captain H. N. Charles
Engineer officer, 56 Squadron, Royal Flying Corps

Well, as time went by, the fighting became more and more desperate. And I shall always remember this about Albert Ball. About three weeks before he was killed, he was so badly shot up that his rigger considered that there were ninety-seven separate bullet tracks through the plane, and the pad for the back of his head was completely blown away. It made not the slightest difference to him: we rigged him up with another machine. As a matter of fact, General Trenchard sent word down to the squadron that he thought Albert Ball should go home on leave for a rest; but Ball decided that the circumstances at the time were against that and that it was his duty to go on. His own machine, 'A', was eventually rebuilt and it was on that that he died in action.

C. K. Shaw (rank unknown)
Engineer Officer, Aircraft Depot, Royal Flying Corps

He had the reputation amongst us, at this aircraft depot, of being, 'Ball? Yes, he goes up and brings down a Hun every morning before breakfast as if it was just the order of the day.' Of course he didn't really do that but that was our opinion of him. And he was so brave, and so completely different – not exactly arrogant, I wouldn't say he was arrogant – from the young man that I saw sitting in my office on one occasion when my mechanics were repairing his SE5: some little thing they were doing to it. When I saw him, I said, 'Cheer up, old boy. What's wrong?' 'Oh,' he said, 'I've got a hunch I don't think I am going to last very long.' I said, 'That's absurd, that's absurd, you'll be here for a long time yet. Don't you worry.' He said, 'I don't think so, I don't think so.' Well, we got his machine repaired and he got into it and that was the last that was seen of him.

Air Mechanic John Boon
Telephone switchboard operator, 9 Wing Headquarters, Royal Flying Corps

The squadron went out at five-thirty. I wasn't on duty when they went out but I was on duty when they were expected back and it was known that there had been a disaster. It was said they had met a Flying Circus [a massed formation of enemy aircraft painted in distinctive colours] and out of the squadron only five had returned, and one of those who hadn't returned was Captain Ball. No one knew what had happened. The other men in due course turned up in hospitals, crashed, killed; but Captain Ball, no one knew what happened. Lewis reported going into a cloud with Captain Ball and when he came out the other side Ball wasn't there. After the war finished I learned that he had landed upside down in the German lines, near a farmhouse, and a young lady came out and lifted him out and he had a broken back and he died in her arms.

Captain Archibald James
Pilot, 5, 2 and 6 Squadrons, Royal Flying Corps
Ball was bound to be killed because he had absolutely no regard for his own safety; whatever the odds, he went bald-headed into the attack. He was therefore bound to be killed.

Major James McCudden DSO MC MM
29, 66 and 56 Squadrons, Royal Flying Corps
60 Squadron, Royal Air Force

James McCudden was awarded the Victoria Cross for 'most conspicuous bravery, exceptional perseverance, and a very high devotion to duty' between August 1917 and March 1918, during which period he accounted for fifty-four enemy aircraft.

Born in Gillingham, Kent, on 28 March 1895, James Thomas Byford McCudden had joined the Royal Engineers in 1910, becoming a member of its Air Detachment from which, in 1912, the Royal Flying Corps was formed. When war broke out he was an aircraft mechanic. After service in France as an observer and gunner he retrained as a fighter pilot and, rising through the ranks, became the highest decorated British Empire pilot of the war, receiving two DSOs, two MCs and a Military Medal in addition to his VC. He died on 9 July 1918 of injuries suffered in an accidental air crash.

Sapper Edward Bolt
Royal Engineers, Farnborough, 1909–1912
I was posted to the Balloon Section of the Royal Engineers in October '09. I went to Farnborough and I was trained as a winch-man and storekeeper for balloons. The two main civilian people there were the two de Havilland brothers, who were experimenting on de Havilland machines; they had their own aeroplane hangar, which could have held four or five

Major James McCudden VC DSO MC MM.

Q 46099

machines. And I remember James McCudden. The first day he came from RE Gibraltar as a bugler boy he went into the de Havilland hangar, switched on one of the machines and swung the propeller and the machine went forward and was only stopped by the doors, when he was sensible enough to switch it off. He was placed under arrest and I was his escort when he was taken in front of Captain Maitland. Captain Maitland said, 'Well, McCudden, this is a bad start to joining the Air Battalion, you should have known better. I know you haven't done a lot of damage, but I can't let you off. Ten days CB [Confined to Barracks]. March out.'

Air Mechanic James Gascoyne
Transport Section, 3 Squadron, Royal Flying Corps, Netheravon, 1913–1915

I was sent with three others to Netheravon where I joined No 3 Squadron; No 3 Squadron and No 4 Squadron were both stationed there. At the time they were living in tents and we stayed in the tents until the manoeuvres when we all went off. I had by that time been allocated to the transport section and I was second driver on a Leyland lorry.

One of the pilots was Sergeant McCudden, not the VC but his elder brother, and he was in charge of the transport section; he was a funny little man but he was very keen and he was rather inclined to be pompous. His brother, Jimmy, came to the squadron after I had joined – about a month after, I suppose – and he had just come out of detention because, in his keenness for flying, he had at Farnborough started up an aircraft and the engine had pulled him into the side of a hangar and broken it up.

He was always a very keen fellow. What I also remember about him was that he had the most wonderful eyesight. With a revolver or a rifle he could always find the target. We used to go on the ranges, firing, mostly for revolver practice, but now and again with rifles. And I think that this wonderful eyesight of his was one of the factors that added to his success as a fighter pilot. Later on, when we got to France, he could always spot a

German aircraft a long time before anyone else, in the air. I liked Jimmy very much.

Second Lieutenant J. C. F. Hopkins
Trainee pilot, Dover, 1917

In 1917 I was training at Dover when he was fighting instructor, I think, for the whole wing. He shared a hut with me – a bedroom – at Dover, just for a few nights. I really didn't know him at all well. He was quite patronising in a way but helpful: he knew I was only a youngster under instruction. We discussed fighting tactics sitting on our beds and talking as we were going to bed. That sort of thing.

He was very abrupt. He had the reputation of having a bit of a chip on his shoulder. Of course he was in the ranks before the war, he was a regular RFC man and he rose up, and I think this rather got him down. Looking back, I gathered from our conversation that he rather resented us young chaps coming in and posing as pilots. I think he looked upon himself as a professional and we were just ruddy amateurs. And I suppose there was a lot to be said for it.

He was a brilliant pilot. Absolutely outstanding. I had enormous admiration for his flying ability and I've seen him do the most hair-raising stunts round the aerodrome when he was demonstrating what a Pup [a Sopwith Pup biplane fighter] could do. His favourite one was to loop directly off the ground when he was taking off and continue looping. On one occasion he looped thirteen times from take-off, just straight off the ground, and when he'd finished he was about five hundred feet high. It was a wonderful piece of flying. And then he used to fly upside down: he'd go up to about a thousand feet, turn the machine upside down, just go round the aerodrome upside down till the engine stopped or something like that – and then he'd go on sliding – and next thing he'd roll it out and get the engine going again and away he'd go. Oh, he was absolutely marvellous, there wasn't a thing he couldn't do with that machine, and we all admired him tremendously.

And I didn't actually see it, but he was at Dover at the time of one of the Gotha Raids on London and, being a fighting instructor, he obviously wanted to go up and tackle these blighters. When the 'readiness' went it was the one time when I was put on home defence duty and I had a dud engine that they couldn't get started, so I never joined the flight. But he went off; he went almost mad rushing round. I believe his Vickers gun was not loaded, the belt wasn't loaded, but he had a Lewis gun on the top plane, which he used to fire. And he dashed round grabbing magazines of ammunition, all he could get from various mechanics, and stuck these in the wire round his cockpit and away he went.

Only afterwards we heard that he'd tackled this Gotha formation before it reached London and he'd dived in amongst them and managed to separate some of the machines and help to break up the formation. He then ran out of ammunition but continued to dive in amongst the formation, further dispersing them: a most outstanding and brave deed for any man to do. This was, to a certain extent, hearsay, but it was what we were all talking about on the ground just at that time on the aerodrome.

Captain H. N. Charles
Engineer officer, 56 Squadron, Royal Flying Corps
We were fortunate that, not very long after the death of Albert Ball, another pilot was posted to us: flight commander of B Flight, J. B. McCudden. Captain McCudden was the son of a regular army sergeant and he'd been extremely strictly brought up from a service point of view. He was punctilious to a degree; he was always very smart on parade; he was a man who kept himself extraordinarily fit and was a very good pilot. But far more than that, he was a shooting genius. And I think it is for that reason that he kept himself so fit, because he realised that the wonderful touch and eyesight that he possessed could only have their full use if he lived in training almost like a competitor for the Queen's Prize at Bisley.

It was just at that time that the SE5 became obsolete and the SE5A, which was a more powerful version with a geared engine, came into use.

Well, it was decided that Captain McCudden should test out this modified version. As time went by, McCudden and I developed this four-bladed type of SE5 and eventually the Germans started to send over high altitude photographic planes and it was decided that an attempt must be made to do something about it. So McCudden and I set about it and we developed his SE5 until eventually he managed to reach a height of 19,000 feet with it. Well, not long after that, he shot down three enemy photographic two-seaters at 18,000 feet, which was the greatest height at which, as far as I know, any successful action by an SE5 ever took place.

Lieutenant Thomas Isbell
Pilot, 41 Squadron, Royal Flying Corps
When McCudden came into the mess, his favoured seat was to sit on a table swinging his legs and sitting on his hands. Now, he was a nice fellow and a good-looking fellow and a young fellow, of about twenty-two, twenty-three. And he used to tell us how he'd led his patrol into a bunch of Huns and how many he'd got down. Lots of people might think that he was big-headed. In fact, the first time you'd see him, until you knew the man, you probably would think that. But it wasn't that. It was that he was brimming over with self-confidence.

The very thing that would strike you from the start, it didn't matter what job he did, was that, when he flew, he flew about three to five hundred feet above his patrol. Now, that may seem odd. It wasn't really, it was a wonderful thing, and he would lead his flight into a bunch of Huns and the flight would know perfectly well that they were as safe as could be as long as McCudden was over the top. He would lead them in and, if one of his flight was getting at a disadvantage with a Hun, Heaven help that Hun because he'd shoot it down: he had such marvellous shooting power.

I've seen McCudden shoot at targets, we'd all go up and we'd fire at the target but McCudden would come down and he'd tear the target to shreds. He had such a wonderful, wonderful way of shooting. He only had to fire a matter of twenty rounds and the machine used to fall to pieces.

You might fly along and fire two hundred bullets at a machine and the machine would still go floating on and not a bit of damage done apparently. So when McCudden was over his flight, everyone had every confidence that as long as he was there they were safe to go into anything. And what a wonderful fellow he was.

Lieutenant Laurie Coombs
Pilot, 10 Squadron, Royal Naval Air Service
Guns: we made no attempt to really take them on the range and line them up accurately and so forth, we left it to the mechanics. I don't think they fired them; they sort of squinted along – 'That's near enough' kind of thing. Many times you fired at aircraft, a lot of rounds, and nothing happened. Now McCudden, he was a marvellous shot with a rifle – they reckoned he could take a .22 and roll a can along the ground by shooting it – but he used to line up his guns very, very carefully. He'd open fire at an enormous range, at least far beyond what the other fellow, a two-seater, would do, so he was right out of range of the rear-gunner, and bring it down because he paid meticulous attention to the sighting of guns and all that sort of thing. He was a very good shot but he also looked after his guns.

Captain John Oliver Andrew
Pilot, 24 Squadron, Royal Flying Corps
McCudden was in my flight for a short time. Came out and did a refresher. Pleasant chap and very determined. A very, very devoted bloke out to kill Germans.

Captain Archibald James
Pilot, 5, 2 and 6 Squadrons, Royal Flying Corps
McCudden fought to kill and not to be killed, and it was a tragedy that he was ultimately killed in a most curious accident. He flew out from England to take command of a squadron, wasn't quite certain where the aerodrome was, landed on the aerodrome my squadron was on at a place

called Auxi-le-Château to enquire, and was told the squadron he was going to was only a few miles away. So he got into his aeroplane, took off, did a circle of the aerodrome and then did the conventional courtesy of doing a dip and a zoom, and his engine cut out at the top of the zoom and he was inevitably killed.*

Major Edward ('Mick') Mannock DSO MC
40 Squadron, Royal Flying Corps
74 and 85 Squadrons, Royal Air Force

A fighter pilot in the Royal Flying Corps and later the Royal Air Force, 'Mick' Mannock, as he was known, was shot down from the ground and killed near Lilles, France, on 26 July 1918. The award of a posthumous Victoria Cross, in recognition of his career and for his 'outstanding example of fearless courage, remarkable skill, devotion to duty and self-sacrifice', came in 1919, following representations from former comrades.

The son of a Scottish soldier, Edward Corringham Mannock was born in County Cork, Ireland, on 24 May 1887. When war broke out he was working in Turkey as an electrical engineer. Interned by the Turks, Mannock's health suffered so badly that he was repatriated. He recovered and was commissioned in the Royal Engineers from which he transferred to the Royal Flying Corps in 1916. Estimates vary, but by the time of his death he had amassed a tally of over fifty victories – probably more than sixty. He also received three DSOs and two MCs.

---

* Other accounts of McCudden's death at Auxi-le-Château claim that he crashed as a result of engine failure caused by a poorly installed carburettor.

Major Edward 'Mick' Mannock VC DSO MC.

Q 60800

Captain Gwilym Lewis
Pilot, 40 Squadron, Royal Flying Corps

When I joined it in December 1917 the squadron was in excellent order. It had done very well on its Nieuports. It hadn't developed during that 1917 period any particular star turn, but a great many of the pilots involved had done well and shot down Huns.

Then Mick Mannock broke through. He started badly, wasn't a very good aerodrome pilot, took time to get going, and then he really started to shoot down two-seaters and had other successes. Within a short time, by January, he had a total of twenty-one Huns, which was remarkable and outstanding.

He was a lot of fun. We remained friends right through after he'd left the squadron. My parents kept an open house in Hampstead and he'd visit there quite often and he knew the rest of the family. He was very musical, he liked to play the violin and liked to sing, and my family was very musical and I think he found a lot of common ground when he was working up to go out with 74 Squadron, which was his next important job overseas. He had very good humour, absolutely popular in the squadron.

He was a few years older. He'd been out in the world, he'd been out in Turkey working with British electrical firms out there, and I think he developed his dislike of the Huns at that time because he was put in prison out there. Eventually he got home and got his commission in the Engineers. His family were a military family; well, his father wasn't so admirable, but anyhow they were a very good crowd.

I remember, before he left us, Mick made a very close association with McCudden, who came down the squadron to meet with him and talk with him. The two of them were tactical experts. They worked out how they should handle the situation in the air. McCudden was particularly brilliant at shooting down two-seaters, which was a very valuable contribution to the war because they were the fellows doing the reconnaissance work and working with their army. And you'd see Mick also adopting tactics as to how to attack two-seaters and he was getting quite a few DFWs [German two-seater reconnaissance aircraft] and suchlike.

There were three great influences on the fighter side of the Royal Flying Corps. There was Ball, who was a fighter-type, pitching in and hitting everything he could see – although there were some skilled operations involved in that too – but a jolly good shot. Then came McCudden, with his thinking and attacking: very seldom had any bullet holes in his aircraft 'cause he was always placing himself in the right position. And Mick Mannock, who was a combination of that and the finest patrol leader that perhaps we ever had. He was always working with his unit, or regularly working with his unit, and they were all taking part in his attacks and he was putting them in the right position for an attack and so on.

Second Lieutenant Laurie Field
Trainee pilot, 74 Squadron, Royal Flying Corps
Mannock used to give us lectures and talk about air fighting. For instance, he would tell you how to attack a two-seater. You see, you would either come up against scouts, like your own machine, or you came up against two-seaters where the pilot could fire, through synchronisation, through the propeller; and the observer could fire, too. And he used to say, if you attack one of those, the safest place would be down below him and on his right. That's what he told us.

He was the life and soul of the mess. I well remember one day – the pilots had one anteroom and the instructors had another one and it used to open out on to our room – and he burst through and said, 'All tickets please!' as though he was on a bus, because he never approved of it. He thought that the pilots and those learning to be pilots ought to be together. Any little difference like that, he made a fuss about.

We used to worship him. We thought he was really the king of air pilots; we thought he was the absolutely ideal man for air scrapping. I think he was also a bit of a mechanic because I remember one day in the mess we all went out because he'd detected something wrong in the running of an engine. Now, I was never sufficiently intelligent to tell when a thing went wrong, but he knew it was wrong and he had the engine stripped right down and he found a bolt that was loose. This mechanic was responsible, it was his fault, and Mannock went very much off the deep end when he found that was it. But he could run an engine and note something a little bit wrong in its tune.

Captain Gwilym Lewis
Fighter pilot, 40 Squadron, Royal Flying Corps and Royal Air Force
I can remember Mick Mannock came over to my farewell dinner with 40 Squadron in July 1918 when I was due to go to Home Stations and brought with him two of his flight commanders from 74 Squadron, which was a nice compliment to me and our friendship. And I remember him telling McElroy [Captain G. E. H. McElroy MC DFC, a famous Irish fighter ace in the RFC and RAF] then, 'Don't throw yourself away. Don't go down to the deck. I hear you're going down to the deck, don't do that, you'll get shot down from the ground.' And ultimately that's what happened to him and indeed what happened to Mick Mannock too. Mick Mannock, in my opinion, had been kept out on the battlefront too long and he'd suffered in losing his judgement, as is likely to happen.

The Western Front, 1917–18

In 1917 the German army withdrew from large sections of the line in France and took up strong pre-prepared positions in what became known as the Hindenburg Line. In April, during the Battle of Arras, British and Canadian divisions had some success in assaulting these positions. Later that year, more huge offensives were launched around Ypres, in Belgium, where the fighting included the Battles of Messines and Passchendaele, and at Cambrai, in France, but neither side looked likely to break the deadlock. However, the United States' entry into the war in 1917 brought a massive input of men, materiel and morale on the Allied side. Hard-won experience in the key battles of that year also provided the British with important tactical and technical advances.

These additional resources and growing expertise only began to make their mark in 1918, but first, in March of that year, the Germans made their own attempt to deliver a knockout blow with a massive offensive against the Allied lines. After initial success, lacking focus and with the German army beginning to overstretch its lines of supply, the attack petered out. In the summer a fresh and effective Allied offensive began. On some fronts Allied troops made deep and rapid inroads into the open land behind the enemy lines. Elsewhere, especially along the Hindenburg Line and in efforts to cross a series of heavily defended rivers and canals, fierce fighting continued until the Germans were finally forced to seek an armistice in November.

Indicative of the scale and intensity of the fighting during this period, more than three hundred Victoria Crosses were awarded to soldiers fighting on the Western Front in 1917 and 1918.

Second Lieutenant Reginald Leonard ('Bill') Haine
1st Battalion, Honourable Artillery Company

Bill Haine was awarded the Victoria Cross for his inspiring example and display of 'superb courage, quick decision and sound judgement' during more than thirty hours of intense fighting near Gavrelle, France, during the Battle of Arras, on 28/29 April 1917.

His citation reads, '2nd Lt Haine organised and led with the utmost gallantry six bombing attacks against a strong point... capturing the position together with fifty prisoners and two machine guns.' An enemy counter–attack then pushed his party back, whereupon, '2nd Lieutenant Haine at once formed a block in his trench, and for the whole of the following night maintained his position against repeated determined attacks. Reorganising his men on the following morning, he again attacked and captured the strong point, pressing the enemy back for several hundred yards, and thus relieving the situation.'

A fellow officer from Haine's battalion, Second Lieutenant Alfred Oliver Pollard MC DCM, was also awarded the Victoria Cross in that action.

Born in Wandsworth on 10 July 1896, Reginald Leonard Haine – always known as Bill – joined the Indian army after the First World War and later won a Military Cross in Afghanistan. During the Second World War he commanded a battalion of Home Guard. One of the

HU 96189

Oppy Wood, France, close to where Second Lieutenant 'Bill' Haine earned his Victoria Cross during the Battle of Arras in 1917.

earliest First World War veterans to be interviewed by the Imperial War Museum – his testimony was recorded in 1973 – he died in 1982.

Second Lieutenant Bill Haine
1st Battalion, Honourable Artillery Company

Right at the start I didn't think that the war would affect me to any extent. As a matter of fact I was in an office in the City, I was an articled clerk to a firm of chartered accountants, and I was due for a fortnight's holiday and I went on that holiday just about 4 August. When I came back from that holiday I went back to the office on the Monday morning and a friend of mine phoned up and he said, 'What are you doing about the war? I've joined my brother's regiment, which is the HAC. If you'd like to come along, I can get you in.' So, sure enough, at lunch time I left the office, which was in Southampton Row, went along to Armoury House, which was at City Road, and there was this chap, my friend, waiting for me. There was a queue of about a thousand people trying to enlist at the time, all in the HAC, right down the City Road. But he came along the queue and he pulled me out of the queue and he said, 'Come along,' so I went right up to the front and into the gates where I was met by a sergeant major at a desk. And my friend introduced me to the sergeant and the sergeant said, 'Are you willing to join?' I said, 'Yes, sir.' He said, 'Well, how old are you?' I said, 'I'm eighteen and one month.' He said, 'Do you mean nineteen and one month?' so I thought a moment and said, 'Yes, sir.' He said, 'Right-o. Well, sign here, please.' And that was my introduction to the army.

For about a week we were at headquarters. We were kitted out in terrible old uniforms; it wasn't modern stuff at all. Within a fortnight we'd been inspected by His Majesty King George V and we went off to Essex, to Aveley, into camp. We were a battalion, I should think, about eleven or twelve hundred strong and most of us, let's be fair, had had OTC experience, we weren't completely green. I mean, we all knew a bit about shooting and parade work and that sort of thing, so we weren't completely green.

The rumour was that we were going to train for six months there and then go to Egypt, but we were at this camp for about a week when there was a panic one evening, when we were on the ranges, and they said, 'Everybody back to camp.' We went back to camp and they said, 'You're leaving tomorrow morning for an unknown destination.' Well, at that time we hadn't got proper rifles; we'd got the long rifle, not the ordinary service rifle. We hadn't got new webbing equipment; this white Slade Wallace stuff [Victorian-era webbing] arrived during the night and we hadn't a clue how to put this webbing together, you know, a lot of us. But at any rate, by about six o'clock in the morning, we were ready to depart and we did depart but without any by-your-leave, without any leave, without saying goodbye to one's family or anything. I remember that I wrote a postcard when I was in the train and chucked it out of the window at the station hoping that it would be delivered to my people at home: that was all. And we arrived that evening at Southampton – that was 18 September 1914 – and we embarked and, well, that was the start of things. I thought the same as everybody else; everybody said, 'It'll be over by Christmas and you've got to get out soon, otherwise you won't see anything.' But when we got into action, which was later on, October/November, one certainly changed one's mind when we found how well-organised Jerry was compared with us, and how thinly we were on the ground, of course.

That first winter, there were the regular divisions who'd been through Mons and that sort of thing and they were reinforced by a certain number of units such as ourselves, the HAC, and the London Scottish and the Liverpool Scottish and I can mention a few other London regiments. We had a terrific line to hold and it was a question of being never out of the war area. The usual thing was four days in the front line, four days in support, and four days in reserve, and you went on until the cows came home, sort of thing, like that. Unless you did a show, we never called it a battle, we always called them a show, and then of course things were a bit different. The winter of '14 was extremely hard, there's no doubt about that. We had no amenities whatsoever; it was just ditches, the trenches were ditches, waterlogged ditches, and one was often up to one's knees in frozen mud and you could do nothing about it at all except stick there. The actual fighting in my opinion was nothing like it was in later years of the war, in '16 and '17, the years I knew most from a fighting point of view, when of course the casualties and everything were terrific.

In 1917, the Battle of Arras started. It was Arras and Vimy, the Canadians were at Vimy and we were on the right of the Canadians in front of Arras, and that started on 9 April. Well, the division went in a few days later and went over the ground which the other divisions had captured. And that was a very hefty show as far as my personal experience was concerned, and also the division's, because we'd bumped up against the dreaded Hindenburg Line. As far as our little sector was concerned, the Hindenburg Line was lying between the villages of Oppy and Gavrelle and had terrific wire and a terrific trench system. The Boche were north of us and the dividing line between us was a light railway. It was a pre-war railway, I think, which ran from Douai or somewhere or other to Arras, I suppose, and this was banked up and the Germans had a terrific strong-point on this thing with several machine guns and all sorts of things.

We were out of the line for about two days and then we were told we had to go back again, but they said, 'Don't worry, you're not in the attack really. All you've got to do is to join up with the troops on your left' – who were going to do an attack where it had failed on 23 April between Oppy and towards Gavrelle. 'All you've got to do is to wait until they get into the trench, you see, and then join up with them.' At any rate, we went along to this blockade where the railway was, this strongpoint, and the attack started and nothing happened. We could see these fellows – fifty yards on our left the nearest of them were – they were a battalion of marines, Naval Division fellows, and I think a battalion of Fusiliers. But they, poor chaps, could not get through the wire. And then Ozzy, Colonel Osmond, our Colonel, said, 'Well, you've got to do something about it,' and I was told to attack.

Well, I tried once or twice. Well, my fellows tried. I mean, I'm talking about me but it was the company; I was no different from anybody else in the company. And eventually we got into this strongpoint and we found quite a lot of German dead there and also a certain number of German living – I think it was about fifty. We got them back and then we pushed along this trench as far as we could, but we'd got very few troops. Then the Boche started a really hectic counter-attack; he was coming up from his own support lines and getting round us. They were Prussian Guards and they infiltrated up the side trenches and I was terrified that we were going to be completely surrounded, so we decided that discretion was the better part of valour and we scrambled back – you can't call it anything else – to the trench where we'd started from that morning. That day they put in several bombing attacks and that sort of thing, but I don't know, we seemed to manage to hold out.

Well, the day wore on – it's very difficult when you're in a show like that to know the time of day or what day of the week it is for that matter – and eventually night fell and things quietened down a bit. I say 'quietened down' but you don't sleep of course; there's no question of sleep at a time like that. And I remember about some time before dawn – I don't know when it was – a runner came up and said the CO wanted to see me. He was in the same trench as we were, it was only a question of going a couple of hundred yards along the trench to the advance battalion headquarters, they were in a dugout there, and I went down there and Ozzy, our colonel, said, 'Well, Bill' – there was plenty of discipline but we were all on very good terms – 'You've got to do it again.' I said, 'Good God.' He said, 'Yes.' I said, 'Well, what about 2 Company?' – because 2 Company had been held in reserve round battalion headquarters the whole time and they were a company intact, you see. I shall never forget him: he said, 'Bill, I dare not risk it. You've got to do it.' So I said, 'Very good, sir,' or words to that effect, and went back.

Well, at dawn we managed to scrape a couple of mortars, Stokes mortars, from somewhere – where they came from, I don't know – and they were some distance behind us of course because we were far too close to the Germans, but they bunged in a few rounds. I thought it was a completely forlorn business. Then we did exactly the same exercise as we did before, we fanned out as far as we could to the wire. And just when these people were mortaring, a big German got up out of the enemy trench – he'd got a bandage round his head, he hadn't got a helmet – and he started running, zigzag, backwards. And the chap next to me got his rifle and aimed at him and for some reason or other – I don't know why – I said, 'Don't.' And I'm certain that that fellow started a panic because, when we went there, these Prussian Guards put up their hands and we captured about fifty of them again, and that was that.

Ozzy immediately sent 2 Company through us with Alfred Pollard. He'd been out since 1914; a terrific individualist, he'd already got a DCM up at Ypres and collected two MCs, he was one of these fire-eating types. And he went through and we passed bombs along to him and his company and he more or less left his company behind and just depended upon half a dozen stalwarts and he bombed and he took two or three hundred yards of trench right the way along. If you were a good bomber with a Mills you could out-range the German stick bomb by a yard or two, five yards possibly, and Alfred took them on and he really got them on the run. Then I had to extend my company out towards him, because we were so thin on the ground again, and he was right up at the danger end of things, towards Oppy Wood. But by the evening we had taken all the ground which these battalions were supposed to have taken on the morning of the 28th – this was the evening of the 29th and it was a two-day show – and that was that. We stuck there and that night we were relieved by another division, it was some Yorkshire regiment that relieved us, I think, and came out of the line. It was quite a show though. From a battalion point of view it was a magnificent show because every chap was a hundred per cent. Being in a regiment like the HAC was not a difficult job for an officer, because, I mean, it didn't matter if you were there or not, really. Any lance corporal could take over or any private for that matter and they were all equally good. So one doesn't take credit on oneself in the very, very slightest for these shows.

Well, we came back that night. I was completely dead. I remember being put on a horse but I can't remember anything more until I found myself in this field outside Roclincourt where we were going to rest and there were tents there. I don't know what hour of the night we got back, we got back some time during the night, and I was terribly annoyed because they woke me and they said, 'The general wants to see you,' you see, and I thought, 'Hell.' But at any rate this figure walked in and it wasn't the divisional commander, it was the corps commander, it was old General Congreve,* he was commanding XIII Corps. And he came and he said, 'Oh, you're the chap...' or 'You're the officer...' or whatever it was 'who was commanding the company which...' I said, 'Yes, sir.' He said, 'Well, tell me all about it.' Well, there was nothing much I could tell him. I said, 'Well, we did it,' you see. And then he said he wanted to see Alf Pollard, so he saw the two of us, and that's all we knew about it. But, oh, about a month later, I suppose, we were in the line and we'd come back to rest outside Arras and the news came through.

There was a thing called the XIII Corps Club and I don't think they had any booze at all left after this because we had a real party, they had the whole division there, and then we both came home in July and had an investiture at Buckingham Palace. King George V was a remarkable man. He had a wonderful memory. There were quite a lot of us at this investiture, there were all sorts of people there; I think there were about a dozen VCs altogether he invested. But when he spoke to us he spoke about the battalion chiefly and it was astounding his knowledge of the battalion and the officers in it, you know, he inquired after individual people; and I met him on several other occasions later on and he never forgot a thing. He never missed a trick, that man.

---

* Lieutenant General Walter Congreve VC (1862–1927), who was awarded his own Victoria Cross for his actions in 1899 at the Battle of Colenso, South Africa, during the Anglo–Boer War.

Second Lieutenant Frederick Youens
13th Battalion, Durham Light Infantry

Born in August 1893 and educated at the Royal Grammar School, High Wycombe, Frederick Youens was working as a schoolmaster and had just gained a scholarship to Oxford University when the First World War broke out. He served in the ranks as a medical orderly, being badly wounded in 1915, before being commissioned in early 1917. He was awarded his Victoria Cross for helping to repel an enemy attack near Hill 60, in the south of the Ypres Salient in Belgium on 7 July 1917. Wounded earlier in the day, he died from subsequent injuries suffered when carrying out the act for which he would receive the VC: picking up enemy grenades that had landed near his position and trying to throw them back over the parapet.

Captain Roderick Sutherland Forbes Mitchell
13th Battalion, Durham Light Infantry

In came Youens, wounded, and we had him in the dugout, dressing him. Then the old Germans came at us – who, we could see in the dark, were four or five times our strength – and Youens went to a Lewis gun post and I went amongst some of the recruits.

The Germans did manage to get a bomb into the Lewis gun post but before it exploded he picked it up and threw it out. But the second or third one exploded just after it left his hand and, believe me, we dressed him and sent him down to the dressing station but he didn't live to get that far.* Being in charge, I'd got to send a report in and, by Jove, I'd have loved to have seen Youens get a DSO, which would have been a lovely decoration for a subaltern. But about a fortnight or three weeks afterwards, the news came through: 'Posthumous VC.'

---

* In fact Youens died two days later.

I wasn't the centre figure. I wasn't Youens. I don't think I would have done what he did, not even in the heat of the moment. A nice lad. A real gentleman. Nothing aggressive.

Second Lieutenant Hugh Colvin
9th Battalion, Cheshire Regiment

Born in Burnley, Lancashire, on 1 February 1887, Hugh Colvin won his Victoria Cross during an attack east of Ypres, Belgium, on 20 September 1917 when he took command of two companies and led them forward under very heavy machine-gun fire. He then went to assist a neighbouring battalion, clearing and capturing a series of troublesome dugouts and machine-gun posts on his own or with his men's assistance, killing several of the enemy personally and forcing others – about fifty in all – to surrender. 'Later he consolidated his position with great skill,' his VC citation concludes, 'and personally wired his front under close-ranged sniping in broad daylight, when all others had failed to do so. The complete success of the attack in this part of the line was mainly due to Second Lieut. Colvin's leadership and courage.' Hugh Colvin survived the war and died in 1962.

Lieutenant John Raymond Mallalieu
9th Battalion, Cheshire Regiment

In the early part of September we got warned about the Third Battle of Ypres. [Our attack] started on 20 September: zero hour was at 5.40. The objective in my opinion was rather a stupid idea. We went down a slope, up a slope and before we got to the top of it was supposed to be our objective, which was all right in its way except that we had quite a lot of officers wounded or killed.

One of our officers, Hugh Colvin, got a VC. He took command of two other companies when their officers were killed or wounded and he organised the position that they'd taken. Then the Welsh on the right were held up and he went over with two other men, one was a man called Gerrard who'd been a company runner, a very fine soldier, and a third man who was killed, and took a couple of dugouts and about twenty prisoners and a machine gun or two which they hadn't been able to take from the front. He took it from the flank and sent various prisoners back.

Marvellous bloke, marvellous. Very capable and a very brave type, too. Before this occurred he came into my little concrete dugout one day and various odd shells were falling roundabout. While he was in there a shell hit the corner outside the dugout, on the concrete, which didn't do a great deal of damage but the place was lit by candles stuck in bottles and of course all the candles went out and there was a general air of fumes and so forth. The ceiling was covered with flies and when we lit the candles again Hugh Colvin was still sitting in a chair opposite and he just looked up at the ceiling and said, 'You know, that didn't even shake the flies off the ceiling.' A very calm character, with no nerves, no imagination, at all.

Lance Sergeant John Rhodes DCM
3rd Battalion, Grenadier Guards

John Harold Rhodes was born in Packmoor, Staffordshire, on 17 May 1891 and went to school in Newchapel before going to work as a miner. He joined the Grenadier Guards in 1911 and served for three years, then returned to work in the mines until he was recalled to the army as a reservist when war broke out. He was awarded the Distinguished Conduct Medal in May 1915 and a bar three months later and received the Victoria Cross for storming an enemy pillbox single-handed and capturing nine prisoners on 9 October 1917, near Ypres, Belgium. He died on 27 November 1917 from wounds suffered in a subsequent action.

Lance Sergeant William Ward
2nd Battalion, Grenadier Guards

Jack Rhodes had been wounded in 1915 and so had I and we arrived back in Chelsea Barracks at about the same time. That was the first time I met him. He was a reservist, he'd been called up when war broke out, and I met him and we palled up and we used to go walking about together. He'd already won the DCM and bar and he used to say to me, 'I'll get the VC – I'm after that.' Just like that! I never thought any more about that.

Then he went back out and I didn't see him again until I met him in the attack on 31 July 1917 when he pinched this bugle off the Germans and he stood up there blowing it. I ran across to see him and he said, 'Hello, Bill.' I said, 'What are you doing? Where did you get that from?' He said, 'Off a Jerry, just down below.' And that was the last time I saw him until I met him on his stretcher when he was dying from his wounds. He didn't know that he'd been awarded the VC.

Lieutenant Colonel John Sherwood-Kelly DSO CMG
1st Battalion, Royal Inniskilling Fusiliers

John Sherwood-Kelly was awarded the Victoria Cross for his actions on 20 November 1917 at Marcoing, France, during the Battle of Cambrai. When his men were held up by heavy fire at the bank of a canal, Sherwood-Kelly led his leading company across and then, under continued fire, reconnoitred the enemy's positions and, manning a Lewis gun, covered their capture by his battalion. Later he led a charge against further enemy positions and captured five machine guns and forty-six prisoners.

Born at Queenstown, South Africa, in January 1880, Sherwood-Kelly had by 1914 already fought in Matabeleland and Somaliland and in the Anglo–Boer War. During the First World War he was wounded and gassed several times, received the DSO for service at Gallipoli and in 1917 was appointed CMG. An outspoken man with a fiery temper, he was court-martialled after the war for a public attack on British intervention in North Russia. Later he stood twice for Parliament for the Conservative Party, again making headlines when he was accused of thrashing some hecklers, and worked in Bolivia and hunted big game in Africa. He died in London from the effects of malaria in 1931.

Private Harry Wharton
12th Battalion, Royal Norfolk Regiment

We had a new colonel when we got over [to France]: Sherwood-Kelly, VC. My God, wasn't he a bugger? Strict; VC; four wound stripes [two-inch brass stripes fastened to the sleeve, typically on the left forearm, to denote a wound]: God, he was a man and a half. Well, we'd always had these gentlemen looking after us till then; he had six of our boys tied up to the damned wheel the first week he was there!* God, he was rum. We were all terrified of this bloke. I had never seen anybody of our regiment tied up to a wheel until Sherwood-Kelly turned up.

But he was a bloody fine soldier, you see. I mean, he got a VC. He was held up in some battle, I forget now which one, and he said, 'Come on!' and he went and took a bloody bridge that was holding up the people ahead of him and went through. Oh, he was a good brave man. He terrified us because when the war finished he went to headquarters and volunteered to take his regiment to Russia, who'd just started the bloody revolution. I remember that so well. Terrible. I didn't want no more of it, I'd had four years of it, I'd had enough.

---

* This was Field Punishment No 1, which involved the offender being attached to a fixed object – often the wheel of an artillery piece – for up to two hours a day and for a period of up to three months.

Captain Cyril Frisby
1st Battalion, Coldstream Guards

Cyril Hubert Frisby was awarded the Victoria Cross for his actions while a company commander leading an assault across the Canal du Nord, near Graincourt, France, on 27 September 1918. His citation explains:

On reaching the canal the leading platoon came under annihilating machine-gun fire from a strong machine-gun post under the old iron bridge on the far side of the canal and was unable to advance, despite reinforcing waves. Capt. Frisby realised at once that unless this post was captured the whole advance in this area would fail. Calling for volunteers to follow him, he dashed forward, and, with three other ranks, he climbed down into the canal under an intense point-blank machine-gun fire and succeeded in capturing the post with two machine guns and twelve men.

By his personal valour and initiative he restored the situation and enabled the attacking companies to continue the advance.

Having reached and consolidated his objective, he gave timely support to the company on his right, which had lost all its officers and sergeants, organised its defences, and beat off a heavy hostile counter-attack.

He was wounded in the leg by a bayonet in the attack on the machine-gun post, but remained at duty throughout, thereby setting a splendid example to all ranks.

Born at Barnet on 17 September 1885 and educated at Haileybury College, he had been commissioned into the Coldstream Guards in March 1917. After the war, he and his brother, who had himself received a DSO and a Military Cross, worked at the London Stock Exchange where they were known by the nickname 'The Cowards'. Cyril Frisby died in 1961.

Second Lieutenant Wilfred Tatham
1st Battalion, Coldstream Guards

27 September 1918: what does that date mean to anyone now? Nothing. But it was the day that the biggest battle of the First World War on the Western Front was fought. On that day the so-called Hindenburg Line was smashed and on that day the defeat of the Germans was made certain. I was there, second lieutenant in a regiment of foot-sloggers; nineteen and three-quarter years old. I am not the hero of this story; I've never aspired to be a hero. My role in the battle was very simple, though not unimportant, rather like that of the man who opens the grand piano for the soloist.

The capture of the Hindenburg Line and the crossing of the dry part of the Canal du Nord was a formidable task. The job of breaking across the canal was given to my battalion. My part was just to find my way to a post in the front line through a network of our communication trenches, scramble out and move down into the canal, which was quite a short way, and behind the leading companies. I still have a slip of paper saying, 'The platoon will improve crossings on battalion front, collect prisoners, direct wounded.'

We were ready to move at 5am summer time. It was quite silent. No one was letting off a gun within hearing distance. A few seconds before zero hour one machine gun went 'Pop-pop-pop!' Then – here I quote from my diary, beginning with its appalling bromide – 'Suddenly hell let loose. Guns every fifteen yards. I stumbled along the trench. I remember laughing with the excitement. The guns made such a din. When we reached the front line, all was confusion.' There usually is with men like Christmas trees trying to pass each other in narrow trenches. In time we sorted ourselves out but it is difficult to give commands in the dark when you can only just hear a man shouting in your ear.

Well, we scrambled over the top and strolled down to the canal. What an innocent I was. I imagined our front companies far in front, whereas there were Germans still holding out only a hundred yards or so to our left.

My job, a mixture between that of a traffic cop and a tourist guide, was easy and pretty safe on the floor of the twenty-foot deep canal. But just on our left there was a bridge over the canal, it had been blown up and one half had collapsed on the German side, and behind a tangle of girders, concrete and so on were two machine-gun posts. They were called Rat and Mouse. It was thought that they had been abandoned; they had not.

Imagine the problem of crossing a dry canal filled with barbed wire, entailing scrambling or sliding down a twenty-foot sloping brick wall, fighting through the wire and climbing up the other side with machine guns not more than thirty yards away. Was it surprising that the front troops hesitated? But the company commander [Captain Frisby] did not hesitate: he knew that the whole operation involving divisions on right and left depended on the kernel of the nut being crushed; he immediately called for volunteers, leapt up and slid down the bank, followed by three equally brave men. Somehow they got through the wire and up the other side and the gunners surrendered. The company commander was an old man, he was thirty-three, and not one of those reckless unthinking youths who do not understand fear. This is the greatest type of bravery. As citations for medals always state, 'Devotion to duty'. He deserved his VC and so did the first volunteer,* who was killed later.

Private William Edgar Holmes
2nd Battalion, Grenadier Guards

Born at Wood Stanway, Gloucestershire, on 26 June 1895 and a former groom on the local estate, William Edgar Holmes was awarded the Victoria Cross for his actions in saving the lives of wounded men while under fire at Cattenieres, near Cambrai, France, on 9 October 1918.

---

* Lance Corporal Thomas Norman Jackson, 1st Battalion, Coldstream Guards.

It was at a time when British forces had broken through the German lines and were advancing at last across open country. 'Pte. Holmes carried in two men under the most intense fire, and, while he was attending to a third case, he was severely wounded,' reads his citation. 'In spite of this, he continued to carry wounded, and was shortly afterwards again wounded, with fatal results. By his self-sacrifice and disregard of danger he was the means of saving the lives of several of his comrades.'

Private Horace Calvert
2nd Battalion, Grenadier Guards
We got out into open country: green fields, no barbed wire, no trenches, nothing. It were beautiful to see it, the green. We'd been told the Germans were retiring and they weren't standing and you needn't worry much and should just keep going. The whole area was farmland more or less, all open country. It were lovely to see it.

It was an attack on a sugar-beet factory; a place and a wood called Cattenieres. I was going across a field of cabbages with the company and this building was fairly substantial. It was built like a tower, to allow traffic to go under and unload, and the Germans were up in the top, they had machine guns, and as soon as we got into the cabbage field to go forward these machine guns opened up.

Chaps were beginning to fall so the officers said, 'Get down and crawl!' Kept on crawling, a little at a time, and then stopping, 'cause as soon as you moved a cabbage you'd get the machine guns going. It took a long time to get through this field and into the sunken road. And when we got together they told us then about the stretcher-bearer of the company, Holmes.

What apparently had happened, he'd gone out to some of our wounded and he'd dragged one in. He'd been hit by a bullet but he went out again and got another one in and then he was hit again. And he went out the third time and he got it through the throat, cut the main vein, and there was no hope for him. Nothing could be done.

I was very sorry when we heard about him. He was a right nice chap. I knew him well. He was a chap about six feet, typical English person, fair hair, blue eyes. I knew him very well. Always a chap to have a joke with.

As a stretcher-bearer he wasn't supposed to carry a rifle, but if one of the chaps on the march didn't feel up to it and was beginning to falter a bit, he, as a stretcher-bearer, like a medical attendant, might go to him and give him a drink of water and then take his rifle. He'd help a chap, look at his feet as well after a march and try to patch them up if they wanted some attention. No, he was a very well-liked chap. He'd struck me as a chap who'd do his duty but he wouldn't risk any more than necessary. As a stretcher-bearer it's your job to look after the wounded, but he went out on his own.

Lieutenant Colonel Dudley Johnson DSO MC
South Wales Borderers
Attached 2nd Battalion, Royal Sussex Regiment

Dudley Johnson was awarded his Victoria Cross for his actions in France on 4 November 1918, seven days before the armistice, while in acting command of the 2nd Battalion, Royal Sussex Regiment, during the crossing of the Sambre-Oise Canal at a point south of Catillon. Under very heavy fire, which caused appalling casualties, he organised and led the assaulting and bridging parties to eventually effect a crossing.

'During all this time Lt.-Col. Johnson was under a very heavy fire, which, though it nearly decimated the assaulting columns, left him untouched,' his citation explains. 'His conduct was a fine example of great valour, coolness and intrepidity, which, added to his splendid leadership and the offensive spirit that he had inspired in his battalion, were entirely responsible for the successful crossing.'

Born in Gloucestershire in February 1884, Dudley Graham Johnson was educated at Bradford College and a regular army officer who had seen action in China in 1914, fought at Gallipoli in 1915 and, in addition to his VC, was awarded two DSOs and a Military Cross. Johnson stayed in the army after the war and retired as a major general in 1944. He died in 1975.

Sergeant Charles Lock
2nd Battalion, Royal Sussex Regiment

I met an officer whom I'd met a number of times on patrol. He disliked trenches, he preferred to walk about in no-man's-land. That was Lieutenant Colonel D. G. Johnson of the South Wales Borderers. The last battle of the war, which I think took place on 4 November, was the crossing of the Sambre-Oise Canal and he was the only senior officer left standing and he quietly led the men who got across the canal. The first ones were decimated, they were either killed outright or they were wounded and fell into the canal and were drowned, but the others got across, he quietly led them into a position where they could resist any counter-attack and for that he was decorated. I can remember him saying that although it was given to him as a personal decoration he would wear it on behalf of the battalion. He was a real cast-iron soldier, a man whom you would willingly follow wherever he went.

Lieutenant Colonel Neville Marshall MC
Irish Guards, attached 16th Battalion, Lancashire Fusiliers

Neville Marshall was awarded a posthumous Victoria Cross for leading his men across the Sambre-Oise Canal, at Ors, not far from Catillon, France, on 4 November 1918. 'Under intense fire and with complete disregard of his own safety, he stood on the bank encouraging his men and assisting in the work,' his citation concludes, 'and when the bridge was repaired attempted to rush across at the head of his battalion and was killed while so doing. The passage of the canal was of vital importance, and the gallantry displayed by all ranks was largely due to the inspiring example set by Lt. Col. Marshall.'

Born at Acocks Green, Birmingham, on 12 June 1887, James Neville Marshall had attended the King Edward VI Grammar School in Birmingham before setting up in veterinary practice. He had friends in Belgium and in 1914 joined the Belgian army, serving in the artillery and being several times wounded, before being discharged in 1915 as medically unfit. After a long convalescence he joined the British Army and fought again on the Western Front, where he collected further wounds and two Military Crosses before being killed in the action for which he received his VC.

An eyewitness, his former adjutant, recalled in 1971 that Marshall died while trying to cross on a duckboard floating on empty petrol tins. 'He was a character of guts and determination, he didn't fear anybody or anything [and] it was a complete tragedy that a man of this quality should have been lost at the end of the War.'*

Lieutenant William Burton Tobey
16th Battalion, Lancashire Fusiliers

Major Marshall was a very famous figure in the brigade. He'd been wounded nine times and he had a chest full of medal ribbons. He used to point to his wound stripes, he had nine wound stripes, and he used to say, 'Two stripes there mean a lot more than three higher up,' meaning of course that a veteran soldier who was still a private was a better proposition than a sergeant. That may be doubted but at any rate that's what he used to say.

---

* Statement by Lieutenant Colonel G. A. Potts in Lt Col J. N. Marshall VC file, Department of Documents, IWM.

Major (later Lieutenant Colonel) Neville Marshall VC MC who was killed in the action in November 1918 for which he would be awarded his Victoria Cross. His many wound stripes can be clearly seen on the sleeve of his left arm.

Q 82346

Major George Horridge
1/5th Battalion, Lancashire Fusiliers

He was a most remarkable chap. He delighted in saying that he thought he was the bravest man in the British Army. He rather enjoyed undressing to show some of the wounds he'd had. On one occasion he made a Military Policeman on point duty march up and down in front of him because he hadn't saluted him, for which he got court-martialled or warned. Another occasion he made some wretched chap who was going over the bridges over the Yser Canal march up and down because he hadn't saluted him.

There was one occasion when our own CO, Colonel Holberton, was in charge of the brigade. The brigadier was away on leave, I think he'd gone home, and the CO and Major Marshall were walking together when the officer who was now in command of our battalion was walking towards these two and a shell arrived very near and the officer who was in command of our battalion fell down – naturally, as I would have done – as the shell burst. Not so Major Marshall. Not so Colonel Holberton. And Major Marshall said, 'Get up. How dare you fall in front of the men? Stand up. Excuse me, Colonel Holberton, for reproving your junior in front of you.' Another occasion he left the front-line trenches while he was with the 6th, with the CO, and went to visit some place in no-man's-land and the only one to come back was Marshall who said he'd had a bayonet wound in the ear.

And finally I must tell the story that was told to me by a fellow called King who had been intelligence officer in the 6th Battalion while Marshall was second-in-command.

They'd got into a new part of the line and King, as was his duty as intelligence officer, had gone up with the troops early one evening to reconnoitre the line and find out as much as he could about it so he could report to the CO. He eventually got back in the evening and Major Marshall said to him, 'Well, King, have you been down the line? You've got to know all about it?' King said, 'Yes, I have,' and Marshall said, 'Well,

87

I'd like to go round too. We'll go round together.' So they started off down the line, and it was dark by that time, and at one point there was a post or something in no-man's-land which King told Major Marshall about, and Major Marshall said, 'Well, King, I'm going out to visit it. I don't suppose you dare come.' King said, 'Well, if you dare go, I dare go an inch further.' So Marshall said, 'Very good, King. Come on, let's go.' And they went out.

Unfortunately, on the way back, Marshall was taken with some internal bleeding from one of these many wounds he had received and they had to lie down in no-man's-land. Marshall thought it was very bad and he was telling King, 'You know, King, if I don't recover from this, I shan't mind very much, but I'm just thinking of little Albert. It's little Albert I keep thinking about.' Anyway, after a time he began to feel better and they went on, they completed their round of the trenches, and Marshall said, 'Now, King, we'll have some breakfast and then we'll go round in the opposite direction,' which they did. And then King told me that he went on leave and went to see Mrs Marshall and told her this story of what happened in no-man's-land. But it were all unfortunate because Mrs Marshall didn't know who 'Little Albert' was.

In the end, Major Marshall was put in command of the 16th Battalion, Lancashire Fusiliers, and a week from the armistice led his troops across a bridge, which was being heavily defended by the Germans, was killed and got the VC.

Private Frank Holding
16th Battalion, Lancashire Fusiliers
We had to go across this canal. It wasn't very wide. The Royal Engineers had built some small bridges to get across, had built about five or six, and our CO, Colonel Marshall, he was always leading the troops wherever he went. Anyway, he was first across this river at Ors, and he was shot clean through the head, and he received a VC for that.

There was more VCs won there at Ors and one was by a Lieutenant Kirk; he was an Oldham man. And I'll tell you who else was there: Wilfred Owen, the poet. He was killed there at Ors and he was buried alongside our colonel and this Lieutenant Kirk. They were buried at Ors.

Russia, 1919

Russia, 1919

Between 1918 and 1939, British forces continued to see action in small conflicts and campaigns around the world and ten Victoria Crosses were awarded. Four of these recognised acts of gallantry on the North-West Frontier, now Pakistan, and one in Mesopotamia, today's Iraq. The first five, however, were earned in 1919 in north Russia, where British forces had been sent to assist the 'White' Russian armies after the Revolution in 1917 had seen their 'Red' Bolshevik opponents overthrow the Tsar and withdraw Russia's forces from the war against Germany. Infantrymen received two of these; the remaining three went to Royal Navy officers for motorboat attacks on the Bolshevik fleet in the port of Kronstadt. One of these officers was Lieutenant Augustus Agar, whose recollections of his time in North Russia were recorded in 1967.

Portrait of Lieutenant Augustus Agar VC.

Q 68014

Lieutenant Augustus Agar
Royal Navy

For much of the First World War, Augustus Agar had served in the pre-Dreadnought battleship, HMS *Hibernia,* in which he saw action in the Dardanelles. Later he served in Coastal Motor Boats (CMBs), which were three-man vessels, very fast and armed with torpedoes, and saw action in the Zeebrugge Raid in 1918 and in attacks on German patrol craft along the Belgian coast.

Based at Osea Island, Essex, Agar was still working with Coastal Motor Boats when, at the end of the war, he was approached by Britain's Secret Intelligence Service to assist in ferrying British secret agents back and forth across the Baltic Sea from Finland to Estonia and the Soviet Union. This was at the time when the British and other western powers, alarmed by the Russian Revolution of 1917, were seeking to confront the fledgling Soviet state and support its anti-Bolshevik opponents. The secret agents working in Soviet territory included the famous Paul Dukes, a thirty-year-old British agent who would be knighted a year later for his daring secret work, whom Agar would know only as ST 25.

By June 1919, Agar had established a secret base for his CMBs at the small Finnish port of Terijoki, close to the Soviet border. Operating in the same area was a detachment of Royal Navy cruisers and destroyers under the command of Admiral Sir Walter Cowan, whose tasks included defending the local sea routes and protecting the independence of Latvia and Estonia. Although he reported occasionally to Cowan, Agar was technically working for the Foreign Office, operated in civilian clothes and ran the risk of being shot as a spy himself if caught.

It was while engaged in this secret ferrying work, which involved crossing minefields and slipping unseen past enemy forts and defence ships, that Agar decided to attack the Bolshevik fleet at the nearby

Soviet port of Kronstadt. And it was for torpedoing an outlying cruiser before escaping under heavy fire on 17 June 1919 that he was awarded the Victoria Cross. He received a DSO for his part in a further raid on Kronstadt, in August, when two more VCs were awarded.

Born in Ceylon on 4 January 1890, Augustus Willington Shelton Agar had entered the Royal Navy as a naval cadet in 1904. During the Second World War, among other appointments, he commanded the heavy cruiser *Dorsetshire* and survived its sinking by Japanese dive-bombers in 1942. He died in 1968.

Today, the boat in which Agar operated in the Baltic and earned his VC, HM Coastal Motor Boat 4, is on permanent display at the Imperial War Museum, Duxford.

Lieutenant Augustus Agar
Coastal Motor Boat commander, Royal Navy
In the spring of 1919 I was serving ashore at Osea Island with our Coastal Motor Boats. These boats were fast motorboats designed by Sir John Thornycroft of a Skimmer design. We carried one torpedo, the bigger boats carried two, and our purpose was to operate in small groups called flotillas against enemy ships and torpedo them. In Russia, they'd lost all contacts with their secret agents and the head of our secret service thought perhaps that these fast boats of ours might help him in getting his agents across into Petrograd, which lay on the River Neva, and I was chosen to handle this job, and take two of our fast boats and their crews across from Osea Island to the Gulf of Finland.

Our boats were put aboard a Swedish coaster, ostensibly for Stockholm, but we offloaded the boats in Finland, all done in the greatest of secrecy and of course with the backing of the Foreign Office behind us with money and influence. We wore civilian clothes. We were told to, and actually did, forget everything about the navy. We took our own money with us: I was given a thousand pounds for our expenses, the first time in my life that I'd ever handled such a sum of money. Our intention was to take these couriers as we called them – they were our secret agents – from the coast of Finland and land them at night across the Gulf of Finland.

The Gulf of Finland is so situated that at the northern end there's a master fortress and at the southern end another fortress, even more powerful, called Krasnaya Gorka. The northern fortress was in the hands of the Finns, the southern fortress in the hands of the Bolsheviks. But it so happened that, on the day I landed a courier in the River Neva, the Estonians mutinied against their guards in the Red fortress at Krasnaya Gorka and hoisted the white flag. The Bolshevik reply to this was of course to send out units of the Red fleet in Kronstadt and bombard the Red fort from the rear. Because the guns of the Red fort only could point to seaward, the unfortunate Estonians in the Krasnaya Gorka fort could do nothing about it except take what punishment was given to them. And this, alas, we watched from Terijoki, from the steeple of our church.

It was a piteous situation. I knew where my duty lay. My duty was with ST 25: contact him in Petrograd or Moscow, wherever he may be, and then bring back my contact, Sokolov, and thus establish this train of communication with London. That was my duty and my job. On the other hand I knew that the Admiral [Sir Walter Cowan] was extremely perturbed about this bombardment of Krasnaya Gorka. His duty was the liberation of Estonia and with Krasnaya Gorka. With offensive intentions on the Russian part, Estonia was threatened on the whole of her frontier. Well, ST 31 [another British agent operating in the Baltic] offered to send a telegram to London and ask permission for me to attack these bombarding ships, which might stop them.

The bombardment went on all day and the next before a reply came back. The reply, to my disappointment, was, 'Your boats should be used for intelligence purposes only, unless otherwise directed by the senior naval officer.' In other words: 'unless otherwise directed by Admiral Cowan.' Well, that's where I saw daylight. The decision had to be taken and the Admiral was at sea, I couldn't communicate with him, but I knew from what he'd told me that he would support me in anything I did. I was absolutely certain of that. So I argued to myself that if I could get Sokolov back and thus establish our contact with ST 25, I could then take fortune in my hands and try to deliver an attack on these Russian battleships, which were quite close to Terijoki. Not more than, I would say, a matter of twenty miles, if that.

The bombardment continued and then came the day for me, as arranged, to bring Sokolov back. Everything went exactly as before. Tension terrific, of course. Hard for me to explain it, one can only imagine one's feelings oneself, but at the same time a certain amount of exhilaration. One felt, at least I felt, that one had a mission to perform, and I was doing it. And we got to the place on the River Neva about the same time, two o'clock in the morning, looked around, nothing to be seen. The waiting in cases like this is appalling. Waited. Five minutes. Ten minutes. Each minute seems an hour. And then I heard a low, what you might call, wail, and the sound of oars: yes, it was him. Then the three flashes – our secret signal. And within a minute, two minutes, three minutes, perhaps, he was alongside, dead beat. The story would come later, the thing was to get him and the little dinghy on board, start up the engine again and away, back through the chain of forts. We successfully accomplished this back to Terijoki, so my mission was finished, accomplished. Now I felt I was more free to give attention to these bombarding ships.

Next day there seemed a lull. We climbed to our church steeple but there seemed to be a pall of smoke, heavy smoke, lying all over Kronstadt. No bombarding ships appeared to be there; they'd gone obviously back to harbour. What had happened? Later on in the day the armoured cruiser, *Oleg*, came out, and in the afternoon started a slow bombardment. It went steadily on till six, seven, eight o'clock in the evening; there was no respite. Well, I decided myself, here was my target and I'd go in and have a crack at it anyway.

I left at slow speed, very slow speed, across the minefield, round about midnight, by which time it was pretty well dark. My crew consisted of Hampsheir, the midshipman; Beeley, the faithful Beeley, the mechanic;

and myself: no one else. We wore our uniforms and I had my little White Ensign which we flew in the boat.

I didn't want to go too fast because of the bow wave, the one thing that would give us away, so I kept a fairly slow speed until I reached the lighthouse, Tolbukhin lighthouse, and it was not far from this lighthouse where the cruiser was anchored. She was guarded by patrol craft and also I first of all had to get through a screen of destroyers. I chose a gap between two destroyers and went for that. Everything had to be done at, say, between twelve and twenty knots so as not to produce a bow wave of any size at all.

Unfortunately, just as I was going through the gap between the two destroyers, I had an accident in the boat. I must explain. The torpedo in our CMBs is fired astern, it's pushed astern by a ram, and then, once it's in the water, an automatic device in the torpedo picks up the speed and revs the propellers at high speed so the torpedo rapidly gathers speed and passes the boat. One must be careful then, immediately after firing, to get out of its way. There's a definite risk of the torpedo hitting the boat if you don't – this must always be expected. The firing of the torpedo, however, is done by means of a cartridge, a cordite cartridge, which is put in a chamber and fired. That cartridge pushes the ram, the ram pushes the torpedo and that's how the business is done. Just after I'd given the order 'Get ready' to the midshipman whose job it is to get the torpedo ready and put the cartridge in, something must have gone wrong as he fired the torpedo by mistake. The whole boat shuddered; it's the most dreadful thing. Luckily again my luck was in, I had the preventive stops down: to prevent the torpedo from moving in the trough, these iron stops are fitted, and, although the cartridge fired the ram, the ram couldn't overcome the stops and the torpedo remained in the boat. It only remained therefore for a new cartridge to be put in. Not so easy when one's at high tension and a choppy sea is running, not a big sea but quite choppy enough to make things most uncomfortable and unpleasant. This occurred just when we were in the middle of passing the destroyers and there was nothing to do but to stop the boat while we reloaded. So I said, as calmly as I could, to Hampsheir and Beeley, 'Put in the spare cartridge and reload.' It seemed to me that that reloading process must have taken three hours, I don't suppose it took three minutes, but they did it between the two of them. And I was so sorry for Hampsheir. One could see he was so shaken. I don't think he ever recovered from the shock.

Anyway, we reloaded the cartridge and I went on to my target. I got the target, as far as I could judge, in my sights and fired at her at a range which I calculated to be between five hundred and a thousand yards, the ideal range for the purpose. And once it was fired I had to get out of the way, turn the boat round and crack on, full speed, and make my getaway. Unfortunately I had been seen before firing the torpedo and had drawn the fire of everything on all sides. I was like a rabbit being chased by all and sundry. There was hardly time to think or look, I had to concentrate on my boat, which now, going at high speed, was sufficient protection against the firing of the forts. I could hear the shells whistling overhead and it's not very pleasant when they splash and one has to send the boat through the column of water the splash throws up, but we got away. I looked behind and I saw that our torpedo had found the mark: a large column of smoke, almost as high as the mast of the ship, shot up, and a big, red flash. There was no doubt about it: I'd hit the target. But whether she would sink or whether she would swim was another matter.

My job now was to get home. Well, we shaped a course, not to Terijoki but out of the Gulf of Finland. I did this so as to leave the impression with the forts and the guard ships that we came from Björkö [an island] and not from the mainland, otherwise I'd be giving the secret of our secret base away. And only when we were well clear, twenty miles at least, did I turn inland and fetch up again at our home in Terijoki.

Next day, as soon as it was daylight, we again went to our observation post at the top of the church steeple. We were there most of the day, watching what was going on, and I could see nothing. The two Russian battleships hadn't come out; they'd remained in Kronstadt obviously. A pall of smoke was hanging over the whole island. All sorts of rumours were flying around that Kronstadt had surrendered. In fact one small boat, one of their patrol craft, did reach Björkö and surrender to the admiral.

Nearby was attached a small Finnish airbase, there were three or four planes. I went there, got a very fine pilot, and he flew me over. I said, 'I want to go as close as you can to Tolbukhin lighthouse,' which he did, and there I could see the *Oleg* at the bottom, quite clearly through the water, lying on her side. She was sunk. That was sufficient for me.

Later I got a boat to the flagship and I reported to the admiral what I'd done. Nobody could have been more pleased, more delighted. He wanted every word, every detail. I told him and he said. 'I admire you, not only your courage but the responsibility you took on yourself. You have helped me, because the Bolshevik fleet will know now that I have a sting and I can use this sting if I want to, whereas before they knew I had only light cruisers to use against their capital ships. Now I have a bit more.'

The reaction at the Admiralty, at first, I understand, was not very good. I am told that it was not very popular as there was a strong party in England, particularly the Labour Party, who, with a certain amount of justification on their side, were using the slogan 'Hands off Russia'. The Admiralty were in a cleft stick: on the one side, politically, they had 'Hands off Russia', and on the other they had the essential purpose of the British fleet, which was to secure the independence of the Baltic States.

The immediate effect upon myself of what I'd done was that I was proud and glad for our team that we'd achieved, first of all, success, and that we'd got out of the way. We'd done something for the fleet, at least the Admiral told me we had, so much so that to my surprise I received a signal from him that I'd been awarded the Victoria Cross. That's what I got it for. And anyone who's been awarded a medal like that will know what it means.

The Second World War

NORTH-WEST EUROPE, 1940

On 3 September 1939, after Hitler's unprovoked invasion of Poland two days before, Britain and France declared war on Nazi Germany. As in the First World War, a British force was sent swiftly to the Continent. This time, however, months would pass – a period that came to be called the Phoney War – before serious fighting finally broke out when the Germans swept into France and the Low Countries on 10 May 1940.

The defending British, French and Belgian forces proved ill-prepared to meet Germany's new *Blitzkrieg* style of formidable and fast-paced warfare and were soon in retreat. By July 1940, having pulled its surviving soldiers out of France via Dunkirk and with its Continental allies having fallen, Britain with its Empire stood defiant but alone. That month the German *Luftwaffe* began aerial attacks on Britain to prepare the way for an invasion and beat the country into submission. These were met with fierce resistance, most decisively from the fighter pilots of the Royal Air Force, and by the late autumn, having failed to secure aerial superiority, the Germans shelved their invasion plans.

Second Lieutenant Richard Annand
2nd Battalion, Durham Light Infantry

The first Victoria Crosses of the Second World War went to officers of the Royal Navy for gallantry during the Norwegian campaign in April and May 1940. The RAF's first VCs were awarded posthumously to the two-man crew of a Fairey Battle aircraft for an attack on the Albert Canal in Belgium on 12 May. The first army action of the war to result in the award of a Victoria Cross was performed, also in Belgium, by Lieutenant Richard Annand on 15–16 May, shortly after the Germans launched their assault on the Low Countries and France.

Annand was in position with his platoon on a bank of the River Dyle, east of Brussels, when German troops arrived on the opposite side and attempted to send a party to repair a blown bridge. His citation reads:

Second Lieutenant Annand attacked this party, but when ammunition ran out he went forward himself over open ground, with total disregard for enemy mortar and machine-gun fire. Reaching the top of the bridge, he drove out the party below, inflicting over twenty casualties with hand grenades. Having been wounded he rejoined his platoon, had his wound dressed, and then carried on in command.

During the evening another attack was launched and again Second Lieutenant Annand went forward with hand grenades and inflicted heavy casualties on the enemy.

When the order to withdraw was received, he withdrew his platoon, but learning on the way back that his batman was wounded and had been left behind, he returned at once to the former position and brought him back in a wheelbarrow, before losing consciousness as the result of wounds.

HU 2124

Second Lieutenant Richard Annand VC.

Born in South Shields on 5 November 1914 and educated at Pocklington School in the East Riding, Richard Wallace Annand was the son of an officer of the Royal Naval Division who would be killed the following year at Gallipoli. Severely deafened in the action that earned him his Victoria Cross, Annand was never again fit for active service and was invalided out of the army in 1948. He devoted much of his later life to helping the disabled and died in 2004.

Second Lieutenant Richard Annand
2nd Battalion, Durham Light Infantry

I was on the Supplementary Reserve when the war started. The function of the Supplementary Reserve was to fill the vacancies for junior officers in the regular battalion in the event of war, and so, as soon as the war began, I went straight to the Second Battalion who I'd done my training with the previous year. I was very enthusiastic. I felt that it justified all the training that one had attempted to do and it was certainly a chance to try to make some little contribution towards the task of defeating the enemy.

Having rejoined the battalion at Woking, I went out with it, on 25 September, to France. We crossed to Cherbourg from Southampton and after a week we were transported by train to the Franco–Belgian frontier, where we remained during the Phoney War for some eight or nine months. While there we were engaged practically all the time in digging what was known as the Gort Line, which was the northern continuation of the Maginot Line.

On the evening before the German attack commenced we had been into Douai for the purposes of watching a show in a theatre. At the end of it we returned to Nomain and during the night I was called out by the company commander to take a detachment to go and search for German parachutists who were reported to have come down in the area. I took my platoon out and we didn't actually find any parachutists. It was possibly a false alarm, I don't know, but anyway we were very soon aware of the

German planes that were flying over. They had been over our position and bombing our rear areas, where our supplies were, further back behind the lines.

We then managed to get right up to take up a position on the River Dyle, in Belgium, which had been planned some time before. We were taken by transport from our positions in the Nomain area over the border, through Tournai and up near Waterloo actually: where we fought on the Dyle was within five miles of Waterloo. Anyway, we got up to our positions on the Dyle without any harassment from the enemy. We met a lot of Belgian soldiers coming back towards us down the line who had been up there before and we took over from them. Our company was on the west bank, with the Dyle flowing northwards, with the company headquarters and the other companies distributed in the area. We were told that the Germans wouldn't be arriving for at least another week. In fact they arrived the day after we did.

Sergeant Major Martin McLane
2nd Battalion, Durham Light Infantry
The River Dyle was a defensive position made by the Belgian army. It was a river with bridges across it and it had a certain amount of pillboxes and wired positions. We were at the foot of a valley and running across the river in front of us was a long bridge. I'd say it was about fifty yards long, it was a walled bridge with ornamental balustrades along the side, and it was about ten, maybe eight, yards wide. It wasn't a massive bridge, it wasn't intended for transport, but it was a straight bridge, absolutely straight, you could see straight across to a crossroads, a busy crossroads, and you could see all the refugees in their carts pushing past by the score, continuous rolls of them.

I saw our vanguard coming back, the lads who had been forward to make contact with the Germans. They said, 'Yes, they're there, they're coming up.' They'd had a bit of a shooting match with them but their job was to report that the Germans were coming and then get across this bridge. Then the Royal Engineers blew the bridge, with a terrific bang, so that they closed the road after the vanguard got over.

Next day the Germans appeared and the shooting match started proper. Their snipers had been out, shooting across, but now the German army proper came up in force. We saw them coming up so I had the mortars ranged on to this crossroads and I fired a couple of warning shots away from there, just so civilians would stop walking round there, to stop the flow of refugees. Then we started hitting this crossroads. We were firing HE [High Explosive] – very, very hard-hitting explosive shells – and they were very, very effective: when they dropped on this crossroads they cleared everybody from there for quite some time. We used to drop a stray bomb over now and again, just to let them know we were still watching that crossroads. We stopped a lot of German traffic that way. We done some good work, I thought, there.

In the meantime, this bridge had been cleared and the Germans had done an attack and they'd got into the riverbed. I looked, and it was too near to our own troops for me to try to drop bombs in. It was only seventy-five to a hundred yards in front of us and the killing power of a bomb is over a hundred and fifty yards, so I couldn't possibly drop them anywhere near our own troops. And then I saw Lieutenant Annand going forward with his hand grenades.

Lance Corporal James Miller
2nd Battalion, Durham Light Infantry
It was getting dusk and the Germans were trying to get a pontoon across the bridge: they were trying to get across. We had grenades there, like, and Annand, he had a sandbag, and he said, 'Put some grenades in this,' and I put about half a dozen in and he went out and he was slinging hand grenades at the Jerries trying to get the pontoon across the bridge. He came back again and I put some more in for him, some more hand grenades. I think he went out three times. He was a brave man.

Sergeant Major Martin McLane
2nd Battalion, Durham Light Infantry

How that man never got hit with all the shooting going on, I don't ever know. It was a miracle, really. I say this honestly, not because I know the man now and we're great friends. He ran across this bridge with his grenades, dodging here and there, ducking and skipping down, moving around, and he got to the edge of this bridge and he just unloaded his grenades and he came back. He caused *devastation* in that area. I don't know who was in there but you could hear them yelling, you know. Don't think that a soldier dies peacefully, they yell when they're hit, the wounded; they scream for their mothers, a lot of them; and you could hear the screams coming from the place of men badly hit. The dead wouldn't have anything to say about it all – they were out of it. And then the Germans attacked again and they got another bridging party in and he did the same thing again with his grenades. He went over again and attacked this position and he destroyed the German post there – it was reputed after the war that he'd killed forty Germans – and the Germans stopped all work on trying to support that bridge. He got wounded on his way back.

Lance Corporal James Miller
2nd Battalion, Durham Light Infantry

Then we got the order to move out. We had to get out of the position, we had to get out quick, and we went up a road and a roll call was made and Sergeant O'Neill, I think it was, said to him, 'Sir, your batman's missing. Joe Hunter, he's back there.' And Lieutenant Annand went back for him and he found a barrow in a barn, there was barn to the right of the trench we'd been in and he found a wheelbarrow in there, and he got Joe back, he wheeled him. That's why they called him 'The Wheelbarrow VC'. Joe was taken to some hospital but later on the hospital was overrun by the Germans and he was took prisoner, but his legs had gone and he died in a prisoner of war camp.

Sergeant Major Martin McLane
2nd Battalion, Durham Light Infantry

He found his batman and he put him in a wheelbarrow and wheeled him up this rugged track, and when he caught up with the troops he collapsed with loss of blood. Well, everybody tabbed on to that and called him 'The Wheelbarrow VC' but King's Regulations state quite firmly, 'An officer who hazards his life for to save a junior rank will not be eligible for an award.' It's the wrong interpretation of him getting the VC entirely, because it was for the brave deed of bombing them Germans when they were bridging.

Second Lieutenant Richard Annand
2nd Battalion, Durham Light Infantry

They saw I was wounded with blood all over and I was ordered by the adjutant into a vehicle to be taken to hospital. I was in hospital in Brussels and then put on to a train, which took me to a hospital near Le Touquet. I remember writing home to my guardian uncle saying that we'd had a go at the Boche and that the Boche had had a go at me and that I was in a hospital miles behind the line – as I thought. But the Germans entered that place the next day and the hospital was evacuated and I was taken on a hospital ship to Southampton.

I was in hospital for about a month after that and then rejoined the battalion, which by that time was reforming at Bridlington on the coast. I rejoined having no idea about the VC until August. It took some time, you see. I think they had to get witnesses and so forth. I don't really know how they work it.

Sergeant Major Martin McLane
2nd Battalion, Durham Light Infantry

One day I was drilling the men in a yard called Marshall's Yard, which opens out on the main road from Bridlington to Hull, and I spotted Lieutenant Annand. I had a lot of time for this officer. He had been wounded and I didn't know he was back with the battalion, and he's standing across the road so I halt the men, tell them they could smoke and I go across and salute him and say, 'Hello, sir. How are you? You got over your wounds all right?' And he got on chatting with us and I said, 'What are you doing here anyway?' If you can imagine a long high wall, like they have round the royalty's estates: he was standing with his back against the wall and there was a farmhouse further along [where the battalion had its headquarters].

And I got on chatting with him and he says, 'Well, sergeant-major, you might be pleased to know I've been sent here to wait for the news reporters.' I said, 'What for?' He says, 'I've been awarded the Victoria Cross.'

Now that's the first we knew about it, that he'd been put in for an award, and I was delighted for him. I said, 'Well, what are you standing here for, sir?' He says, 'They've had me in to headquarters and told me that I'm due for a VC, that the reporters are coming to meet me and that I should wait outside.' I said, 'They never sat you down and gave you a cup of coffee or tea or made you at home?' He said, 'No.' He was standing on his own outside! So I got the men around and told them about him, a lot of them knew him, and they were delighted to know he'd got the VC. But for a man who'd really fought and made history for the regiment, which everybody's so proud of now, to be left standing on his own in a lone country road with no traffic passing, just on his own till we went over and spoke to him…

Second Lieutenant Paul Armstrong
2nd Battalion, Durham Light Infantry
His ears were very badly damaged and he very rapidly learned lip-reading. Regrettably, his injuries were so bad that if another subaltern was drilling and Richard couldn't see by his mouth what order he was giving, he was caught out, and it was found that he couldn't hear and so he was sent to the training battalion, much to his annoyance.

Terribly popular, one of the nicest people one could ever meet. I think, without exception, everyone in the battalion tried to cover up for him as long as they possibly could, until it was obvious that it would be unfair on him to let him continue in a battalion that was likely to go abroad shortly.

Private James Watts
2nd Battalion, Durham Light Infantry
He was an excellent man. He was exceptional. He was well loved, was Dick, because he was a human being.

Lance Corporal James Miller
2nd Battalion, Durham Light Infantry
He was one of us. He was great. I admired him. He saved his platoon.

Captain Marcus Ervine-Andrews
1st Battalion, East Lancashire Regiment

The British Army received five Victoria Crosses in France and Belgium in 1940 before the evacuation. The first to be officially announced in the *London Gazette* was that of Captain Marcus Ervine-Andrews for his actions in holding back a German attack on the Dunkirk perimeter on 31 May–1 June 1940. His citation reads:

Captain Ervine-Andrews took over about a thousand yards of the defences in front of Dunkirk, his line extending along the Canal de Bergues, and the enemy attacked at dawn. For over ten hours, notwithstanding intense artillery, mortar, and machine-gun fire, and in the face of vastly superior enemy forces, Captain Ervine-Andrews and his company held their position.

MH 9417

German troops crossing the river Meuse during their advance through France, 1940.

H 2611

Captain Marcus Ervine-Andrews VC.

The enemy, however, succeeded in crossing the canal on both flanks; and, owing to superior enemy forces, a company of Captain Ervine-Andrews' own battalion, which was despatched to protect his flanks, was unable to gain contact with him. There being danger of one of his platoons being driven in, he called for volunteers to fill the gap, and then, going forward, climbed on to the top of a straw-roofed barn, from which he engaged the enemy with rifle and light automatic fire, though, at the time, the enemy were sending mortar-bombs and armour-piercing bullets through the roof.

Captain Ervine-Andrews personally accounted for seventeen of the enemy with his rifle, and for many more with a Bren gun. Later, when the house which he held had been shattered by enemy fire and set alight, and all his ammunition had been expended, he sent back his wounded in the remaining carrier. Captain Ervine-Andrews then collected the remaining eight men of his company from this forward position, and, when almost completely surrounded, led them back to the cover afforded by the company in the rear, swimming or wading up to the chin in water for over a mile; having brought all that remained of his company safely back, he once again took up position.

Throughout this action, Captain Ervine-Andrews displayed courage, tenacity, and devotion to duty, worthy of the highest traditions of the British Army, and his magnificent example imbued his own troops with the dauntless fighting spirit which he himself displayed.

Born on 29 July 1911, Harold Marcus Ervine-Andrews had seen active service before the war on the North-West Frontier. He left the army in 1952 with the rank of lieutenant colonel and went to farm in Devon. He died in 1995.

Captain Marcus Ervine-Andrews
1st Battalion, East Lancashire Regiment

I was born in Cavan, in Ulster, in Ireland. My father was a bank official and the family lived very much a country life; we always lived in the country rather than in towns. And from an early age, I don't quite know why, I suppose the influence of the First World War, I thought I'd like to be a soldier.

I went to school at Stoneyhurst in Lancashire and after that I went to Sandhurst and joined the East Lancashires. The East Lancashire Regiment had looked after the Officers Training Corps at Stoneyhurst and I'd been very much associated with the regiment. And apart from that we had quite a number of men from my area of Ireland who were in the regiment, there were quite a number of families who'd had army connections in the area, and it was like going home in many ways.

I'd been abroad for seven or eight years and I was due for eight months' leave and I'd just come home and was fishing in the west of Ireland when the war broke out. I was due to go up to fish for salmon in Lapland and the War Office wouldn't allow me to go, so I realised something serious must be happening. Shortly after that I got a telegram telling me to report to the home service battalion in Northern Ireland.

We went across to France in about March or April 1940. We went down first of all to an area near Paris and from there we moved up to Armentières and we stayed there until the balloon went up on 10 May. Then we moved up to Tournai where we took up a defensive position to wait for the Germans, who arrived to meet us on 20 May, and from that point we fought a rearguard action right back to the beach at Dunkirk. Then we were ordered to go back and take up a position on the Canal de Bergues, which, I suppose, was the perimeter. I went up there on the evening of 31 May to relieve D Company of my regiment.

We were very short of ammunition, because we had been told to abandon all our heavy vehicles on the way back and we were ready to embark at Dunkirk when we were suddenly whipped up and ordered back into the line, and as we went back we had to go along and search for ammunition: we were searching dead bodies to try and get ammunition. We knew we were in for an attack the next day because all that day D Company had been having it pretty hard. And at dawn on 1 June the enemy attacked.

There was a tremendous barrage of artillery and mortaring before and during the attack, which went on, I suppose, for two or three hours. During the course of the morning, most of my forward positions were pretty well all right, they'd had the odd casualty here and there, but one position was in desperate straits. They'd had a tremendous onslaught on to them, they were running very short of ammunition and they'd sent back and asked for urgent help. And I looked round, I had no reserves whatsoever, so I looked to the few soldiers who were with me in the company headquarters and said, 'Look, I'm going up, who's coming with me?' And I picked up a rifle and some ammunition and every single man came forward with me, went up and took over the position.

I suppose it was rather like going forward on a training scheme. There was a job you had to do, you were trained to do it, we had to get that position and we knew we had to get there, because if we didn't get there the Germans would have come across, so we had to go and fill the gap. Luckily I had some excellent men with me and we were able to do the job, I had a corporal and six or seven men. The terrain was pretty good: low-lying land, intersected by dykes, with a very, very, very few farm buildings here and there and a few folds in the ground, but a very open area, which gave me personally a very good field of fire. We could see quite a lot of them; they were right out in the open when we got into this forward position.

Lieutenant Joe Cetre
1st Battalion, East Lancashire Regiment
He dashed off and I saw him dash off. He said, 'Look after things' – I was his second-in-command – 'I'm off to the forward section.' And I remember him slinging his rifle and away. The barn that contained the section

was blazing, the roof anyhow, but without any regard to himself at all he clambered up and from his vantage point there he saw the German first line coming and picked off seventeen of them with his rifle. But he was a crack shot and shooting and fishing were his passions and he put his shooting nous to very good purpose and that put a bit of a stop to them.

Captain Marcus Ervine-Andrews
1st Battalion, East Lancashire Regiment

We were so short of ammunition that I took it on myself to do most of the firing. Even though I say it myself, I was an exceptionally good shot and my men knew it and they realised it was much better that I should do the shooting rather than waste ammunition. It was all very, very quick. You're firing ammunition and if you fire accurately and you hit men the others are discouraged. It's when you fire a lot of ammunition and you don't do any damage that the other chaps are very brave and push on; but when they're suffering severe casualties they are inclined to stop, or, as in this case, they move round to the flanks. Because you've no point in going up and getting a bloody nose if you can avoid it.

Private Frank Curry
1st Battalion, East Lancashire Regiment

They sometimes made an attempt, where the trees were thicker, to come over in little rubber boats and we repulsed them, it was as simple as that. We just riddled them like stupid. They were like suicide squads. This went on for hours, hours. Andrews spent a lot of the time on top of the barn, on top of the straw, and he could see and shout. 'There's enemy troops coming on the far left! On the far right!' It was advance warning to us. Over on the right were small groups who Andrews took care of, if I'm not mistaken. It was like a shooting gallery to him. You'd see one or two fall on their own, they weren't machine-gunned, and we realised it was probably Marcus picking them off, being a good shot. Odd ones were dropping without the burst of machine-gun fire.

Captain Marcus Ervine-Andrews
1st Battalion, East Lancashire Regiment
We had no dive-bombing but they were shelling us and mortaring us the whole time: I think most of the casualties I had were the result of mortar bombs or shells. Then I eventually realised that we were getting desperately short of ammunition, so I gathered up all the ammunition and I sent away all my surplus men and I kept eight men with me and I kept a Bren gun carrier to get away on. We then held a final little position from which we held up the Germans for as long as we could.

When I came to get away, I had two wounded men and my intention was to tell them to stay there because the Germans could look after them better than we could, but they said they would like to be evacuated. I said, 'All right,' and I looked at my other men and I said that we'd put the wounded men on the carrier that we'd kept for ourselves. My men were quite happy, there were no qualms about it, and I said, 'We'll make our way as best we can.' I got my men into the canal and we waded back and that was that.

Lieutenant Joe Cetre
1st Battalion, East Lancashire Regiment
[Colonel] Pendlebury was at the checkpoint to see the companies through into Dunkirk proper, and Marcus, with his ragged little band – unwashed, unshaved, stinking – marched past the CO and Marcus gave the order to march to attention. They did it as if they were on parade and that indicates their morale. I think they were rather proud of themselves having done what they did.

Captain Marcus Ervine-Andrews
1st Battalion, East Lancashire Regiment
We got back into Dunkirk itself, we found a good safe cellar to sit in and we reported to the CO. We were told to wait and in due course we were told that a destroyer was coming along and that we were to go to the end of the pier and get on it and that was it. I was flat out until somebody

woke me up and said, 'You're in England.' I was absolutely flat out. I'd been in constant action for ten or eleven days with very little sleep.

The VC was quite a bolt out of the blue to me. I was sitting in a restaurant about 29 July, some six to eight weeks afterward, and it appeared on the nine o'clock news. I was of course completely shaken, surprised.

Lieutenant Joe Cetre
1st Battalion, East Lancashire Regiment
Marcus was a very generous man, always, and he always said, 'Of course, my VC belongs as much to the men who were with me as to me.' And that has a certain amount of truth in it, because without their support and their co-operation that wouldn't have been achieved; but on the other hand, he was the inspiration. That's leadership.

Captain Marcus Ervine-Andrews
1st Battalion, East Lancashire Regiment
I always hold that men will go through hell – you can lead them through hell – but you can't drive them across the road unless they want to go. It's a question of building up confidence and knowing that you have confidence in them and, much more important, they have confidence in you. I was terribly lucky, I had a wonderful crowd of men, we worked as a team and without them I could have done nothing at Dunkirk, nothing at all, absolutely nothing. They were splendid. Their morale was high, they fought and fought, they gave everything they had to give; many of them gave their lives. I will never forget them.

Leading Seaman Jack Mantle
Royal Navy

The only Victoria Cross ever to be awarded for an act of valour in British waters was received by Jack Mantle during a devastating attack

HU 1914

Leading Seaman Jack Mantle VC.

by enemy Stuka dive-bombers on HMS *Foylebank* in Portland Harbour, on the south coast of England, on 4 July 1940. Mantle, whose award would be posthumous, was in charge of the ship's starboard 20mm pom-pom gun.

'Early in the action his left leg was shattered by a bomb,' his citation explains, 'but he stood fast at his gun and went on firing with hand-gear only, for the ship's electric power had failed. Almost at once he was wounded again in many places. Between his bursts of fire he had time to reflect on the grievous injuries of which he was soon to die; but his great courage bore him up till the end of the fight, when he fell by the gun he had so valiantly served.'

Born on 12 April 1917, Jack Foreman Mantle had been brought up and schooled in Southampton and joined the navy at the age of sixteen. Before the action in Portland, while on convoy protection duty, he had already received a mention in dispatches for his gunnery aboard a French ship under attack, becoming one of the first naval gunners to have brought down an enemy aircraft.

Able Seaman Ronald Walsh
HMS *Foylebank* (Royal Navy anti-aircraft ship)

The captain cleared the lower deck and said, 'Right lads, our job from now on is that we're going to be at Portland as a harbour defence ship. We're going to be moored in Portland Harbour very close to the docks so that we are an anti-aircraft ship for Portland until they can build up their own defences.' So off we went down to Portland.

Foylebank looked like a big merchant ship. At the base of her she was long, big, and of course the upper deck, the derricks and all that lot, were gone. Some of the holds were retained, others were mess decks, and the whole of the upper deck was built up to take four anti-aircraft mountings plus multiple pom-poms, starboard and port sides, plus 0.5 machine guns – we had the lot.

My action station was on the starboard gun of X mounting, which was 3.5 ack-ack, down the stern end about twenty feet above the deck. I was the range-setter. On 4 July, I and my mate, who was on X gun with me, we'd scrubbed out the mess, it was all nice and clean, the whole mess deck was bright and shiny, and then all of a sudden they sounded Action Stations. And I looked at my mate and I said, 'Well, I suppose we'd bloody better get up there, hadn't we?' He said, 'What else? Let's go.'

He went out first and as I was stepping over the combing there was an almighty bang and I found myself flying across the canteen flat on me face. I got up, went back to the mess and looked in and there was all the hammock nettings burning; the double ladders that go up and down were all twisted with blokes in them; the tables that we'd just scrubbed, their legs were all twisted. It was a terrible sight. We went down the port side, we got about half-way down and they dropped one down the funnel and blew the side of the ship out and we could see the docks just out there.

We got down then to the aft end of the ship where the sick bay flat was, a big flat where all the non-combatants were mustered: writers, sick-bay attendants, wardroom stewards. Although they had action stations, they hadn't been able to get to them and they were all mustered in the sick bay flat. There was a ladder going up to X gun from that, a straight ladder up, and I said to my mate, 'We'd better make our way up there.' We're going up the ladder, I'm up and he's below, he's behind me, and then there's an almighty bang. They'd hammered one through the upper deck into the sick bay flat. Well, that cleared that lot in the sick bay flat, including the mate behind me.

I got up the ladder on to the upper deck and then I looked. The Stukas were coming down, mast-height, dropping their bombs. You saw them. None of my gun's crew was there. The guns were all bent to hell.

Then I heard someone shouting about and I went and looked over and there was old 'Badger' Ottley, a leading seaman, and he was going to town there, he had his gun going – he was the captain of X gun – and it was a sight. He had two crew there and the coconut matting around the gun was all on fire and he was saying, 'Give us some ammo! Give us some ammo!' and they were saying, 'We can't, we've only got that practice there.' And he said, 'Well, give us that then,' and rammed it up: a practice shell! There was a plane coming down and he wanted to get a crack at it and he poked this practice shell in and hammered that up. Whether it did anything or not, I didn't stop to see.

I looked over the front of the gun deck and I was looking down from about fifteen feet on to the upper deck, which was littered with bomb holes and bodies and all sorts, twisted metal, and then a voice shouted up, 'Anyone up there?' I looked over and it was the first lieutenant. I said, 'Only me, sir. There's no one else.' He said, 'Right, you'd better get down. We're on fire aft and we're going to abandon ship shortly.' He said, 'We're abandoning over the bows,' because the back end was all burning and smoking, and I got on the upper deck to the passage leading forward, it was about eight to ten foot wide.

I got nearly along to the starboard pom-poms and there was a body of men all piled up there. And I looked at them and the POGI [Petty Office Gunnery Instructor] was stood beside the pom-poms and he said, 'Go on, push your way through. Walk over them, they're all dead. Get up here, because I want you here.' And I got up there and he said, 'Right, stay there. Mantle's still firing and when he's finished we'll have to get him down.' And I stood by, watching, and Mantle was on his gun. There was a plane that had dropped a bomb and it had hit his gun crew and killed his gun crew and shattered his left leg, but he'd pulled himself up on the gun.

Able Seaman Francis William Pavey
HMS *Foylebank* (*Royal Navy anti-aircraft ship*)

I was up forward when the first bang and the first bell sounded, so I galloped aft, grabbed my lifebelt and tin hat from the chief's pantry, up the ladder, and I was having to jump over bodies to get to my action station on the starboard pom-pom on the ammunition hoists. Half of them were sprawled about dead, then. To me, the *Foylebank* sinking, it was like Dante's Inferno. I was only, what, eighteen and a half? And I just didn't believe things like that could happen.

The whole attack apparently only lasted eight to ten minutes. They reckoned there were about twenty-six bomb holes in the ship, which worked out that we were getting a bomb about every forty seconds, so it was all over before it started even though it seemed like a lifetime. At one stage, I always remember, someone screamed out 'Gas!' Because of the strength of the high explosive, they thought it was gas. All I had was a tiny scratch across my shin where a little shrapnel splinter must have gone across and yet there were blokes around me with heads off, arms off, legs off.

Jack Mantle, he was badly wounded. During the action he'd been hit early – I could see him – and three or four of the crew were down on the deck wounded or dead. One leg was shattered and he was down to a stump, the electrics had gone and he clutched a handle – you had a couple of handles and each revolution fired a round. The gun was jammed obviously: chunk, chunk, chunk, he just churned them out by hand.

Able Seaman Ronald Walsh
HMS Foylebank (Royal Navy anti-aircraft ship)
He was having difficulty getting the changeover lever on the top from electrics to hand, it was slightly bent and he was getting it bit by bit, at the same time cursing and swearing at a plane that had gone out over the bay, turned round and was coming back in over the mole. And he got the lever back at the same time as the plane opened up, they opened up together: him with four barrels of pom-pom and the plane with machine guns. What happened to the plane, I don't know, it just seemed as if it all blew apart, and Mantle flaked out on his gun. He'd been hit across the chest by the machine gun.

The PO sent someone up to help get Mantle down and then he said, 'Right, I want the rest of you to get the wounded and anyone you can into all these boats that are alongside and I want somebody to go down below with the first lieutenant.' I thought, 'I ain't going round picking up them' – our surgeon lieutenant was sat on a bollard with his guts in his hands – I thought, 'I'll go below,' so I went down below with the first lieutenant and we had a look round what we could. A lot of places were flooded. There was a couple sort of sat against the bulkhead; the first lieutenant went over and said, 'Come on,' shook their shoulders, and they fell apart, so nothing we could do there. We went back up on deck and by then they'd got Mantle down. I gave them a hand, we lowered him into a boat alongside, and we made our way up on the forecastle and went over, down ropes, into the boats that were waiting. They took us ashore, we all mustered in Boscawen, part of the dockyard, and then the postman had the mail, called out the names. You only got a few answering.

Flight Lieutenant James Nicolson DFC
249 Squadron, Royal Air Force

During the Second World War, only one Fighter Command pilot was awarded the Victoria Cross. That pilot was Flight Lieutenant James Nicolson, who earned the medal for his actions in the air over Southampton on 16 August 1940 at the height of the Battle of Britain.

Born at Hampstead, London, on 29 April 1917 and educated at Tonbridge School, Kent, Eric James Brindley Nicolson had joined the Royal Air Force in 1936 and been posted to 249 Squadron as a Hurricane fighter pilot in 1940. After recovering from the injuries and burns he had suffered when earning his VC, he was posted to India in 1942 and flew Bristol Beaufighters over Burma in 1943–44, operations for which he was awarded the Distinguished Flying Cross.

Nicolson was killed on 2 May 1945 when a B-24 Liberator in which he was flying as an observer crashed into the Bay of Bengal. He recorded the following account for broadcast in December 1940.

Flight Lieutenant James Nicolson
Hurricane fighter pilot, 249 Squadron, Royal Air Force
The sun was shining from a cloudless sky and there was hardly a breath of

Flight Lieutenant James Nicolson VC DFC.

CH 1700

wind anywhere. Our squadron was going towards Southampton on patrol at 15,000 feet when I saw three Junkers 88 bombers about four miles away, flying across our bows. I reported this to our squadron leader and he replied, 'Go after them with your section,' so I led my section round towards the bombers. We chased hard after them but when we were about a mile behind we saw the 88s fly straight into a squadron of Spitfires. I used to fly a Spitfire myself and I guessed it was curtains for the three Junkers. I was right and they were all shot down in quick time with no pickings for us. I must confess I was very disappointed for I had never fired at a Hun in my life and was longing to have a crack at them. So we swung round again and started to climb up to 18,000 feet over Southampton to rejoin our squadron.

I was still a long way from the squadron when suddenly, very close, in rapid succession I heard four big bangs. They were the loudest noises I had ever heard and they had been made by four cannon shells from a Messerschmitt 110 hitting my machine. The first shell tore through the hood over my cockpit and sent splinters into my left eye. One splinter, I discovered later, nearly severed my eyelid. I couldn't see through that eye for blood. The second cannon shell struck my spare petrol tank and set it on fire. The third shell crashed into the cockpit and tore off my right trouser leg. The fourth shell struck the back heel of my left shoe, it shattered the heel of my shoe and made quite a mess of my left foot, but I didn't know anything about that either until later. Anyway, the effect of these four shells was to make me dive away to the right to avoid further shells. Then I started cursing myself for my carelessness. 'What a fool I'd been,' I thought. 'What a fool.'

I was just thinking of jumping out when suddenly a Messerschmitt 110 whizzed underneath me and got right in my gunsights. Fortunately no damage had been done to my windscreens or sights and when I was chasing the Junkers I had switched everything on, so everything was set for a fight. I pressed the gun button when the Messerschmitt was within nice range. He was going like mad, twisting and turning as he was trying to get away from my fire, so I pushed the throttle wide open. Both of us must have been doing about 400 as we went down together in a dive. First he turned left, then right, then left and right again. He did three turns to the right and finally a fourth turn to the left. I remember shouting out loud at him, when I first saw him, 'I'll teach you some manners, you Hun!' and I shouted other things as well. I knew I was getting him nearly all the time I was firing.

By this time it was pretty hot inside my machine from the burst petrol tank. I couldn't see much flame but I reckoned it was there all right. I remember looking once at my left hand, which was keeping the throttle open. It seemed to be in the fire itself and I could see the skin peeling off it, yet I had little pain. Unconsciously too I had drawn my feet up under my parachute on the seat, to escape the heat, I suppose.

Well, I gave the Hun all I had and I gave him a parting burst and, as he disappeared, started thinking about saving myself. I decided it was about time I left the aircraft and baled out, so I immediately jumped up from my seat but first of all I hit my head against the framework of the hood, which was all that was left. I cursed myself for a fool, pulled the hood back – wasn't I relieved when it slid back beautifully – and jumped up again. Once again I bounced back into my seat because I'd forgotten to undo the straps holding me in. One of them snapped, so I had only three to undo. Then I left the machine.

I suppose I was about 12,000 to 15,000 feet when I baled out. Immediately I started somersaulting downwards and after a few turns like that I found myself diving headfirst for the ground. After a second or two of this I decided to pull the ripcord, the result was that I immediately straightened up and began to float down. Then, an aircraft, a Messerschmitt I afterwards heard, came tearing past me. I decided to pretend that I was dead and hung limply by the parachute straps. The Messerschmitt came back once and I kept my eyes closed but I didn't get the bullets I was half-expecting. I don't know if he fired at me. The main thing is that I wasn't hit.

While I was coming down like that, I had a look at myself. I could see the bones of my left hand showing through the knuckles. Then for the first time I discovered I'd been wounded in the foot: blood was oozing out of the lace holes of my left shoe. My right hand was pretty badly burned too. So I hung down a bit longer and then decided to try my limbs just to see if they would work. Thank goodness they did. I still had my oxygen mask over my face but my hands were in too bad a state to take it off. I tried to, but I couldn't manage it. I found too that I had lost one trouser leg and the other was badly torn and my tunic was just like a lot of torn rags, so I wasn't looking very smart. Then, after a bit more of this dangling down business, I began to ache all over and my arms and legs began to hurt a lot.

When I got lower I saw I was in danger of coming down in the sea. I knew I didn't stand an earthly if I did, because I wouldn't have been able to swim a stroke with my hands like that, but I managed to float inland. Then I saw a high-tension cable below me and thought it would finish me if I hit that. Fortunately I was travelling towards a nice open field. When I was about a hundred feet from the ground I saw a cyclist and heard him ring his bell. I was surprised to hear the bicycle bell and realised I had been coming down in absolute silence. I bellowed at the cyclist but I don't suppose he heard me. Finally I touched down in the field and fell over. Fortunately it was a very calm day: my parachute just floated down and stayed down without dragging me along as they sometimes do.

I had a piece of good news almost immediately. One of the people who came along and who had watched the combat said they had seen the Messerschmitt 110 dive straight into the sea. So it hadn't been such a bad day after all.

AFRICA, 1940–42

Fighting spread to North Africa after Fascist Italy declared war on Britain in June 1940. In August, Italian forces from Italy's possessions in East Africa then invaded British Somaliland. Before the end of the year, British counter-attacks from their own bases in Egypt had turned the tide in East Africa. By the end of May 1941 the Italian colonies of Somaliland and Abyssinia had surrendered.

In North Africa, however, the arrival of General Erwin Rommel and major German forces to assist their struggling Italian ally soon forced the British, after initial successes, on to the back foot. Battling eastwards from Libya, Rommel's forces crossed into Egypt in the summer of 1942 and the British retreated beyond Mersa Matruh, over one hundred miles inside the Egyptian border. Only in late 1942, with the British victory at El Alamein and the American-led invasion of Morocco and Algeria, would the Allies begin to deal fatal blows to Axis forces in North Africa, which finally fell under Allied control in the spring of 1943.

Captain Eric Wilson
East Surrey Regiment, attached Somaliland Camel Corps

Eric Charles Twelves Wilson earned the Victoria Cross during the
Italian army's opening attack on British Somaliland. The commander
of a Somali-manned Vickers machine-gun company, he succeeded in
maintaining his position in the Golis Hills and holding off the enemy
from 11 to 15 August 1940 while under very heavy fire. As his citation, printed in the *London Gazette* in October 1940, describes:

The enemy attacked Observation Hill on August 11th 1940.
Captain Wilson and Somali gunners under his command beat off
the attack and opened fire on the enemy troops attacking Mill
Hill, another post within his range. He inflicted such heavy
casualties that the enemy, determined to put his guns out of
action, brought up a pack battery to within seven hundred yards,
and scored two direct hits through the loopholes of his defences,
which, bursting within the post, wounded Captain Wilson
severely in the right shoulder and in the left eye, several of his
team being also wounded. His guns were blown off their stands
but he repaired and replaced them and, regardless of his wounds,
carried on, whilst his Somali sergeant was killed beside him.

On August 12th and 14th the enemy again concentrated field
artillery fire on Captain Wilson's guns, but he continued, with
his wounds untended, to man them.

On August 15th two of his machine-gun posts were blown to
pieces, yet Captain Wilson, now suffering from malaria in addition to wounds, still kept his own post in action. The enemy
finally overran the post at 5 p.m. on the 15th August when
Captain Wilson, fighting to the last, was killed.

Captain Eric Wilson VC.

E12315

In fact Wilson had been captured, wounded but alive, and was freed a few weeks later when his prison camp in Eritrea was liberated. He served subsequently in the Western Desert with the Long Range Desert Group and in Burma with the King's African Rifles. Retiring from the army in 1949, he joined the Overseas Civil Service, serving in Tanganyika until 1961. Later he was for many years warden of a foreign student residence in London and honorary secretary of the Anglo-Somali Society. He died in December 2008 at the age of 96.

Captain Eric Wilson
East Surrey Regiment, attached to the Somaliland Camel Corps

I was born in Sandown, Isle of Wight, in 1912. My father was a clerk in holy orders, an Anglican clergyman in other words. By the time I went to school we'd moved to Southampton, my father was away at World War One as a chaplain to the forces, and I went to a prep school in Dorset and then I went to Marlborough from which I went to Sandhurst.

I was a rather academic boy. I was in the classical side of the school and for six generations back my forebears had been Anglican churchmen and I would have been the seventh generation had I followed that so Sandhurst was something of a culture shock. I found myself about the only cadet there who wore spectacles. Looking back on it, I think it did me a lot of good, certainly physically it did, but I would very much like to have gone on to Oxford and not gone into the army. That's what I would have liked to have done.

I was commissioned in February 1933, I went into the East Surrey Regiment, and in 1937 I went on secondment to the Nyasa battalion of the King's African Rifles stationed in Tanganyika. The battalion companies were on a tribal basis and I found myself in the Yao Company. After I'd been eighteen months with the KAR I went as a non-volunteer, though I was very pleased to be sent, to take command of the Yao Company of the Somali Camel Corps in Somaliland. In February 1940 I landed down in Berbera and I was telephoned that I ought to form, train and command a Somali Vickers machine-gun company. While I was sorry to leave the Yaos, it delighted me, as I was an experienced machine-gunner and this was something interesting and new; and that was the start of my close and short and violent involvement with Somalis. A few weeks later we assembled and began an intense period of training, they were very quick at learning, and then by August we were in action: our first and last battle.

The divisional plan for the defence of British Somaliland relied quite a lot on the French: the French in Djibouti had more forces than we had and more prospects of reinforcements. But shortly before the Italians started their advance from Abyssinia the French in Djibouti packed it in, so then the Italians realised they only had the British to deal with. They desperately needed a propaganda victory and they massed immense forces, by our local standards, and they attacked.

The main British position was in the Tug Argan Gap, which is on the way from Abyssinia down to the port of Berbera. My company was supporting and under the command of the 1st Northern Rhodesia Regiment. Our position was based on four hills, they all looked down about a mile to a *tug*, a dry riverbed, and the Italians were forming up, hidden, protected, in this *tug* bed. Before the battle started I sat out on the hill in the evening and there was a non-stop revving of engines: there was obviously a tremendous gathering, massing, of forces; occasionally I even saw a light. I thought, 'We're for it tomorrow.'

Fairly soon after sunrise we got our first target. We were rather pleased we had something to hit but of course once you start opening fire with machine guns you draw the attention of enemy artillery, which we did in a big way. We got a number, two or three anyway, direct hits into the embrasure. One knocked the machine gun over and didn't hit any of us, I think. Well, as the day went on we got two or three other direct hits. One killed my sergeant instantly and I've still got three bits of that same shell in me, minding their own business. One bit broke my spectacles, which was a bit distracting.

Manual machine-gunnery lays down three rates of fire: slow, medium and rapid. Well, we were firing well beyond rapid and the gun [a water-cooled Vickers machine gun] would boil, we'd take the top off and there'd be a lot of steam and we'd refill and on we'd go. Well, in the afternoon, we saw, coming out of the *tug* bed, a mounted battery of the enemy, mule-borne. I remember thinking they were being very brave because we had their range and we hit a couple of the mules at least. But they succeeded in spite of our fire at a range of only 1,500 yards in setting up and firing directly at us. We were shooting back at them of course but they had their gun shields, which must have protected them sufficiently. Looking back on it, I don't think at that moment our prospects were good. But we had a Kenyan battery of seventeen-pounders and by the grace of God they got a direct hit on to the mountain battery. Then there was a tremendous African tropical downpour and then dark. So we were alive.

Well, the battle went on for another four days. The Italians had suffered such tremendous losses the first day – we'd really hit them – that they didn't try that again, they were much more cautious and they'd try and work along the *tug*, and nothing on the same scale happened. Then on 15 August the brigade commander gave the order that our position should be abandoned, at four o'clock or some specific time. I never heard that order. I think I was a bit knocked about, though I did notice there weren't many people about. Eventually with another chap I got down from the hill and we spent the night in the open but the next day I got picked up and I was a prisoner of war then.

After about four months in a prison camp in Eritrea, an airman who'd been shot down came in and he said that he'd read in the paper that I'd had a Victoria Cross. Well, I don't remember it making any impact on me at all. I don't remember if I believed it or not. I don't remember any of my fellow prisoners ever mentioning it. It was really brought home to me when, as our troops advanced through Eritrea, the guards all scuttled and we were free, we had nowhere to go but we were free, and very soon an armoured car of the Sudan Defence Force appeared. It happened that I was at the entrance to the camp and before the officer got down from the car he called out, 'Who's the man with the Victoria Cross?' I said, 'I believe I am.' Later I discovered that it had been posthumous.

Sergeant Nigel Leakey
1st/6th Battalion, King's African Rifles

Born in Kiganjo, Kenya, on 1 January 1913 into the famous East African family of naturalists and archaeologists, Nigel Gray Leakey was posthumously awarded the Victoria Cross for his actions in Italian-occupied Abyssinia (now Ethiopia) during the final stages of the East African campaign in May 1941.

As British forces sought to advance, his battalion, in which he was a mortar platoon sergeant, encountered strong opposition and was faced with a sudden Italian counter-attack by tanks. Leaping on to one of the tanks, he wrenched open the turret and, with his revolver, shot all of the crew except the driver, whom Leakey then made drive the tank into cover. Unable to get the tank's cannon to work, Leakey dismounted, ran across bullet- and shell-swept ground and, with three African troops, began to attack other tanks. He had jumped on to one, opened the turret and shot one of the crew when he was killed by the machine gun of another tank coming up behind. His body was never recovered.

Lieutenant Philip Arthur Thorne
1/6th Battalion, King's African Rifles

We were marching down this road to the Bilate River, where there was a bridge blown at this village, Kulito, and we got shelled and we disappeared into the Indian corn at the side of the road. Then there was an O-group, Colin Blackden held this O-group, and Ted Onslow came back and said, 'Right. We'll move on a compass bearing. Two platoons are going to cross the river.'

Actually, two platoons on one side and two platoons on the other side to give covering fire was a pretty silly idea because it wasn't bush such as the Somali bush, it was pretty thick. Not jungle as such but great big kind of bush-trees and tremendous anthills going up to twelve, fifteen feet, which the Italians had made into machine-gun posts: good shelter and jolly good camouflage as well.

Well, by that time my platoon strength was down to fifteen Africans. I was just behind them and they came to this river and they didn't like the look of it and I didn't like the look of it either. My platoon sergeant had the sense to make a kind of human bridge across and we got to the other side and we weren't being fired on at that time, thank God. Well, we couldn't see anybody, the bush was very thick, and somebody opened up on us. We silenced it, then we went on to the next machine-gun post. I sent my platoon sergeant, Sergeant Rose, back to see if he could find a better way of crossing and bring the rest of A Company and C Company.

We came to this road. I was told to take up a position on this road. There was an awful lot of milling about and people disorganised and one thing and another and somebody started firing at us from the side of the road. I said, 'All right, I'll go and get him,' I saw this bloke and fired at him, but I'd got an empty cylinder – click! And he got me; he shot me in the hip.

Corporal Issa wouldn't leave me and we got to this ditch at the side of this road and we heard tanks coming down the road. Blackden, who ought to have got a DSO, was standing in the middle of the road with a fly-whisk in his hand, no equipment, ordering people about the place. He said, 'Sorry to see that you've been bashed, we'll get you out in a minute,' not taking any notice of any of this dirt flying about the place, all these tanks coming down the road. This was the Italian counter-attack coming in and catching us very disorganised on the wrong side, the enemy side, of the river.

And that is where Sergeant Leakey did his stuff. He'd fired off all his mortar bombs and he'd joined A Company – I saw him flitting past me – and we didn't know for some time afterwards that he'd opened the first tank's turret, shot the commander, leapt off that one, leapt on to another and was never seen again. And he got a posthumous VC for that. Of course, a tank coming down these narrow roads would have gone over me and that would have been that, so I can quite definitely say that he saved my life.

Captain Charles Upham
New Zealand Forces

One of only three men to be awarded the Victoria Cross twice, Charles Hazlitt Upham was born in Christchurch, New Zealand, on 21 September 1908. After school and agricultural college he became a sheep farmer and from 1937 valued farms for the New Zealand government. He joined the New Zealand Expeditionary Force when war broke out and sailed for the Middle East in late 1939.

Upham earned his first Victoria Cross in May 1941 during the German assault on Crete. Commanding a platoon in the defence of Maleme airfield, he destroyed a series of enemy posts with grenades, carried an injured man to safety and, though wounded, continued to kill German soldiers in skirmishes around the airfield and later, when covering his retreat, shot a further twenty-two with a Bren gun.

After being evacuated from the island and recovering from his wounds, Upham rejoined his men and earned his second VC on 15 July 1942 during the defence of the Ruweisat ridge in the first battle of Alamein, lobbing grenades into a truck of German soldiers, crossing bullet-swept ground to deliver information and, though wounded, leading an attack on an enemy strongpoint. He continued to direct his men until he was wounded again and unable to walk. Eventually he was taken prisoner.

Charles Upham saw out the war in Colditz Castle, Germany. After the war he returned to New Zealand to farm. He died in 1994.

Captain Charles Upham VC and bar.

E 6066

Lieutenant Corran Purdon
Royal Ulster Rifles, attached No 12 Commando, prisoner in Colditz Castle, 1943–45

I got to know Charles very well because Dick Morgan and I messed with him – just the three of us – for a bit. Victoria Cross and bar: one VC in Crete and one in the desert. The most modest man you could ever meet; but then most Victoria Cross holders are modest men, at least all I've met. Bit careless in his appearance. I mean, clean, but I seem to remember Charles never did his boot laces up.

He also didn't like the Germans at all and I remember walking round the courtyard chatting one day and a little twit of a German major came out wearing a cloak, he may have been the paymaster, and as we went by he said, 'Salute!' So of course we took no notice at all. And then we came round again and on the way round I said, 'That little something-or-other,' and Charles said to me, 'What was he saying? What did he want?' I said, 'He wants us to salute him.' So Charles waited and then we walked past again and this chap barked out again for us to salute, so Charles in a loud voice said to me, 'WHAT'S THAT PRICK SAYING?'

Really, he was just a nice, down-to-earth guy, never talked about himself apart from sheep farms in New Zealand and so on, never ever talked about himself, and I don't think I ever saw him wearing his Victoria Cross ribbon on his battledress blouse.

Private Adam Wakenshaw
9th Battalion, Durham Light Infantry

Adam Herbert Wakenshaw was posthumously awarded a Victoria Cross for his actions on 27 June 1942 at Point 174, south of Mersa Matruh, Egypt, during the German army's eastward push towards Cairo and the Suez Canal.

Born in Newcastle upon Tyne on 9 June 1914, he had gone to work at Elswick pit at the age of fourteen. A pre-war soldier in the Territorial Army, he had been mobilised when war broke out and fought in France in 1940 before being sent with his battalion to North Africa. After taking part in the Battle of Gazala where the British, spread out across the desert in defensive 'boxes', had tried to hold off the German advance, the battalion pulled back and halted at Mersa Matruh.

Point 174 was a small stony plateau on which Adam Wakenshaw's company had scraped a position with soldiers behind boulders and hastily built stone walls. The company's two-pounder anti-tank gun, whose crew included Wakenshaw, was out in front on a gentle forward slope. As the citation for his VC then explains:

Shortly after dawn the enemy attacked and an enemy tracked vehicle towing a light gun was brought to within short range of the position. The gun crew opened fire and succeeded in putting a round through the engine immobilising the enemy vehicle.

Another mobile gun then came into action. All members of the crew manning the two-pounder including Private Wakenshaw were killed or seriously wounded and the two-pounder was silenced. In this respite the enemy moved forward towards their damaged tractor in order to get the light gun into action against our infantry.

Realising the danger to his comrades, under intense mortar and artillery fire which swept the gun site, Private Wakenshaw crawled back to his gun. Although his left arm was blown off above the elbow, he loaded the gun with one arm and fired five more rounds. These succeeded in setting the tractor on fire and damaged the light gun. A near miss then killed the gun aimer and blew Private Wakenshaw away from the gun giving him further severe wounds. Undeterred he slowly dragged himself back to the gun, placed a round in the breach, and was preparing to fire when a direct hit on the ammunition killed him and destroyed the gun...

This act of conspicuous gallantry prevented the enemy from using their light gun on the infantry company which was only 200 yards away. It was through the self-sacrifice and courageous devotion to duty of this infantry anti-tank gunner that the Company was enabled to withdraw.

The battle-scarred anti-tank gun manned by Adam Wakenshaw stands on display today in the DLI Museum in Durham.

Corporal James Wilkinson
9th Battalion, Durham Light Infantry

He was a good soldier in the soldier fashion but he wasn't a smart soldier. He wasn't one of these regimental bods. He was down to earth and you might think he was a little bit slovenly, not a guardsman-type if you know what I mean. We often used to talk, 'cause I think Adam was the same nature as me, really; we got on like a house afire when we saw each other. He was a very nice lad. Quiet. He wasn't very talkative; he was sort of selective, because he thought some people thought themselves better than him. He was a very nice lad. He'd worked in the pits for a bit. I liked Adam.

Private Richard Atkinson
9th Battalion, Durham Light Infantry

He was a smashing bloke. If you were going out at night-time he looked rough and ready and you might go, 'Keep clear of him' – he looked that type. You'd say, 'Keep clear, he's a right handful, a rough 'un.' But he was exactly the opposite; he had a heart of gold. If you stayed out, he'd stay sober to make sure you got back. Things like that. He looked after you, he was that type of a lad; if you looked at him you got the completely wrong impression. A nice lad altogether. Oh yes, I knew him well, Wakenshaw.

He could look after himself, he could handle himself, he could be handy with his fists and things like that, but not vicious, you know what I mean? If there'd been a boxing competition, he'd win it hands down.

Private John Rodgers
9th Battalion, Durham Light Infantry [for Africa]
We were in Tiverton to prepare for embarkation. We had all kind of jobs to do, like stencils on kitbags, preparing stores for the embarkation, but we spent a nice time there. We were in a town and out of the field and they used to organise dances at night-time and the company used to organise impromptu concerts. And there's one thing in particular I'd like to mention about Tiverton. We had been out for a drink and we'd come out at night-time and we were walking back to the barracks and there were two chaps in front of me and one of them was called Wakenshaw. And we passed some scrimmages going on over by the side of the road, kind of a fight, soldiers were crowded round, and he turned back to go to them. I shouted to him, I said, 'Wack!' – we used to call him 'Wack' for short – 'It's got nothing to do with us, you carry on, man!' He said, 'No, not on your life, that's a Durham in there,' and he walked in and he sorted the whole lot out. I've never seen anything like it in all my life. Scattered the whole crowd. He picked the fella up who was being punched by another fella, put his hat on and just walked him away and put him out in front of him and walked behind him on the way back to the barracks.

He was just a kind of rough diamond type of a lad. He was just a hard man; he had been brought up hard. He used to box for Murphy, the showman, used to go three rounds with him. I think he'd lost a son. We had a long talk when we had a bit of a scheme [an exercise] before we went to Bir Hakeim, I had a long chat to him about his home life, and he was a bit of a lad at school, you know. They used to tell his mother and his mother used to go up and see the teacher; and he said it was his own fault, he'd really been in trouble, but you know how mams and dads are, they try to go and sort the teachers out. And he said, 'I don't even go to church and I see you going when you're having your Mass and I see the lads going and I always want to go. I cannae buck up courage.' I said, 'There's no reason why you shouldn't. I'll go and see the padre and tell him and you'll be OK.' He said, 'Would you?' He was having that feeling that he wanted to attend to his religious duties again. So I took him up to see the padre and the padre said, 'Leave him with me,' and he must have made his peace with God and he come back and he was happy.

A new anti-tank company was formed, it must have taken place in the Gazala Box, and I was then given the job of storeman and when this company had been formed some of the soldiers were left over and one of them come to me. It was Adam Wakenshaw. He'd been missed off the gun crew and was surplus to the make-up of the new anti-tank platoon that had formed, so he come to me and he said he'd been posted. He said, 'I've been with the Territorials, in D Company, all the time the war's been going on and I'm going to be sent back now, there's no room for us on the guns.' I said, 'What do you want me to do?' He said, 'You're well in with these people' – the officers – 'can you not see me kept in the battalion?' Major Woods was the company commander then and he was a person that you could approach without any worries, so I said, 'Hang on and I'll go and see him,' and I went and saw Major Woods. He said, 'The company's made up, what do you want me to do?' I said, 'He's out there, he's never been out of D Company, he's nearly in tears. Before we get much further up there somebody's going to go down with sandfly fever or something like that and you might need somebody else for the gun crew.' So he said, 'Well, can you find him a job?' I said, 'I can find him a job all right'. He said, 'Right, just hang on to him for a bit.'

So poor old Adam Wakenshaw might have been posted, might have been sent away, but he was kept in the battalion. Next time I saw him, he said he'd been taking training for the gun and he was delighted. And I saw him again, later on, after that, and he come and told me especially: he said, 'I'm on the gun crew!' And it was his own doing, he used me as an instrument and Major Woods had to make the decision, but it was his own decision, he wanted to be on the gun, and he was granted it and it worked out that he won the Victoria Cross. But it might have been different. He might have been sent away somewhere else.

And before moving up – we knew we were going up to some kind of action – the C of Es were having a service in one place and the RCs were having another one, 'Abide With Me' was ringing out in the distance, and I saw Adam Wakenshaw coming back from Holy Communion. After that, I never saw him again. That was the last time I saw him.

I would say he was just a kind lad, rough and ready. I don't know if he would be the best of soldiers but he'd been in the Territorial Army and that was his life. He wouldn't let anybody down. He proved it to me in the early days when we were at Tiverton. If you were a Durham, that was it. And that was why he was crying, he didn't want to leave the Durhams, he'd been with them all the time. He was wrapped up in the Durham Light Infantry and he thought it was sacrilege that Adam Wakenshaw had to be posted away from it.

Private Richard Atkinson
9th Battalion, Durham Light Infantry
We came down to Mersa Matruh, we stopped and they said, 'We're going to make a stand here and get organised.' You could see the coast road and the sea, by this time it was getting dark, and we just sort of stopped on an escarpment, a ridge thing like a hillock. And that's when Wakenshaw won his VC, that night.

Nobody knew what was happening, we'd just sort of stopped, and Adam Wakenshaw was with us with the anti-tank gun and three or four vehicles and some men behind him – I think they must have been mostly transport. And the next thing we knew, this stupid Ned Sparks was shouting in the middle of the night, 'Is that the 9th Transport?' Well, Jerry was about twenty yards behind him and fired at him and hit us. And that's when Wakenshaw started firing back.

By this time it was breaking daylight and Wakenshaw was firing at them. I was lying about ten yards behind Wakenshaw at the time, he had the top of his head off, his arm was away and he was blind and that, and his two mates was dead, and he was just shouting, 'Left a bit! Right a bit! Up a bit!' and he was firing and he knocked this armoured thing out and this car and that. And then, boof, he got it.

Lance Corporal William Ridley
9th Battalion, Durham Light Infantry

I didn't see Wakenshaw but we were getting the flak from the guns and what have you. I went up to one of the officers and I said, 'Could you tell us what's happening, sir?' and he says, very tearfully, 'It looks like the last glorious stand.' I said, 'It's nae good crying about it, like,' and I crawled back.

All of a sudden somebody shouted, 'Every man for himself!' so I gets up and, as I got up, wallop, I got one right in the arm and a spurt of blood about fifteen-foot come out of me arm. I knew at least one artery had gone – as it happened there was two arteries gone – and I thought, 'I've got to stop the blood.' I put the heel of me hand into the hole in me arm and I come off the ridge and Andy Davies, the sergeant, come up and he says, 'What's the matter with you?' I says, 'I've been hit.' He says, 'Well, get on the truck.' I says, 'I daren't leave loose of this, otherwise I'm a dead man.' So him and another sergeant slung us on to the truck. The driver got in and all he done was set the motor away, got a hold of the wheel and sat on the accelerator, like, and he belted out. Of course he wasn't watching where he was going and hit every hole and trench and every time he hit a trench my arm came away and the poor guy sitting next to us was saturated in blood.

When I was in Cairo hospital, a doctor in the ward came in and he told us the state of the battalion, you know. He also told us that one of our lads had been recommended for a VC. I says, 'What did they call him, like?' He says, 'I just can't remember. It was Wake-something. Wakehall or Wake-something.' I said, 'It wasn't Wakenshaw, was it?' He says, 'Yes, it was.' And that was the first time that I heard Wakenshaw had been recommended for the VC.

Corporal George Lambert
9th Battalion, Durham Light Infantry
Somebody had the bright idea of us going back to the wadi at Mersa Matruh. I think the officer's name was Pickering. He'd been in charge of some money, supposed to be around six hundred quid or something, he'd dropped it and buried it and somebody had the bright idea of going back to see if there was a possible chance of finding a needle in a haystack. And when we got there, that's when we came across Adam Wakenshaw.

He hadn't been buried. Well, he was still lying exposed, half-buried, so we buried him and two more lads beside him, just where they were. Course, it knocked all the stuffing out of trying to look for anything. After we'd done that we went back to the battalion and I got a cross made up. Normally numbers were stamped on, transferred, but for that particular cross I got a lad called Dave Walton, who was a sign-writer in the platoon – he was an old TA lad, came from Blaydon or Dunstan – I got him to paint everything on. He put the DLI badge and '9th DLI' and his name all painted on. And we took that back and we put it where he was buried.

Lance Corporal William Ridley
9th Battalion, Durham Light Infantry
I remember when we were in England I was on an exercise and one officer told us to get our groundsheets out of our packs and Wakenshaw didn't have his in his pack, which he should have done. And this officer turned round and he said, 'Wakenshaw, if you live till you're a hundred you'll never make a soldier.' And I always wonder what that officer thought after he won the VC.

CROSS-CHANNEL RAIDS

Britain's wartime commandos were a highly trained volunteer force conceived in 1940 as a means of launching raids into enemy territory. Two of the most famous raids in which they took part were the attacks on the French ports of Saint-Nazaire and Dieppe.

The aim of Saint-Nazaire raid, which was carried out on the night of 27–28 March 1942, was to destroy the port's dry dock, the only one on France's Atlantic coast that was large enough to accommodate the German battleship *Tirpitz*. The attacking force suffered very heavy losses – of the 611 commandos and sailors who took part, 169 were killed and 200 captured – but the dock was successfully put out of action for the rest of the war. Five Victoria Crosses were awarded after the raid, three going to the Royal Navy and two to commandos.

The attack on Dieppe, on 19 August 1942, was a larger affair. The aim this time was to attack Dieppe's port facilities and destroy installations and gather intelligence. The principal raiding forces were five thousand Canadian troops and one thousand British commandos of No 3 and No 4 Commando, the latter units being given the task of destroying enemy gun batteries north and south of the port. Again casualties were very high – the Canadians alone lost nine hundred killed and nearly two thousand taken prisoner – and the attack has long been criticised as poorly planned and overly ambitious, though important lessons were learned in advance of D-Day. Three VCs were earned at Dieppe, two by Canadians and one by a British officer of No 4 Commando.

Sergeant Thomas Durrant
Royal Engineers, attached No 1 Commando

Born at Green Street Green, near Farnborough, Kent, on 17 October 1918, Thomas Frank Durrant was the son of the village carpenter and had joined the Royal Engineers as a regular soldier at the age of twenty. An early volunteer for the commandos, with whom he had seen service in Norway, he was posthumously awarded the Victoria Cross for his actions in the early hours of the morning of 28 March 1942 during the British raid on the port of Saint-Nazaire, France.

Having withdrawn from Saint-Nazaire, the small wooden motor launch (ML 306) which Durrant was aboard came under very heavy and close-range fire from a German minesweeper, the *Jaguar*. Although wounded earlier in the raid while firing at onshore searchlights and gun positions, Durrant, manning a twin Lewis machine gun, now kept up a continual fire at the enemy vessel's bridge, drawing heavy fire, and was wounded again several times. 'Despite these further wounds he stayed in his exposed position, still firing his gun, although after a time only able to support himself by holding on to the gun mounting,' his citation reads.

After a running battle and several calls from the enemy captain to give in, to which Durrant responded with further bursts of fire, the survivors aboard the ML surrendered. Shot through the head, arms, legs, stomach and chest, Durrant died soon afterwards. The captain of

A 13626A

Motor launch (ML) of the type in which Sergeant Thomas Durrant received the Victoria Cross for his actions during the raid on the French port of Saint-Nazaire, March 1942.

HU 2014

Sergeant Thomas Durrant VC.

the *Jaguar*, Kapitänleutnant Fritz Paul, later commended Durrant's gallantry to the commandos' commanding officer, when the latter, Lieutenant Colonel Charles Newman, who was himself awarded the Victoria Cross for his own part in the raid, was being held in a prisoner of war camp.

Lance Sergeant Ernest Chappell
No 1 Commando, aboard ML 306
The idea of the raid was to destroy the dry dock at Saint-Nazaire. The thinking was that, if the Saint-Nazaire dry dock was destroyed and *Tirpitz* did come out into the Atlantic and she was damaged, she would need to run the gauntlet of the English Channel to get to a dock – possibly in Norway – and could be intercepted and caught on the way.

Additional to the dry dock, it was expedient that we blow the lock gates entrance and make the basin tidal. If we made the dock basin tidal, obviously this made the off-loading and loading of shipping within the basin that much more difficult, because the ships in the basin would rise and fall with the tide and not remain at a pre-determined level. Parties were therefore designated the jobs of blowing various installations: the pump-house, which was necessary to pump water out of the dry dock after the ship had entered, pump water out of the lock and so on; the power station; the gates themselves.

The *Campbeltown*, which was an ex-US destroyer, was equipped with about six tons of explosive cemented in her bows, the idea being that she rammed the main caisson and gate of the dry dock and explode at a pre-set time, later. Motor launches would be following the *Campbeltown* and we would land at pre-set points and make our way to our individual targets and, to the best of our abilities, destroy these things.

At Falmouth we were introduced to the various motor launches which would transport us to Saint-Nazaire and became acquainted with the crews. Each motor launch carried, basically, one demolition party assigned to one task: in my own case, the lock.

We sailed on a very calm night, thank the Lord, for Saint-Nazaire, by a tortuous sort of route, down into the Bay of Biscay to cross a few sand-banks, then back up and entered the Loire, which we entered some time after midnight on 27/28 March 1942. Our target, the dock, lay some six miles up the river, up the estuary. We hoped to make the biggest part of the six miles without being discovered to be who we were and, to this purpose, our destroyer, the *Campbeltown*, which was in the van, flew the German flag, which was quite a legitimate ploy of war providing she didn't fight under it.

We'd had a fairly uneventful trip up the Loire for three or four miles when we were confronted from the Saint-Nazaire bank with searchlights and a short burst of fire. Our destroyer answered this with signals. He told the Germans that we were in fact a German force who had encountered action in the Bay of Biscay and were making our way into Saint-Nazaire to repair damage and that we had casualties on board. Could they please meet us at the quay with ambulances? This seemed to pacify the Germans for a time, they ceased fire, and we made progress up the river without problems for probably another quarter of an hour, when again we were challenged from the shore, and this time it was a heavier challenge. *Campbeltown* was fired on heavily, and we saw the German flag come down on the *Campbeltown* and the White Ensign go up. Then we came under terribly heavy fire from both banks and from various ships in the harbour. *Campbeltown* made her way up towards the caisson, which she had to ram, and she actually rammed at 01.34am.

The motor launches were coming up in two columns astern of the destroyer and obviously we were under the same fire, and we were firing back. We were equipped, the motor launches, with two Oerlikon guns, pretty heavy automatic guns, one fore and one aft. We were equipped with Bren guns and with twin Lewis guns.

MLs were very vulnerable because of the petrol tanks which were built on deck and several caught fire and were burning in the river and this made it rather impossible for us, coming up in the rear, to reach our landing point. In my own case we were supposed to land at the old mole and make our way to the dock entrance to do our job, but when we got to the old mole there was a motor launch there well alight. The sea was alight. I think one of the most pitiful things was to see a fellow swimming in the burning water and having to pass them by. They were screaming in the water and we had to shout at them, 'We'll pick you up on the way back' – which we knew damned well we couldn't.

We tried several times to get in, but couldn't. Ronnie Swayne, our army commander, implored the captain of our motor launch, a fellow called Lieutenant Henderson, great fellow, to run his boat ashore so that we could jump in on the mud somewhere, or on the bank, and get ashore that way, but he wouldn't sacrifice his boat. I don't blame him for doing that. His first concern was his boat at that stage. So, after several attempts to land, it became obvious that the situation was hopeless as far as we were concerned. We couldn't make it. We had to turn tail and run the gauntlet back down the Loire, where again we came under terrifically heavy fire, and eventually we passed the coastal batteries on the mouth of the Loire – who gave us a good pounding but fortunately didn't hit us – and we got out into the bay.

We were now intent on making our way back to Falmouth under our own steam. This was somewhere, presumably, about three o'clock in the morning, and still very, very dark, very calm. We were very, very annoyed and mad at ourselves that we hadn't been able to get ashore to do our job.

At this stage we became obsessed with the fact that we'd have to make Falmouth in daylight and we thought we would be surely spotted from the air, so we now engaged in loading magazines and preparing ourselves for what we considered imminent air attack during our trip back.

Durrant and myself and several others were on deck, loading Oerlikon magazines, when Henderson came down off the bridge and said, 'Be quiet, lads, we're surrounded by shipping. We don't know whether it's our ships coming out of Saint-Nazaire or whether it's in fact Germans.' The wake of our ship was glowing like neon lights with phosphorescence, and this of course was how we could discern the shipping around us, we could see the bow waves glowing like neon lights. Henderson decided to stop our boat and just let her drift – see if we could dispel this wake and not create such a fluorescence in the water. And we were just lolling around in the water with no engines running when we saw one of these bow waves detach itself from the others and come towards us.

We were still not too sure whether this was a German or a British vessel. But after a very short time, it must have been only a matter of seconds, the ship approached us, put on a searchlight which fell directly on us, and the searchlight was immediately followed by a burst of fire. So we were now no longer in any doubt as to what the ship was that was coming towards us; it was in fact a Möwe-class minesweeper, which is equivalent to a light destroyer. And she came bearing down on us at full speed with the bow silhouetted in her own searchlight. It was like watching a great carving knife come down.

Able Seaman Ralph Batteson
Oerlikon gunner, ML 306

We thought they was all going past, they was just far enough away for us not to be seen, or so we thought, but there was another one following up behind and he must have spotted something. In the accounts of the Germans after the war, Captain Paul, the skipper of the German *Jaguar*, said he thought he saw a shadow so went back to investigate and came back straight towards us, switched the searchlights on and opened fire straightaway. And of course we had a go back at him. Soon as we could see we were going to be fired on, we weren't going to sit there and let him knock us out of the water without any effort.

Every gun that we'd got was firing back at them. But the severity of the fire from the German destroyer was putting people out of action, people were getting killed second by second not minute by minute, people were getting mown down. They was that close they was within shouting distance and if you're within shouting distance and they can fire at you with an Oerlikon gun – they'd got similar guns to the Oerlikon if it wasn't the Oerlikon – you knew you was in trouble.

Quite a number of commandos had got killed; one or two in our wheelhouse had got killed. And when our man on the twin Lewis gun got knocked out of action and fell away from the gun, Tommy Durrant shouted for some of the lads to get some more magazines and come and load him up on the Lewis gun. And he was having a right go at 'em, all the time.

Corporal Glyn Salisbury
No 1 Commando, aboard ML 306
They came around the port side and fired a salvo at us and it came through the funnels and I had shrapnel then all over me back. The lad that was at the side of me, a sailor, he had his leg off; he had his wellies on and his trousers were ripped and all the blood was going into his wellies. Tommy was firing away at them *all* the time, you know.

Lance Sergeant Ernest Chappell
No 1 Commando, aboard ML 306
We suffered some pretty heavy casualties. Henderson himself was mortally wounded. He was shot through the legs and I think he had a leg blown off. I myself was hit about the legs at that time and found myself with my legs dangling over the gunwales slipping through into the sea, until I was pulled back by some colleagues on board – couldn't say who – and rested against the stack of our boat, where I managed to fire a Bren gun from the feet of Durrant who was above my head on a twin Lewis.

Shortly afterwards, a small explosive bullet hit the smokestack above my head and shrapnel penetrated my tin helmet. I was hit in the head and to all intents and purposes lost consciousness, was out of action from then on, although I do remember snatches, I remember little bits and pieces. I can remember the fight continuing although I don't remember detail. I remember the German boat circling us and the German captain or one of his minions calling out in English, 'Have you had enough? Have you had enough?' and he was answered each time with a burst of fire from Durrant.

Lieutenant Ronald Swayne
No 1 Commando, aboard ML 306

A lot of the soldiers on deck were killed or wounded. Then the destroyer went off a little bit and I went down below to see what was happening and I saw holes appearing simultaneously in the sides of the ship, a hole there and a hole there, and one or two soldiers were dead down below. Then I went on deck again and the destroyer came in, it couldn't have gone away very far, and it tried to ram us and gave us a glancing blow and it was still shooting at us. And Tom Durrant all this time was on the twin Lewis – of course the regular soldiers were trained in them in the 1930s and he knew all about those guns and he was rather glad, I think, to get on this – and he'd been shooting away at the destroyer regardless of anything that was shouted at him by the Germans. I started parleying with them and I think it was at that point that Durrant gave the Germans another burst at the bridge and they really let him have it. But he went on shooting until he absolutely dropped on the floor, terribly badly wounded.

Able Seaman Ralph Batteson
Oerlikon gunner, ML 306

While Durrant was firing the twin Lewis guns he was getting hit all the time; they was concentrating on him because the other guns, people with machine guns, handguns and things like that, were gradually getting knocked out. They could more or less concentrate on Durrant because his was about the only gun left that could fire. He was absolutely riddled.

He could speak good English could Captain Paul and he said, 'Surrender!' I can't remember the words but Swayne must have said, 'We can't carry on any more,' and the Germans said, 'Well, no tricks now, no messing about,' so we more or less surrendered. They could have blown us out of the water. The commandos were mostly dead or wounded and we had no more guns to fire; there were dead and wounded all over the ship.

After we'd surrendered, they drew up alongside us and dropped these rope ladders down the side of the boat and we were trying to get the wounded up off our boat on to the German *Jaguar*. And I went round and there was Sergeant Durrant laid out at the foot of the gun and he was absolutely covered in blood and bullet-holes and things. I tried to pick him up, he was a bigger man than I was, and I just couldn't manage it. He was still conscious and he said, 'Go and help some of the others. I'm finished anyway, go and help somebody else.' He'd stopped that many bullets, he must have known he was going. It showed what a brave man he was, to say, 'Go and help somebody else.'

Lieutenant Ronald Swayne
No 1 Commando, aboard ML 306

Paul wouldn't tell me at the time how many casualties he'd had but there were certainly quite a few of the crew of the destroyer who were wounded or killed because there was a lot about when we went on board. And they took us on board and then they were absolutely wonderful. The Germans really looked after the wounded beautifully. Durrant was enormously badly wounded, he was wounded all over, and I nursed him for some time. Then we gave him some morphia.

I kept on getting requests to go and see Paul, the German captain of the ship. I was very irritated and I sort of said, 'Fuck off,' you know. And eventually the No 1 came along – previously it had been a sailor – and said to me in very good French that the captain really did want to have a word with me. I said, 'I'm not going to be questioned by the captain,' and he said, 'No, he wants to give you a glass of brandy.' I said, 'Well, that's different. When I finish what I'm doing, I'll come along.' I went along and I had a long chat with him. He was very nice and he later came to the prisoner of war camp which I was in to inquire how we were getting on. After the war he became a friend.

I went back to the wounded and then Captain Paul came down to see me. And just as he was talking to me – we'd come into port, actually, I think the ship must have been tied up – an enormous explosion took place, and this was the *Campbeltown* going up. We went running up together on deck to see what had happened and the *Campbeltown* was coming down as we arrived on deck, pieces were banging around all over the place. It was very exciting and we knew we'd succeeded then. Then eventually they got us all off the ship. It was all done with great courtesy and kindness and when we were going over the side, on to the shore, Captain Paul drew the whole ship's company to attention and saluted us, and I didn't know what to say to thank him.

Able Seaman Ralph Batteson
Oerlikon gunner, ML 306

While we were in the prison camp at Rennes, a German officer came on a big horse. He came into the camp and he said could he see Colonel Newman. So they led him in to see Colonel Newman and he said he wanted to make it known that one of the commandos on my boat was worthy of a good award from the British Government, a good award for bravery. Finally it finished up that Tommy Durrant got the VC and I think it was through this German recommending him to Newman. It was a good thing, really, for the German to do that.

Captain Patrick Porteous
Royal Artillery, attached No 4 Commando

Born at Abottabad, North-West Frontier on 1 January 1918, Patrick Anthony Porteous was educated at Wellington and Woolwich and commissioned into the Royal Artillery in 1937. He fought in France in 1940 and, later that year, joined Lord Lovat's No 4 Commando. He was awarded the Victoria Cross for his actions during the raid on Dieppe on 19 August 1942. Promoted to the rank of major soon after the events that earned him the medal, his citation reads:

Major Porteous was detailed to act as Liaison Officer between the two detachments whose task was to assault the heavy coast defence guns.

In the initial assault Major Porteous, working with the smaller of the two detachments, was shot at close range through the hand, the bullet passing through his palm and entering his upper arm. Undaunted, Major Porteous closed with his assailant, succeeded in disarming him and killed him with his own bayonet thereby saving the life of a British Sergeant on whom the German had turned his aim.

In the meantime the larger detachment was held up, and the officer leading this detachment was killed and the Troop Sergeant Major fell seriously wounded. Almost immediately afterwards the only other officer of the detachment was also killed.

Major Porteous, without hesitation and in the face of withering fire, dashed across the open ground to take over the command of this detachment. Rallying them, he led them in a charge which carried the German position at the point of the bayonet, and was severely wounded for the second time. Though shot through the thigh he continued to the final objective where he eventually collapsed from loss of blood after the last of the guns had been destroyed.

Major Porteous's most gallant conduct, his brilliant leadership and tenacious devotion to a duty which was supplementary to the role originally assigned to him, was an inspiration to the whole detachment.

Pat Porteous went on to land on D-Day as second-in-command of No 4 Commando. He survived the war and remained in the army until 1970, retiring with the rank of colonel. He died in 2000.

Captain Patrick Porteous
No 4 Commando

My family had all been soldiers for several generations. My father was a Gurkha officer and I originally intended to go into the Gurkhas myself but shortly before I left school my father said, 'I wouldn't advise you to go into the Indian army because I think it's going to come to an end before very long, so I should try a British regiment instead.' I was fairly good on maths so I decided I'd try for Woolwich and I passed in there at the beginning of 1936. I had eighteen months there and then went on to Larkhill for the young officer's artillery course.

I started the war with an anti-aircraft regiment, went to France, came out through Dunkirk, then joined a training regiment at Oswestry. That was in about September 1940. While there I saw an ACI asking for volunteers for special service. I went up for an interview in due course and just before Christmas I was ordered to report to the RTO in Glasgow. I was bored with sitting on an anti-aircraft site, we'd been posted to Glasgow and there couldn't have been a more boring spot, so I volunteered for something a bit more interesting. And I was told to report to the RTO at Glasgow who said take the ferry to Arran and report to Colonel Lister who was commanding No 4 Commando.

We trained in Troon for two and a half years. During that time the Commando took part in special operations: the Lofoten Raid; there was an unsuccessful raid on Boulogne; there were one or two minor raids; and we also sent some of our officers and men on the Saint-Nazaire raid with 2 Commando. I did not go on any of those.

In about mid July 1942, the whole unit was sent on block leave for about a fortnight. On returning from leave there was a commando parade at which the CO, Lord Lovat, said that we were about to take part in an operation. He didn't tell us where it was or what it was about at that stage, but that we were leaving in two days' time to go down to do some special training at Weymouth, which we duly did. And we did intensive boat training in LCAs, Landing Craft Assault, and cliff assaults along the Dorset coast at various spots.

About the seventeenth, we were all loaded into trucks, driven up to Southampton. We spent a night in a transit camp in Southampton and went on board the following evening – that was the evening of the eighteenth – and joined a convoy going across the Channel. We didn't know at all, in the Commando, the junior ranks, what the operation was or where it was. All we were told was that it was supporting a major landing and that our job was just to knock out the battery.

The main assault was to go in on the main beaches of Dieppe itself. On either side of Dieppe there are big headlands where there were known to be German batteries and a battalion, roughly, on each headland. So there was a right-hook, at a village called Pourville, carried out by the South Saskatchewan Regiment and the Canadian Camerons. They were to come up on to the west headland and try to knock out the defences there. And then the Royal Regiment of Canada were to come in on the left hook, at a village called Puys, and do the same on the eastern headland. About two or three miles beyond those landing points there were two heavy gun batteries which were covering the approaches into Dieppe. No 3 Commando was detailed to destroy the one on the east, at Berneval, and No 4 Commando, which I was with, to destroy the battery at Varengeville.

The plan that Lord Lovat adopted was to divide the Commando into two parties. One party of eighty men was to land at the foot of the cliffs immediately facing the battery and try and get up one or other of two narrow little gullies that went up the cliff. The rest of the Commando, which was about another two hundred men, was to land about a mile further west, near the village of Sainte-Marguerite, and were to make their way inland, swing left and come round at the back of the battery. That was the plan.

We set off, just before dark, with an enormous convoy. Hundreds of ships, as far as one could see: landing craft; Landing Craft Tank; destroyers; minesweepers who went ahead and cleared a gap through the German minefield, which was about ten miles offshore, roughly. We got to the lowering position at about four o'clock, having had a good night's sleep and a nice breakfast of stew. Grenades had been primed, magazines filled; everything was all ready. Soon as we got to the lowering position, we were lowered away.

It was about a two-hour journey in. Luckily the sea was very calm, very clear. After we'd been going about half an hour or so, we suddenly saw some fireworks going on, way out on the east, to our left flank. This was No 3 Commando, who had been going for the other battery at Berneval, who had bumped into a German naval convoy coming down and there was quite a firefight. The landing craft of 3 Commando were all scattered; several of them were sunk. The whole thing was a bit of a shambles there.

In the meantime, the main body was coming in at Sainte-Marguerite. About a couple of hundred yards offshore they started opening up with machine-gun tracer, which luckily was aimed high and it all went flying over the top of us and did no damage. Then we hit the beach, which was a steep shingle beach, with a belt of about three or four yards of wire at the top of the bank and a steep drop down the other side. We knew this was there from air photographs and every boat had some rolls of ordinary chicken wire which we rolled over the barbed wire, which made a sort of bridge which one could stagger over. While we were getting that on, the Germans opened up with mortars, which they had obviously ranged very closely on to the beach, and caused about a dozen casualties.

The whole training had been to get off the beach as quickly as possible, regardless of anything, so we left a medical orderly with the wounded who were on the beach and we got off the beach. And under cover of a fold in the ground, where they couldn't machine-gun us any more, we formed up along the bank of a little river, which came in more or less at right angles to the beach. The bank to that was fairly high and completely screen-less from the German positions up on the hill above Sainte-Marguerite.

We went along the bank beside this river. We were wading most of the way because the Germans had flooded the valley there, and it was fairly heavy going for about a mile directly inland. Then we swung left across open ground behind the German defences – we had no opposition at all crossing that bit of ground – which brought us round to a little wood at the back of the battery we were to assault. The battery had barbed-wire entanglements around it but there was a spot where the German soldiers had been coming home late from leave, or something of that sort, and had trampled a path through the barbed wire at the back, and we managed to get in without any problem at all.

As we got into this area of the battery, which was typical *bocage* country – masses of hedges, farm buildings, bushes: very close country – we bumped into a truck of German soldiers who were just disembarking. Obviously they'd come up from Sainte-Marguerite, somewhere from that direction. We managed to knock them off before they got out of the truck. Killed the lot of them, virtually, with tommy guns.

Private Peter Fussell
No 4 Commando
The OC that led us in, he was killed. The subaltern was killed. The sergeant major took over and he was killed. This was where Pat Porteous came in. He was the liaison officer who was liasing between the two groups. He came over because there were no officers, no NCOs, no warrant officers or anything to lead us. He himself had been hit in the hand by a German defender and had killed this German and several others.

Sergeant Irving Portman
No 4 Commando
They sent Captain Porteous over to regroup the troop and make sure that we got through to our objective. And he came over and he said, 'Try the hedge, sergeant,' so I dived through this hedge and that's when I got a lump of grenade in my eye. I dived behind this tree and a guy flung another grenade – he was in a hedge about twenty yards from me – and it landed in the tree and a few little bits went in my backside. I was

Commandos returning to Newhaven after the raid on Dieppe, August 1942.

H 22604

frightened to death. I looked left and saw something moving in the grass and there was this Jerry just poking his head out and I pulled round at him and knocked him off, got him straight through the middle of his forehead. And I went forward and there was another guy in the same slit trench looking through and he didn't realise his mate was dead – there was so much noise, banging going on, grenades flying – so I managed to put a couple into him. Then we moved on from there across this orchard, it was all sort of open, and we came behind these guns. We lay on the bank there, we were on the edge of a lane, and Pat said, 'Right, let's go in.' So we rushed the guns. I was so excited, I was really rushing forward, and I tossed a grenade into one gun pit and there was a big 'Whoof!' – a lot of cordite exploded. I jumped into the gun position and, when I got in there, two Jerries were dead, got no clothes on – all their clothes had been burned off.

Lieutenant Donald Gilchrist
No 4 Commando
In came F Troop from the front led by Pat Porteous who'd win a VC. And then in came B Troop, Gordon Webb leading them with one hand dangling but carrying a revolver in his left. And then there were bad moments with the bayonets while we overcame the guns.

Private Clifford Leach
No 4 Commando
Hectic. Very hectic. There was a tremendous amount of firing going on, people darting all over the place. We did have to fix bayonets and charge the position finally, under the orders of Captain Porteous. As we did the charge he got hit again, in the thigh, and bowled over.

Corporal William Spearman
No 4 Commando
Captain Porteous was on the other side with F Troop and he got a VC for what he did. It was total confusion really because anybody who wasn't a

commando you recognised, you just killed them. People were running out of buildings, running into buildings. Some of them were quite brave, they were trying to put up a fight, but they really didn't get a chance because there must have been a hundred finely trained troops attacking what must have been nearly three hundred Germans, artillery people, whose job was to fire guns. And they were all embedded in these sand-banks and we just went through from one building to another, from one sandbank to another.

Captain Patrick Porteous
No 4 Commando

The first gun pit I came to was just full of corpses. I staggered on to the next gun pit and then I rather gave up the ghost after that. I'm glad to say I didn't actually bayonet anybody, I couldn't have done because my rifle had been smashed, and my pistol had run out of ammunition and I wasn't able to reload it with one hand. Then a couple of my chaps came along and they hauled me out while the demolition team went into the gun pit I'd just fallen into. We had a team of chaps with made-up charges: all you had to do was open up the breech of the gun, shove this in, close the breech and put the delay mechanism on.

Having blown the guns, that was our job completed and the only thing to do then was to make a quick withdrawal. I was loaded on to a door somebody had pulled off a shed somewhere and carried by two German prisoners down the gully which the other party had just forced their way up. The Germans didn't like it at all because they had laid all the mines there and they weren't quite sure where they were and they were very nervous.

The destroyer I was on went on trying to pick up all the awful mess that was going on outside Dieppe, the wounded people. Landing craft were being sunk. An absolutely appalling shambles. We were loaded with wounded, we had one bomb very near us from a German Junkers or some-thing, I was on a stretcher in the wardroom and all the lights went out and it was all rather frightening. However, it didn't seem to do any serious damage to the destroyer and we eventually returned to Portsmouth at about one o'clock the following morning, having started off, well, about twenty-four hours before, roughly. And I was carted off to a Canadian hospital at a place called Bramshott, between Liphook and Hindhead, where I spent the next six weeks or so. Then I had a month's sick leave. Then I went back to full duty.

Sergeant Irving Portman
No 4 Commando

He was a very brave man was Pat Porteous and when we came back from Dieppe and went back up to Troon, up in Scotland, I fiddled the orders a bit to get posted to his troop. I was in E Troop at the time, which was the demolition troop, and because I was senior sergeant on E Troop I fiddled the orders and posted meself to D Troop. Pat was away then, he was too wounded, and when eventually he came back he was my troop leader and eventually he made me sergeant major. He was a great guy. I mean, he was my officer, but he was a great friend of mine. Oh, we'd have followed him through hell and high water, old Pat Porteous. He was a very, very brave man.

Captain Patrick Porteous
No 4 Commando

I was very lucky, I think, extremely lucky, to get the award of the VC. The citation said that I'd been wounded in my hand and then led this bayonet charge against the guns, got wounded again and carried on. But I felt as though it was rather like being in a rugger scrum: you got kicked about a bit and the object was to get over the line, which was all that we did do, in fact. One was scared stiff but there was nothing you could do about it, you had to press on regardless. I was scared from the moment we started getting shot at; or before that, as soon as we realised we were going on an operation, which was all rather frightening. It has to be. I don't think there's any man on earth who is not frightened if he's going into an operation unless he's absolutely bone-headed.

THE WAR AT SEA

The role of the Royal Navy during the Second World War took many vital forms, from maintaining crucial lines of supply to hampering enemy efforts at shipping men and supplies to support their own war effort. The navy bombarded enemy onshore positions as well as protected the Allies' own harbours and bases. Ships, submarines and aircraft were heavily engaged throughout the war and made a crucial contribution in every theatre.

Twenty-three Victoria Crosses were awarded to men of the Royal Navy during the Second World War. Three featured here went to submariners for actions in the Mediterranean and two to the commanders of tiny X-craft submarines for a daring long-range attack on the German battleship *Tirpitz*. Also described are the actions of a destroyer captain who was awarded the VC after the Arctic convoy he was escorting to North Russia came under heavy enemy attack.

Lieutenant Commander David Wanklyn DSO
Royal Navy

The first submariner of the Second World War to be awarded the Victoria Cross, Malcolm David Wanklyn was born in India on 28 June 1911 and joined the Royal Navy in 1925. He served on submarines from 1933 and took command of HMS *Upholder* in 1940. Patrolling out of the Royal Navy's submarine base on Malta, he received the VC for intercepting a strong enemy convoy and torpedoing a troopship, the 18,000-ton former liner *Conte Rosso*, on 24 May 1941 south of Sicily.

Observation was difficult, the submarine's Asdic listening equipment was broken and Wanklyn had only two torpedoes remaining. Despite this, as his citation describes,

Lieutenant-Commander Wanklyn decided to press home his attack at short range. He quickly steered his craft into a favourable position and closed in so as to make sure of his target. By this time the whereabouts of the escorting Destroyers could not be made out. Lieutenant-Commander Wanklyn, while fully aware of the risk of being rammed by one of the escort, continued to press on towards the enemy troop-ships. As he was about to fire, one of the enemy Destroyers suddenly appeared out of the darkness at high speed, and he only just avoided being rammed. As soon as he was clear, he brought his periscope sights on and fired torpedoes, which sank a large troop-ship. The enemy Destroyers at once made a strong counter-attack and during the next twenty minutes dropped thirty-seven depth-charges near *Upholder*.

The failure of his listening devices made it much harder for him to get away, but with the greatest courage, coolness and skill he brought *Upholder* clear of the enemy and safe back to harbour.

A 7293

Lieutenant Commander David Wanklyn VC DSO, left, with his First Lieutenant, Lt J. R. D. Drummond.

Whenever in action, the citation adds, Wanklyn carried out his attacks 'with skill and relentless determination... [He] has also sunk one Destroyer, one U-boat, two troop-transports of 19,500 tons each, one tanker and three supply ships. He has besides probably destroyed by torpedoes one Cruiser and one Destroyer, and possibly hit another Cruiser.'

In terms of tonnage sunk, Wanklyn, who also received three Distinguished Service Orders, was one of the Royal Navy's most successful submariners. One account transcribed below is a broadcast made by Commander Anthony Kimmins describing his experiences of Wanklyn at work, patrolling, in the Mediterranean after he had been awarded his VC. A vivid account of life in a submarine at war, it was recorded not long before Wanklyn and his crew were lost in April 1942 on *Upholder*'s twenty-fifth patrol. The precise fate of the submarine remains uncertain.

Petty Officer Gordon Selby
Second Coxswain, HMS Upholder (Royal Navy submarine)
I was drafted in September 1940 to Barrow-in-Furness to stand by *Upholder* as second coxswain. Now, that was quite exciting because it was the first time that I'd ever been in a brand new submarine. We sailed from Barrow in our trials in October 1940, went up to the Clyde area to do our trials, did one shake-down patrol in the North Sea, nothing happened, came back to Portsmouth and sailed from Portsmouth on 10 December 1940 for the Mediterranean. Our captain, who was a lieutenant at that time, was Wanklyn. He was promoted lieutenant commander very shortly afterwards.

He was what I would classify as a gentleman. He was a delightful person himself and gave everyone a feeling of confidence in him. We were very fortunate in *Upholder* that all the crew except one were regular servicemen, we only had one Hostilities Only rating, a young ordinary seaman, and it stayed that way nearly all the time *Upholder* was in commission. Officers, we had regular RN officers except one: our naviga-tor was an RNR, a Merchant Navy man. The crew itself didn't change very much during commission but the officers changed quite consider-ably. In fact only the captain remained of the original officers that commissioned *Upholder*.

We sailed from Gibraltar early in January '41 and arrived at Malta around about the first week in January and we did our first patrol towards the end of January. I can't remember anything outstanding about it except that everyone was naturally calm. There was no real excitement. The captain was a very quiet person, he never shouted, he never dashed around, etc, and I think that sort of set the pace for everyone else. After that we just carried on patrolling from Malta.

Patrols would last anything up to fourteen days; sometimes they only lasted three or four days. We didn't have very far to go to get to our patrol billet and it was a matter of diving the minute we got out of harbour. We used to go to sea in the evening, late evening, and we used to arrive back in harbour early morning so that we could remain dived for the maximum amount of time. On patrol it was a matter of being dived all day and then surfaced all night for charging batteries. You always expected to see something. I don't think there was very many patrols when we didn't see anything.

We really started to have success from about April onwards. We had two or three patrols to begin with where the captain hadn't really got his eye in. But once he'd got his eye in, which would be about April or May, then we started to have a great deal of success, and in fact he finished up by being the top-scoring Allied submarine commander.

He was awarded his VC for an attack we did in May. That was quite a hectic one, it really was. We had no Asdics and we only had two tor-pedoes left, we were just in the last couple of days of our patrol, and he sighted this convoy coming out from the Straits of Messina: I suppose three troopships escorted by half a dozen destroyers. And he attacked without any Asdics to assist him and sank *Conte Rosso*.

Lieutenant Michael Crawford
First Lieutenant, HMS Upholder (Royal Navy submarine)
We'd already had two attacks and only had two torpedoes remaining, Asdics were out of action so we couldn't hear things coming, and we were patrolling and it was just beginning to get dark. I happened to be on watch and I just saw a dark shape and so called the captain to the periscope and he took over and did a most remarkable attack. The citation for the VC really says it all. He had destroyers coming at him at very close range but he managed to just dodge them and fired two torpedoes and sunk this 18,000-ton liner, the *Conte Rosso*, with considerable loss of life to the enemy. We then naturally had a pretty heavy depth-charge attack after that and you could hear the destroyers' propellers passing overhead and instinctively all the crew sort of bent their knees, waiting for the crunch. But fortunately we didn't suffer any damage and got away and were able to return to Malta.

Commander Anthony Kimmins
Broadcast correspondent with the Royal Navy, reporting his experiences of patrolling in HMS Upholder in 1942
The captain of our particular submarine was a young lieutenant commander. He's got a certain 140,000 tons of enemy shipping to his credit and probably a good deal more. He's tall and lanky, with a keen studious face and a rather untidy black beard, which gives him a definitely biblical appearance. At sea, he wears one of the most disreputable uniforms I've ever seen, torn and patched with only a few wisps of what had once been gold lace hanging from his sleeve. He wears no medal ribbons but on his smarter harbour uniform he's worn for some time the DSO. Now there's an additional ribbon, a crimson one, with a small bronze cross in the centre: the VC. His name is Wanklyn. And it will always be one of my proudest memories that I've been out on a job with Wanklyn and his crew, who, in their ship, *Upholder*, have written such a glorious page in submarine history.

Once at sea we soon went to diving stations. All on the bridge, with the exception of Wanklyn and one signalman, disappeared down the conning tower hatch and, in doing so, said goodbye to daylight for many days. From now on, we'd be cooped up in a steel shell with a cross-section about that of the inside of a London Tube. But here, most of the space is taken up by engines, torpedoes, periscopes, pipelines, bells, dials and so on. In *Upholder*, the only release from this maze of machinery, the only human reminders of the outside world, are two very lovely signed photos of the King and Queen.

At the moment it was all rather noisy and confused. Being still on the surface, the diesel engines were at full ahead and the boat was pitching into the swell. Various orders were being shouted and then suddenly, above the general din, there was a hoot from the diving klaxon. In a flash, the whole atmosphere changed. The noise and the vibration of the diesels stopped and gave way to the quiet hum of the electric motors. The only sound to be heard was the first lieutenant giving his trimming orders. 'Pump on A. Stop the pump. Flood Z. Shut Z.' And so on. As the needles of the depth-gauges passed the twenty-foot mark, we lost the effect of the surface swell. The boat stopped creaking and settled down to her steady underwater course. The sudden silence was quite uncanny.

For the first few days while on passage to the prearranged position, there's little excitement to break the monotony. The crew work in three watches: two hours on and four off. In most surface warships, they work four-hour shifts; but in a submarine the job is too concentrated for a man to do more than two hours at a stretch. Besides, the comparatively short time off doesn't allow him to get into too deep a sleep in case of an emergency.

The routine seldom varies. Sleep, eat, a spell on duty, sleep and eat. The only differences between day and night are that during the daytime, while you're running submerged and clear of the effect of the waves, it's all very still and quiet. At night, when you surface under cover of darkness to charge the batteries, you're rolling and pitching to the sea. There's the noise and vibration of the diesels and, the conning tower hatch being open, you can smoke. The amount of sleep you put in is quite amazing.

It's largely the lack of oxygen when submerged. You don't notice it much at the time but if you strike a match towards the end of the day you'll find it just flickers and goes out. There's of course no exercise to be had in the terribly cramped quarters and during the twenty-four hours you probably only move a few paces, and yet you're always tired and always hungry and oddly enough, at the end of a patrol, you've probably lost weight.

The whole business of submarine attack is rather like stalking big game, only about a hundred times more exciting. Sound travels a long way underwater and in one corner of the control room an operator is rotating a dial and listening out for enemy ships. He suddenly concentrates on one bearing, then raps out a report: 'Ships. Bearing green 20.' The captain immediately decides to have a look and motions to the first lieutenant to take her up to periscope depth. A few sharp orders and the boat starts to rise. When they're at the depth at which the top lens of the periscope, when fully extended, will break surface, the captain orders, 'Up periscope.' A slight swishing noise and the periscope shoots upwards. The captain bends double, meets the eyepieces as they rise between his feet and straightens up with his eyes glued to them and with his hands grasping the handles on either side. With a flick of his fingers the periscope stops dead with its top lens just clear of the surface. A quick glance round for aircraft and then he searches the horizon. As he concentrates on green 20 he clasps the two handles just a little tighter. His back suddenly stiffens. Yes, there it is. Smoke on the horizon. That's all he wants to know for the moment and he's not going to stay up a second longer than necessary. 'Down periscope. Fifty feet.' For a moment, the captain considers his plan and glances to the compass. His hand reaches out to a buzzer: action stations.

That buzzer starts the quickest move I've ever seen. There's no noise, no scramble; the men just appear. Many of them were fast asleep but before you can say 'knife' they're at their stations. There's never a yawn or a rubbing of eyes. They know that buzzer and they know that when the captain presses it he means business. By now it's time for another look. A nod to the first lieutenant, a few quiet orders as tanks are blown, a nod to the periscope operator and again that lanky figure is uncoiling itself as the periscope rises. A quick glance round for aircraft and he swings on to the target. Then, with the quiet confidence of the expert, he raps out the details: course, speed, bearing, range. At each report, another officer sets various dials on a large box attached to the bulkhead. Finally he pulls a handle at the side which coordinates all these settings and produces the vitally important answer: the torpedo firing angle. Needless to say, this box is known as the fruit-machine. By now they're down deep again and the captain discloses the good news of what he alone has seen: two transports, four destroyers. There's no undue excitement; but, standing in the gangway, you can see it being whispered down to the ends of the boat: 'Two transports, four destroyers'; 'Two transports, four destroyers.' Meanwhile, the captain has finally decided on his plan of attack. As the enemy draws closer, he has just one more look through the periscope to check his bearing and make sure they haven't zigzagged off their course. No, everything's going to plan. The leading destroyers are drawing near by now and he decides to dive underneath and get a close shot on the important target: the transports. 'Down periscope. A hundred feet.'

Once settled at depth there's a tense silence. A distant rumble heralds the approach of the destroyers. It grows louder and louder, until, with a deafening din like the roar of an express train, their propellers go racing overhead. The captain is a picture of cool confidence. He's got every move fixed in that clear, calculating brain and nothing's going to deter him. Neither is there a sign of anxiety amongst the officers or crew. They know that this is the big moment but they've got complete confidence in each other and particularly in the man in command. At exactly the moment when he's calculated he's clear of the enemy destroyer screen and almost in the firing position, he gives a familiar sign. Back swings the death needle: eighty, seventy, sixty, fifty... This time, he's almost lying flat on his stomach as the eyepieces come up. There's no time to swing round the horizon now. Anyhow, his periscope is fixed at the firing angle and he's only waiting for the target to come into view. For a moment, it's an empty horizon; and then, suddenly, there comes into his field of vision a transport bow. As it passes the centre wire, her foremast is coming in. 'Stand by. Fire one.' A fraction's pause and then a slight jolt and recoil as the torpedo leaves the tube. 'Fire two. Fire Three.'

There's no hesitation about his next order: 'Down periscope. Go deep.' This time the needle fairly races round. The captain is eyeing his watch closely. From the range he can estimate almost exactly when his torpedoes will cross the enemy's track. Those two or three minutes put years on his life. The suspense of whether he's hit or missed is the worst part of the whole business. Fifteen seconds to go. Ten. Five. He's missed, something must have gone wrong, the gyros must have failed, they... Suddenly there's a crash which shakes the whole boat and sends a couple of light brackets clattering down: there's an unmistakable sound when a fish hits, there's a distinct metallic ping of impact followed immediately by the explosion. A few seconds later there's another, then silence. Two hits. Well, that should be good enough to do the trick. There's no cheering, no whoop of joy, only grins and rubbing of hands and dead silence, except for a whispered remark from the first lieutenant: 'Nice work, sir.'

Silence is essential at this moment. From now on, they're no longer the hunters, they're the hunted. Sound travels fast and loud underwater and the dropping of a spanner or anything like that might easily spell disaster. 'Crash!' There come the depth charges: one... two... three, four, five. The petty officer telegraphist is jotting them down in his log as casually as a grocer checking the empties. As they get closer, the submarine is shaken more and more violently. It's a terrific noise, one that gets you not so much in the ears but in the pit of the stomach. The hunt may last for half an hour, an hour and often much longer. But when it eventually dies away and the captain's reasonably satisfied that it's over, he'll return to periscope depth to have a look at the damage and the possibility of other targets. Very often, of course, the torpedoed ship will have sunk by now. But if she hasn't yet foundered and there's no danger around he lets some of his crew have a look through the periscope before she goes. If it happens to be anyone's birthday, it's his privilege to have the first dekko.

And so the patrol goes on. Blank, boring days, desperately exciting days and tense, snooping days creeping round the enemy's coast, watching him through that little eye above the surface, until, at last, it's time to go home and refuel. On reaching harbour, the crew are fallen in on the fore and aft casings. As they pass and salute the other ships, the side is piped and they come smartly to attention with all the pomp and ceremony of peacetime. But if you look closer, you'll notice that the men's long, white submarine sweaters are grimed and dirty. Their chins carry many a day's growth of beard. Their eyes are heavy and blurred at the unaccustomed glare of daylight. And on the stump mast above the conning tower flies the Jolly Roger.

Petty Officer Gordon Selby
Second Coxswain, HMS Upholder (Royal Navy submarine)
You can be the most efficient CO under the sun but if the targets don't come you can't sink them. But he had a very clear mathematical mind. I'm sure he didn't depend entirely on what we called the fruit machine for carrying out his attacks; I think he knew exactly what he was going to do and he knew exactly how to do it. I think also that, certainly after the first couple of attacks and patrols, he had the confidence in himself; I suppose you would say he had his eye in. Luck naturally does have to play a part in it and I suppose we were lucky on one or two occasions, but you can't be lucky all the time, there has to be some skill involved in it.

Commander Philip Francis
Royal Navy submarine captain, 1938–42
He was a star. He was very quiet, you wouldn't have known he was such a great man. He was lucky in that he had plenty of targets but he was a very good shot to start with, which is very important. He was the best submariner we've had.

Lieutenant Peter Roberts
Royal Navy

Petty Officer Thomas Gould
Royal Navy

Peter Roberts and Thomas Gould were both awarded the Victoria Cross for their actions in the Mediterranean on 16 February 1942 in dealing with two unexploded enemy bombs left lying on the casing of their submarine, HMS *Thrasher*. One bomb had in fact penetrated the casing and was rolling loose on the pressurised inner hull.

'This deed was the more gallant as HMS *Thrasher*'s presence was known to the enemy; she was close to the enemy coast, and in waters where his patrols were known to be active day and night,' their joint citation ends. 'There was a very great chance, and they knew it, that the submarine might have to crash-dive while they were in the casing. Had this happened they must have been drowned.'

Born at Dover on 28 December 1914, Thomas William 'Tommy' Gould had joined the Royal Navy in 1933 and served in submarines since 1937. He had joined HMS *Thrasher* as second coxswain after service in the Far East. Peter Scawen Watkinson Roberts, born in Buckinghamshire on 28 July 1917, had joined the Royal Navy in 1935 and was *Thrasher*'s first lieutenant.

Peter Roberts retired from the navy in 1962 and died in 1979. Tommy Gould returned to civilian life soon after the war but maintained strong links with the navy, serving for many years as president of the International Submarine Association of Great Britain, and was an active member of the Victoria Cross and George Cross Association. He died in 2001.

Lieutenant Hugh ('Rufus') Mackenzie
Commanding Officer, HMS Thrasher (Royal Navy submarine)
We were attacking a heavily escorted ship in flat, calm conditions,

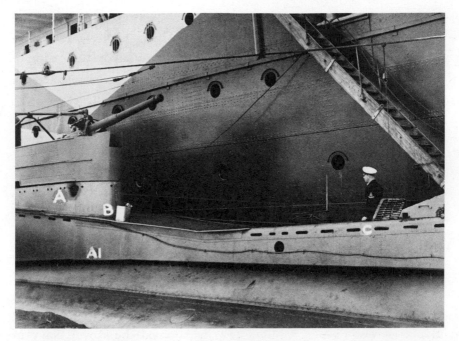

In a photograph taken in 1942 of *HMS Thrasher* moored against the side of a larger ship, Petty Officer Tommy Gould stands in the hatch through which he and Lieutenant Peter Roberts crawled to retrieve an unexploded enemy bomb that had penetrated the submarine's casing. The hole made by the bomb can be clearly seen at 'A'. It came to rest, within the casing, at the spot marked 'A1'. 'B' indicates the position, represented in the photograph by a white tin, where another bomb was discovered lying on the casing. For their gallantry in disposing of these bombs, Gould and Roberts each received the Victoria Cross.

brilliant sunshine, in the clear waters of the Mediterranean: the worst sort of conditions for a submarine to do an attack. I knew perfectly well that at periscope depth any aircraft flying over us could see us as clearly as if we were on the surface. Sure enough, just as I fired my torpedoes at this ship, which was escorted by five or six surface escorts and three aircraft flying round it, as I put the periscope down I heard what was undoubtedly machine-gun bullets hitting the water followed by a fairly loud explosion close to, so I reckoned we'd been spotted by an aeroplane. Anyway, I'd fired my torpedoes so we went deep to avoid the inevitable counter-attack by the surface escorts, which followed in due course, but no great damage was done and eventually we got away.

Much later that day, when we were on the surface, in fact at about midnight, we were just clearing the western end of Crete and we ran into a slight swell, which caused the submarine to start rolling. I was asleep in my bunk and I was woken up by something going, 'Bonk, bonk, bonk,' overhead: clearly something rolling about in the casing. Well, this was anathema to any submariner, something making a noise like that, which would give your position away to anybody listening for you. So I told the officer of the watch on the bridge to send somebody down to see what it was, if he could find out what it was, and to secure it to stop it rolling about.

I got a rather startled report back that there was what appeared to be a bomb lying on the fore casing just under the gun. And there was a hole in the casing by the gun, which seemed to indicate that something had gone into the casing and which might be causing this noise. I went up on the bridge myself and went down to investigate and, sure enough, there was a bomb lying on the casing, about two feet long I suppose. I reck-oned about a fifty-kilogram bomb, a hundred-pound bomb, and there was a hole in the side of the gun casing that looked as if it had been made by another bomb, by its size. So I sent for the first lieutenant and the second coxswain, who were the people normally concerned with the housekeeping and husbandry of the casing anyway.

Petty Officer Thomas Gould
Second Coxswain, HMS Thrasher (Royal Navy submarine)

It wasn't really a case of volunteering, it was my job: the outside of the ship was my responsibility and my part of the ship was untidy. I was a petty officer and the second coxswain, then. The second coxswain's the senior seaman; he's the man who's the senior sailor on board, responsible to the first lieutenant. Roberts was the first lieutenant. He and I were working together.

The first one was just laying there. We don't know why it hadn't fallen off into the drink, we had no idea why that didn't happen; it was there and it was rocking, it was incredible. We wrapped a sack around it and with a couple of heaving irons we went forward with it, lowered it gingerly over the bows, gave a dim flash of light to the bridge for the skipper to go astern, and we laid flat waiting for the explosion, which didn't occur.

Lieutenant Hugh ('Rufus') Mackenzie
Commanding Officer, HMS Thrasher (Royal Navy submarine)

The bomb inside the casing was a much more difficult problem. The two men concerned had to get into the casing by the fore hatch and then crawl aft, on their stomachs, to get to the bomb. Then they had to drag it back with them to the only opening where they could get it out, which was by the fore hatch, a matter of thirty feet or so, on their stomachs or on their hands and knees, dragging this damned thing. And of course, the whole time they were there, if we happened to be surprised by an enemy patrol we'd have had to dive and they'd have been drowned, which was not an easy thing for me to contemplate standing on the bridge.

Petty Officer Thomas Gould
Second Coxswain, HMS Thrasher (Royal Navy submarine)

The second one – we knew it was there because of the hole in the super-structure – it had gone in and laid down on to the hull and was making that noise: it was rolling when we were rolling.

Down we went. I went first and I crawled through. We got through, I went through, got hold of the bomb, pointed it at the hole that it had made to get in there but it wouldn't go back so I had to pass it through to Peter. That allowed me to get through to where he was. Then I took it from him, laid down, put it on my stomach, crawling headfirst on my back and he was giving me a bit of help by pulling my shoulders.

Inside there, you see, you've got angle irons to hold the casing together, to give it some kind of strength; then there's battery ventilations in there; there's also drop bollards: all that you've got to get by in darkness, there's not much room. And every time we moved there was a twanging noise as if of a broken spring, which was a bit upsetting, from inside the bomb. It sounded like a loose spring.

They say, 'It must have been frightening,' but I don't think it was because we had a job to do, we were doing a job, and I don't think we gave any thought, at least I didn't, to the fact that it might go off at any minute. The first one didn't go off, why would this? That would be the subconscious thought. I don't think we gave any conscious thought to it at all; our consciousness was all on the work we were doing.

I think the people who suffered were those down in the boat who knew what was happening. 'Hurry up you silly buggers' was probably what they were saying; they were conscious of the time, we weren't. They were also thinking that the old man might have to dive at any minute but we didn't even give that a thought. But the point was, had the enemy seen us, the captain would have dived to save the boat: he'd got a crew to think about.

It took over an hour. The first lieutenant got out first, Lieutenant Roberts. I was left with the bomb then and I passed it up and it was received by him and Sub Lieutenant Fitzgerald. Then, when we got up there, we wrapped it in cloth and put a couple of heaving irons around it and Roberts and I took it forward and the sub lieutenant went back to the bridge. We did the same thing with the same results: it didn't go off either.

Lieutenant Charles Fetherston-Dilke
Anti-submarine warfare officer, Royal Navy

In 1950 I went down to HMS *Osprey* to qualify in anti-submarine warfare, it's a training establishment at Portsmouth, and we had two very highly decorated officers on our course. One was Lieutenant Peter Roberts, who'd won a Victoria Cross in a submarine in the Mediterranean during the war, and the other was Lieutenant Commander Christopher Dryer, who had a DSO and two DSCs, I think, which he'd got largely in coastal forces during the war.

We had these tactical games which the Wrens used to do and I saw one of these Wrens looking intensely at Peter Roberts and eventually she plucked up courage and went up to him and said, 'What's this first medal ribbon you've got there?' And he said, 'It's the Victoria Cross'. And she said, 'Oh, go on. You couldn't get a Victoria Cross.' And Peter Roberts didn't react to this at all and she wandered away.

But I could see that a worm of doubt was at work in this Wren's mind and eventually she could contain herself no longer and she went up to Christopher Dryer and said, 'What's that first medal ribbon that that officer's wearing?' He said, 'It's the VC.' She burst into tears and left the room in a hurry, poor girl.

But Peter Roberts was such a modest officer. He didn't look the sort of swashbuckling type, which indeed he wasn't. He was a very, very gallant submariner.

Captain Robert Sherbrooke
Royal Navy

Robert St Vincent Sherbrooke was awarded the Victoria Cross for his actions while in command of a force of destroyers escorting an important convoy for North Russia on 31 December 1942, in an engagement that became known as the Battle of the Barents Sea.

Encountering a vastly superior enemy force, which included the German heavy cruiser *Admiral Hipper*, Sherbrooke marshalled his ships so well that four enemy attacks were turned away and the convoy escaped, though several of the protection vessels, including Sherbrooke's HMS *Onslow*, were badly damaged and two sunk. Sherbrooke himself was seriously wounded in the face, losing his nose, an eye and a cheekbone. 'His courage, his fortitude and his cool and prompt decisions inspired all around him,' his citation reads. 'By his leadership and example the convoy was saved from damage and was brought safely to its destination.'

Born in Oxton, Nottinghamshire, on 8 January 1901, he had attended the Royal Naval Colleges at Osborne and Dartmouth and joined the Royal Navy in 1916 as a midshipman. He served throughout the Second World War in destroyers and survived to retire from the navy with the rank of Rear Admiral. He later became Lord Lieutenant of Nottinghamshire and died in 1972.

Lieutenant Peter Joseph Wyatt
HMS Onslow (Royal Navy destroyer)

Convoys were always very long, very slow, and an awful lot could hit you in the way of aeroplanes, U-boats and of course surface craft: there'd be battleships and German cruisers sitting in the Norwegian fjords. So they were always a bit worrying.

I think one of the things we were very conscious of was that there'd been a big summer convoy, PQ17, which was one that came under air and U-boat attacks, so there was, in the back of one's mind, 'There is going to be another surface attack by the Germans.' One was always looking back to PQ17 when the convoy scattered and the navy was supposed to have abandoned the Merchant Navy to its fate. And at the conference at Loch Ewe you could see it amongst some of the merchant skippers, you know. They were talking an awful lot about the defence of the convoy: 'What are five or six destroyers against the might of the German navy?' One had this feeling.

Anyway, we set sail. Quite nice weather when we joined. Nothing much happened. But on about the third day we were getting up fairly far north and we started to get into really bad gales, very bad gales in fact. Temperature was low. A lot of icing: as you do, you collected an awful lot of ice up there with the spray and you get a thick coating of it; the whole ship gets covered in it and gets a bit wobbly because of the weight of the ice. And there were one or two contacts with Asdic and reports of U-boats in the vicinity but we didn't lose anyone. I think the weather was too bad for that: the submarines were having to keep down and not come near the surface. And then we turned the corner, going east across the top of Norway, and the weather started to ease up a bit.

By the thirtieth of December, the weather was moderating quite a lot and we had an awful lot of ice, so all the ship's company were chipping ice, getting rid of it off the guns, off everywhere. It was thick and took an awful lot of getting off. By dusk we were fairly clear, we were having trouble with one or two of the guns because they get a bit iced up too, the breech-blocks and things. Although they're heavily greased up and everything else, there's one little bit will get iced up and you can't get rid of it – you can't even see where it is.

Anyway, everything was quiet. The wireless was quiet. Some little signal came through in the night that indicated that the German forces in Norway were agitating – in other words, there was something going on – but nothing definite at all.

Next morning, in the dim twilight, we as usual were up about seven at action stations. And at about half-past seven or eight o'clock we said, 'Well, let's get hands to breakfast and fed. Good time to do it.' 'And,' said, the captain, 'tell the ship's company to change their underwear.' It was an old Nelson one: 'Clean underwear won't dirty your wounds.' And we'd just got back from breakfast and changing our underwear when three unknown destroyers were sighted astern of the convoy by one of our screens. We told her to go and investigate, so she dashed back behind the convoy to see what it was. They may have been Russian destroyers, we weren't quite certain; they sometimes appeared but very seldom and we were due to get some Russian destroyers to help us. However, only a quarter of an hour had gone by when suddenly gunfire started back there. *Obdurate* said, 'Enemy destroyers firing.'

Lieutenant Commander Hudson
Australian officer, HMS Obedient (Royal Navy destroyer)

It was about nine o'clock when they were first sighted: three dim shapes coming up the right flank of the convoy at high speed and then turning away back into the mists astern. 'Destroyers, sir,' I reported to the captain. 'Sound the action alarm,' ordered the captain. 'Both engines to full speed. Hard to starboard.' The engines chattered and roared in rising crescendo as the ship, turning sharp right, increased speed with surprising rapidity. There was much scuffling and swearing on deck as ice-covered muzzle and breech covers were removed from the guns.

Then came a wireless message from Captain Sherbrooke: 'Enemy in sight. Destroyers join me. Am attacking enemy.' HMS *Onslow* was tearing through the convoy, a great bow wave almost obscuring her from sight. Through the icy spray flying up over our forecastle a number of fast-disappearing German destroyers could now just be seen in the mists ahead. The three we had encountered were evidently only a scouting force. Huge gun flashes suddenly appeared in the murk behind the German destroyers, obviously from something very much larger. Veiled in the distant mist, the outline of a heavy German cruiser was just discernible.

HMS *Onslow*, with thin orange flames spitting from gun muzzles, was now racing across the convoy's rear. Following closely in her wake were the other British destroyers. Great columns of smoke from their funnels were enveloping the convoy in a thick smokescreen. Again and again came the gun flashes from the enemy cruiser, their shells straddling us as the destroyers crossed and re-crossed the convoy's rear. Again and again did our own small four-inch guns strive to hit back at the enemy, but we were well out-ranged by the enemy's 8-inch guns. The convoy was protected, though, behind our smokescreen.

Sub Lieutenant James Cockburn
HMS Orwell (Royal Navy destroyer)

Our Captain D [Captain Sherbrooke] ordered his destroyers to follow him in single line ahead and he went straight for the Germans, his tactics being to threaten them with a torpedo attack but not to fire the torpedoes because once we'd fired the torpedoes we'd have no means of keeping them away from the convoy. It was a feint, steering toward them at full speed as if we were going to make a torpedo attack, and this turned them away. And having turned them away, we withdrew and prepared to make another dummy torpedo attack. Both sides were firing guns throughout these actions, and I saw, on the *Onslow*, which was Captain Sherbrooke's ship, B-gun going up in flames. A rather traumatic experience because I was standing on B-gun on *Orwell* at the time.

Lieutenant Commander Hudson
Australian officer, HMS Obedient (Royal Navy destroyer)

We watched *Onslow*, as, with all their guns blazing, they dashed gamely away, drawing, as they did so, the whole of the enemy's fire. Then someone exclaimed, 'They've hit *Onslow*!' *Onslow* was hit all right but she hadn't faltered and, firing savagely, was leading forward under a shower of salvos. Suddenly she shivered and a swift arc of flame shot up somewhere near her bridge. She lurched sideways viciously as she met the full force of another salvo. Then an extraordinary thing happened: the massive enemy ship turned away. Captain Sherbrooke's determined approach had shaken the confidence of the German admiral. *Onslow*, though, was in real trouble. Through my glasses I noted the heavy list; stabs of flame from aft demonstrated her stern guns were still firing. Captain Sherbrooke, though badly wounded, was continuing to fight his ship without the slightest let-up. *Onslow* turned about and came slowly toward us. Through a hole in her side a great fire could be seen.

Lieutenant Peter Joseph Wyatt
HMS *Onslow* (*Royal Navy destroyer*)

The *Hipper* locked on to us and started pounding us. We turned to dodge the shells but it was all rather close range and so she started to hit us. Very luckily she was using the wrong shell. She was using high explosive, which, I suppose, against a merchant ship is probably a useful thing, it goes off on impact, as opposed to a semi-armour-piercing shell, a normal warship's shell, which would go inside the ship, perhaps through the ship, and explode. But anyway these were exploding on the outside and although they were doing an awful lot of damage – you know, spreading muck through the mess decks and things – they weren't making vital holes in the ship and I think that's why we survived.

They were mostly up forward, the shells, in the forecastle and B-gun deck, down there. Then they got one which exploded on top of the funnel. The shrapnel spray from that went right through the radar room where the radar operators were and through the back of the bridge and it was a bit of metal from that shell that hit Sherbrooke on his left eye and gouged it out. We lost our radar and we lost our radio too, more or less, and the ship was on fire forward and we more or less had to leave, we were just about to sink. We thought, 'Honour satisfied. We'd better really dodge the next one.'

The *Obedient* carried on with the other two ships making smoke and they were still engaging the *Hipper* while we went and joined the convoy. A- and B-guns were both out of action, X was out of action, and we thought we'd better retire for a bit to get the ship going again because it was in a mess. Then the weather rather closed down and the *Hipper* was lost in the middle of a snowstorm and although one had had her aerial knocked away by the *Hipper* there was no serious damage done to the other destroyers.

It was decided by the torpedo officer, who'd taken command of *Onslow* because Sherbrooke had been persuaded to at last go below and have his wounds mended, that we'd better go back to Murmansk.

A 22903

A Royal Navy X-craft underway in Loch Striven, near Rothesay, Scotland, with its commander on deck by the conning tower.

A 21692

A Royal Navy X-craft midget submarine in Holy Loch, Scotland.

Ordinary Signalman Richard Ashton
HMS Onslow (Royal Navy destroyer)

Thick black smoke was pouring out of us. Flames. All the guns were out of action. We were listing badly. And the noise from the siren, which was broken by the shells, was absolutely deafening. A terrible experience, really, and there was lots of dead on board. We were sewing the dead bodies up in the hammocks – we were full of rum to do it – and then there was a burial at sea: I think there was forty killed or thereabouts. There's not much room on the bridge of a destroyer and it's open, you're open to all the elements, and it was just luck that I wasn't hit: there was all kinds of shrapnel and bits and pieces blowing about. Captain Sherbrooke was the only one who got hit on the bridge, he was just unlucky, but he got the Victoria Cross for his trouble.

Lieutenant Godfrey Place DSC
Royal Navy

Lieutenant Donald Cameron
Royal Naval Reserve

Godfrey Place and Donald Cameron were both awarded the Victoria Cross for their role as commanders of separate X-craft midget submarines during a daring attack on the German battleship *Tirpitz*, moored in the protected Norwegian anchorage of Kåfjord, on 22 September 1943. Their joint citation paid tribute to their 'courage, endurance and utter contempt for danger in the immediate face of the enemy'.

Born at Little Malvern, Worcestershire, on 19 July 1921, Basil Charles Godfrey Place had joined the navy at the age of fourteen and been serving in submarines since 1940. In 1942 he had been awarded the Distinguished Service Cross for his part in sinking an Italian submarine off Sicily. Donald Cameron, born on 18 March 1916, came

Lieutenant Godfrey Place VC DSC (second from left, standing) and the crew and passage crew of his midget submarine X-7, prior to the attack on the *Tirpitz*.

A 19636

from Carluke in South Lanarkshire, Scotland. He had joined the Royal Navy after six years in the Merchant Navy and became a submarine officer in 1940.

Both men were captured after the raid. Both also remained in the navy after the war. Cameron died aged forty-five in 1961. Place, who transferred from submarines to the Fleet Air Arm and saw action in Korea as a Sea Fury pilot, retired from the navy in 1970 with the rank of Rear Admiral and served for many years as President of the Victoria Cross and George Cross Association. He died in 1994.

Lieutenant Godfrey Place
Commander, X-7 (Royal Navy X-Craft submarine)

I'd just got back from the Mediterranean in an ordinary submarine and I was sent for by the Captain of Submarines, in what was then the 5th Submarine Flotilla in Fort Blockhouse in Gosport, who just blandly said, 'How would you like to sink the *Tirpitz*?' I just said, 'Yes.' He didn't give very much explanation of what was required to be done but I inferred that it was a small submarine venture. I then left my old boat and went up to the northern base for a little bit of learning about the boat and then went back and took on the second prototype which was being built in Portsmouth dockyard at the time. And after trials in the dockyard I went back to Scotland and ran that as a training boat, while Vickers-Armstrong were building in Barrow the first six operational boats.

An X-craft was a small submarine originally devised by a Commander Varley with the idea of penetrating enemy harbours, but it also had an engine and a considerable amount of fuel which meant it wasn't limited to short-range attacks. In fact, in the final version, the range would have been of the order of 1,200 miles on the surface and a matter of 150 dived. The original and in fact the later method of attack was to go under an enemy ship in harbour and for a diver to go out and attach limpet mines to the hull of the enemy ship. Later this was given up in favour of simply detaching large side charges, as the explosive mines were called, on the bottom of the sea directly underneath the enemy vessel. The plan of attack was to be towed to a target by ordinary submarines on the surface when out of sight of enemy air-reconnaissance, and dived when closer to the enemy targets. The X-craft towed best when dived all the time at a depth of about sixty to eighty feet, or less if the water was shallower.

Because of the passage envisaged being fairly long and the boats being usually damp, somewhat tiring, difficult to sleep in and so on, a passage crew was embarked for the passage and a change-round was to be made one or two days before release for the actual operation. The necessity for a reasonably long dive range was that the *Tirpitz*, which was the principal target, and the other German heavy ships were most of their time either in Trondheim Fjord or Altafjord, and both those two approaches involved something of a seventy- or eighty-mile trip up from the open sea.

We had hoped to do the operation about March but the first of the first three boats didn't come off the stocks until mid-February and by the end of March there would be too much daylight to do the operation, so it was decided to put it off till September. We spent the summer working out various things and generally speaking working up, and then, I think it was in late August, the *Malaya*, an old but still well-in-commission battleship, was anchored in one of the Scottish lochs and all boats attacked. There were six boats by then and all six came in and out, they all attacked without any difficulty at all in fairly accurately simulated conditions. So of course there was a good deal of confidence among the individual crews. And immediately after that the boats were brought inboard for final checking over and loading with the live side charges. We were briefed about three weeks before the operation, early September, and it was very well done. The intelligence that they'd got was very thorough. From about 5 September till about the end of the month, PR [Photo Reconnaissance] Spitfires did a daily reconnaissance over the area, operating from the Shetlands and landing in North Russia to refuel and return.

Each submarine went a different path up to the dropping position, so boats set off from about 10 September, over as much as forty-eight hours, in turn, going along their allotted route until well north of the Shetlands on the surface, and then dived. There were particular instructions to the towing machines that only capital ships were allowed to be attacked, which was unfortunate because *Stubborn*, towing my X-craft, saw a U-boat on the surface going along quite gently and had an excellent opportunity to attack had they been allowed to.

There were two particular disasters in the tow going there. The first disaster really was when X-8 had been out of communication and was signalled to come up. There was no sign of the boat so the submarine stopped and hauled in the tow and there was absolutely nothing at the end of it, and X-8, I'm afraid, was never seen again.

The other one was when *Stubborn*, towing X-7, my boat, saw another X-craft on the surface at night – remarkable because they're very small – and signalled to it and it signalled back. It had lost its towing submarine, so *Stubborn* waited by it and sent a signal to the towing submarine to come and try and pick it up. But by then the buoyancy chambers in one side of the X-craft had got so loose from bumping against the hull in the very heavy weather that one of the seams had undoubtedly cracked and flooded, so the boat had a list of something like thirty degrees. They released that charge and unfortunately, for no known reason, the charge exploded, oh, about five, ten seconds after being released. They were going along at the time and the damage was not all that severe but the X-craft was really in such a hopeless state that it was decided to abandon it and the passage crew was taken off into the towing submarine. So that left only four boats in a position of being capable of attacking.

The weather had been fairly poor for the first four or five days but three nights before slipping – the slipping date was 20 September – we decided that the weather would probably improve. So, in X-7, the passage crew went into the towing submarine and I and the operational crew went into the X-craft.

We came to the slipping position in masses of time and finally slipped at eight o'clock on the evening of the twentieth. X-5, X-6, X-7 and X-10 all slipped within a relatively short time of each other, all making their independent way in to Stjernsund over a declared German minefield. We deemed it wisest to go in on the surface because it would be a defensive minefield against submarines, the German heavy ships being able to go over the top of it. We made a fairly steady passage up Stjernsund into Altafjord proper, coming up to periscope depth every so often but otherwise had a quiet day dived deep – at about ninety feet I thought we'd be out of sight – in really very pleasant weather indeed. We saw the *Scharnhorst* in Altafjord. Altafjord is something similar to Scapa Flow and is obviously used for minor fleet exercises, sub-calibre shoots, anti-aircraft exercises, those sort of things, and the *Scharnhorst* was obviously out doing that.

We surfaced just after dark, which was something about eight-thirty or nine o'clock, among some small islands, outside the main fleet anchorage and a little way away from the auxiliary fleet anchorage where they hold all the store ships and oilers and those sort of things. It's very steep too all the coast there, so we were right behind some rocks to avoid being seen and charged the batteries to get a full charge. We had a little bit of a problem with the exhaust but we got that fixed and dived the following morning, at I think half-past one, two, to make the passage through the anti-submarine boom up to the *Tirpitz*, which was lying at the head of Kåfjord. The boats were not expected to see each other or coordinate their attacks at all.

We hung about a little bit to make sure it was fully daylight before going through the opening in the boom – there was an anti-submarine boom across the neck of Kåfjord – and then wasted a little while because there was an empty anti-torpedo boom with no ship inside but forming a square and we ran into this. It took quite a while to get out, with rather a lot of pulling and pushing and blowing a little. I don't think we broke surface actually but certainly I was a little bit cautious that we'd probably

HU 50728

Hitler mounting the podium before the launching of the German battleship *Tirpitz*, 1 April 1939.

HU 50983

Tirpitz at anchor in Kåfjord, Norway, July 1942.

revealed our presence. However, we went on, and then, at about a quarter to six, we had our first view of the target, the *Tirpitz*, quite plainly, very clear. And we approached, fixed ourselves, and then went deep at about two hundred yards', three hundred yards' range to go under the anti-torpedo nets that were surrounding the ship.

All our information about German anti-torpedo nets had been based on either air reconnaissance or our knowledge of our own nets. Our own nets don't go below forty or fifty feet at the most and are rather like chain mail, heavy steel rings interlocking. But in fact the Germans' nets weren't like that at all, they were very fine four-inch mesh, criss-cross material with this very thin wire, and they did go undoubtedly a great deal deeper so it did take us a considerable time to get in. In fact, having tried it all depths, I thought, 'Well, we're just simply going to have to come up to the surface and have a look properly through the night periscope.' Miraculously, at that moment when we came up to the surface, there was no intervening net and the *Tirpitz* was a matter of fifty, sixty feet away.

So we went down as fast as we could and collided with the ship's bow at, I think, about twenty-five feet and slid on gently underneath in the full shadow of the hull. We were by then in an ideal position for attacking and dropped the first charge, as I estimated, under 'A' turret and went towards the stern of the ship and dropped the other charge under 'X' turret. And being somewhat in doubt as to how we'd got in, I thought I'd go back to the point where we'd penetrated the nets. But it's very difficult in a very small area – the nets came to within ten yards of the bow of the *Tirpitz* and within that area it's very difficult to pinpoint yourself absolutely precisely – so in fact we spent most of the next three-quarters of an hour trying to find a way out. I think we went into quite a number of positions, passing under the ship two or three times to try various bits.

Our charges were set for an hour and now it occurred to me that we needed to take somewhat drastic measures to get out. So in fact we did a sort of 'flop' operation: hitting the net, holding ourselves down, blowing the bow tank to absolutely full buoyancy, going as fast as we could, so that you came up at a terrific angle, and at the same time going full ahead on the motor, and we scraped over the top of the net and got out.

Lieutenant Donald Cameron
Commander, X-6 (Royal Navy X-Craft submarine)

We had pretty much the same experience as X-7 during the inward passage and left our charging position among the islands at half-past one in the morning of the 22nd to make our attack on *Tirpitz*. A flooded periscope and starboard charge, which gave me a decided list, caused a certain amount of inconvenience. At five o'clock we passed through a gap in the defence nets in the inner fjord and headed for our target. Vision through the periscope was very poor and our course very erratic but somehow we managed to remain undetected by all the anchored shipping and patrol craft.

At seven o'clock we found ourselves outside the boat entrance in the anti-torpedo net defence around *Tirpitz*. The boat entrance was a narrow gap where the net had been drawn back to enable small craft to pass through, going to and from the *Tirpitz*. We wormed our way through this but just inside ran aground on a shoal. It wasn't so good, but we managed to drag ourselves off, though stirring up a certain amount of mud. This seems to have escaped unnoticed. The lookout who reported the disturbance was told not to be a bloody fool, it was only fish: I learned this later, during interrogation. This little mishap, however, sent our gyrocompass off the board and we were now without any idea of direction.

Heading in the direction I thought the target to be, I found myself caught at seventy feet in the anti-torpedo net. After some very awkward moments, by which time the enemy was sitting up and taking notice, we shot to the surface, stern first, out of control. Fortunately for all concerned, we were so close under the bow of the *Tirpitz* that she was unable to bring her heavy armament to bear and had to be content with hand grenades, small arms and light flak. This was extremely noisy but not very dangerous.

A 19625

Aerial reconnaissance photograph showing the German battleship *Tirpitz* at anchor in a Norwegian fjord. Note the L-shaped torpedo net around the ship.

It was quite obvious that we had no chance of escaping so I decided to lay myself alongside the target, drop my charges and scuttle the craft on top, to prevent her falling into enemy hands. We proceeded to do this. The enemy had stopped firing immediately the hatch was opened and we stepped off into a motor pinnace as X-6 disappeared.

Our reception aboard the *Tirpitz* was rather frigid. They would not believe we were British and maintained we were either Russian or Norwegian saboteurs. We were interrogated and my engine room artificer and myself were on our way below when the charges exploded. It was an extremely unpleasant few minutes before the enemy regained his composure and shepherded us back on deck again. *Tirpitz* had now a slight list to port and oil fuel was spilling over the water. Meanwhile, Place was trying to escape after making his attack.

Lieutenant Godfrey Place
Commander, X-7 (Royal Navy X-Craft submarine)
The explosions went up, with quite a considerable amount of noise, and really rather too close to us for any comfort, although by no means lethal. The after hatch lifted and quite a volume of water came in, there were one or two spurting leaks but nothing very dramatic round and about.

Unfortunately, in the next half an hour, we were unable to maintain any sort of depth. There was so much water inside the boat that as soon as you got the bow-up angle it all washed down to the end and you came up to the surface, and as soon as you got a bow-down angle it switched down to the other end and of course you went rocketing down to the bottom again. We were fired at on the surface and when we lost the night periscope we had a little conference and decided we'd really better bale out.

We considered going up by Davis Escape Apparatus [emergency breathing equipment] but really concluded that it was better for one person to wave a white flag on the surface and be picked up. Then, if the boat went down, it would give an opportunity for the others to make an escape, or he could perhaps warn the enemy not to go attacking them. There was quite a lot of firing going on, so it seemed logical that I should go outside and wave a sweater.

Unfortunately, the boat by then had so little freeboard that it started to fill up. I hastily shut the hatch and the small amount of water that it took in was in fact enough to put it back down to the bottom again, where the other three, as we'd worked out, were to wait about an hour until the worst things had stopped up top and then make a Davis Escape. A Davis Escape, I suppose, is always very risky, although 110 feet of water, as there was then, is not a huge amount. But unfortunately something occurred and two of them got stuck in the boat, I think probably they were overcome by oxygen poisoning, as it was called, before they got a chance to flood it up, and only one of them escaped. He was picked up like myself about an hour or so later. We were taken to the *Tirpitz* and eventually taken to Germany.

Of the other boats, [Lieutenant] Ken Hudspeth, in X-10, the fourth boat that went in, had so many defects that he had to lie up for about four or five days and try to cure, remake, the gyro compass. He was lying up in a deserted part of Stjernsund and didn't get into the target area until ten days after slipping. By then the place was so teeming with small boats that he didn't really have a chance of getting in at all so he went back and was picked up by *Stubborn*.

X-5 got into the vicinity of the target: Cameron saw it after he was on the deck of the *Tirpitz* and the rest of his crew did as well. Whether he attacked or not, we don't know, and I think probably it is impossible to tell. Some years later, a very, very thorough search was made of Kåfjord and his boat was not found, although Cameron was of the opinion that the boat he saw was sunk at that time. All we know is that Henty [its commander, Lieutenant Henty-Creer] was a very, very 'press on' sort of character and that he would have done everything he possibly could.

THE WAR IN THE AIR

Early in the war, the British identified strategic bombing as one of the few available means of delivering serious blows to the heart of the Third Reich. Flying from bases in Britain on raids against Nazi Germany, Fascist Italy and the occupied countries of Europe, the aircraft of RAF Bomber Command – the body that controlled Britain's bomber squadrons – focused initially on military targets. Many of the early operations were flown in daylight, but over time, and as the scale of operations intensified, more were flown at night. Objectives also changed: civilian morale became an additional target.

Enemy fighters and anti-aircraft fire took a tremendous toll of aircraft and the casualties suffered by Bomber Command were extremely high: out of 125,000 aircrew, 55,000 would be killed. By 1943, just one in six airmen could expect to survive a tour of thirty operations and just one in forty to survive a second. By 1945, Allied control of the skies over Europe was growing and daylight raids, escorted by fighters, were common again, but the dangers remained.

Nineteen Victoria Crosses, nine of them posthumous, were awarded to Bomber Command during the Second World War. Airmen of RAF Coastal Command, which was concerned largely with anti-submarine operations, the defence of Allied supply lines and attacks on enemy shipping and harbours, earned a further four.

Flight Lieutenant Roderick Learoyd
49 Squadron, Royal Air Force

Roderick Alistair Brook Learoyd was awarded the Victoria Cross for a low-level attack on the important aqueduct carrying the Dortmund-Ems canal over the River Ems, north of Münster, Germany, on the night of 12–13 August 1940. His citation added that in this and other raids he had 'repeatedly shown the highest conception of his duty and complete indifference to personal danger in making attacks at the lowest altitudes regardless of opposition'.

After the war, Learoyd returned to civilian life, working first as a pilot and later in the motor industry. He died in 1996.

Flight Lieutenant Roderick Learoyd
Hampden bomber pilot, 49 Squadron, Royal Air Force
I was born in Folkestone, Kent, in 1913, the fifth of February. My father had been in the army but otherwise he didn't do anything. He became secretary of a golf club at Littlestone, that's all; otherwise he was a gentleman of leisure, I suppose you might call it. I went to a prep school near Hastings and then to Wellington College. I was only there for a year, Wellington; my mother and father hadn't got very much money so I was withdrawn. After that I went to the Argentine, I'd got a lot of relations in the Argentine, I went to an uncle's fruit farm up in the foothills of the Andes and I was there for a couple of years. Then I came back and I went to an automobile engineering training college in Chelsea for a couple of years and then I got one or two jobs in the motor industry and then decided I'd go in the RAF.

Flight Lieutenant Roderick Learoyd VC.

CH 13631

C 2092

Aerial reconnaissance photograph of the damaged twin aqueducts carrying the Dortmund-Ems canal over the Ems river near Münster, Germany, after the low-level attack by RAF Handley Page Hampdens on the night of 12–13 August 1940. For making a particularly determined attack in his badly damaged aircraft during this raid, Flight Lieutenant Roderick Learoyd of 49 Squadron was awarded Bomber Command's first Victoria Cross.

I tried to get in when I was twenty-one but I was turned down. My father, who knew the Minister for Flying in those days, wrote to him and said something about it. He came back and said, 'Roderick was turned down because the level of his education was not high enough; and, on application to his headmaster, his headmaster was very reticent on the subject. But if he crams he could get in.' So I crammed, went to a crammer, and then I got in, in March 1936.

I got trained at Hamble, near Southampton. Passed that all right, I think. And then we went to Uxbridge, which was the induction centre for short-service officers where we learnt how to be an officer, really: which knives and forks to use and things like that. Then I went off to Wittering before going to my first squadron, which was No 49. The whole squadron got transferred up to Scampton in Lincolnshire and after a period there we got issued with the new Handley Page Hampden.

When war broke out we did mining in the Skagerrak – an awful lot of mining – dropping mines at low-level in the shipping lanes, entrances to harbours and that type of thing. We used to drop propaganda stuff, messages to the German public – 'Give up' and that sort of thing. And we did a lot of bombing of railway marshalling yards, tunnels, to try and cause disruption there. And of course the idea of the Dortmund-Ems canal business was stopping armaments from the Ruhr up to the northern ports. It was a really well-used canal and the target was actually an aqueduct over the Ems River, near Dortmund.

Well, there were five of us, some aircraft from 83 Squadron and some from 49: they were both on the same station. I was detailed to be the fifth aircraft and the timing was a two-minute gap for each aircraft. The delay on the explosive device – it wasn't a bomb or a mine but a cross between the two – was a ten-minute delay, so the last one had to be out in proper time or else he might get blown up by the number one.

Pilot Officer George Frederick Reid
Hampden bomber observer, 49 Squadron, Royal Air Force

It was murder all the way through these sorts of raids, these low-level raids. You're flying at very low level, you see, in order to drop a mine, a soft-skinned mine; to not break up, it had to be dropped from a height of a hundred feet. And you came in along the canal to drop it because there was really only one approach, you had to approach from the north to the south because of the terrain and the Germans knew it as well as we did and they'd kept intensifying the number of guns they had, so you were literally flying into almost parallel flak as it came up towards you. It was a *very* unpleasant raid. Certainly for the last three-quarters of a mile or so, they really gave you a very rough time. 'Bomber' Harris was not at all keen on this sort of thing; he considered at the time that this was almost an act of madness rather than an act of war, that you were asking people to carry out almost suicide missions.

Flight Lieutenant Roderick Learoyd
Hampden bomber pilot, 49 Squadron, Royal Air Force

Gradually we lost height as we came along the canal, following its course all the time. The navigator was in the nose of the aircraft doing the bomb-aiming. Everything was quiet until we got to a point where the canal forked, just before the two aqueducts. I was doing the run-up to this point and then the navigator was taking over the directing. We must have gone off a bit to the left, 'cause he called out, 'Right!' and, immediately after, when we'd turned a bit to make the correction, he called out, 'Steady!' Then suddenly everything started at once: searchlights and all the anti-aircraft fire.

Unfortunate from our point of view of course was that the enemy knew pretty well the direction from which we were going to attack and they had disposed their defences so that they formed a sort of lane through which we had to pass. It seemed to me that they had strengthened these defences a great deal since the first raid. The searchlights were blinding and we were flying entirely on the bomb-aimer's instructions. I had my head down inside the cockpit, trying to see the instruments, but the glare made even that difficult. Our instructions were not to rush it too much 'cause of the need for extreme accuracy. Before we started, the rear-gunner had asked if he could fire at something or somebody and he was shooting at the searchlights as we went past. Almost at the same moment as we bombed, I felt a thump and the aircraft lurched to the right. A pom-pom shell had gone through the starboard wing. Then another shell hit the same wing between the fuselage and the engine. They were firing pretty well at point-blank range.

It was all over in a few seconds. The navigator called out, 'OK, finished!' Then we turned away again. The ground defences were still after us but the tracer was dying out by this time. When we had got away and set course for base, the rear-gunner reported that oil was coming into his cockpit. Then the wireless operator reported that the flaps were drooping. I tried to raise them but found they wouldn't come up; what had happened was that the hydraulic system had been damaged. We discovered too that the undercarriage indicators were out of action. Not having landed without flaps before, I didn't like to try it at night with a crew aboard, so we cruised around for a bit doing a few local cross-countries for about two and a half hours; we waited until dawn, and then we came in all right.

Pilot Officer George Frederick Reid
Hampden bomber observer, 49 Squadron, Royal Air Force
I believe that 'Babe' got his VC because, on that particular raid, the leader went in and it was well over six to seven minutes before Learoyd came along to drop his mine. I'm convinced he knew that there was every chance that the [leader's] mine was going to go up underneath his aircraft.

'Babe' was a nickname from his school days. He was a blonde, blue-eyed, chubby-cheeked lad, looks which must have been even greater when he was a small schoolboy: probably that's why he was called

'Babe'. Incidentally, he was about six-foot-two and he played quite a formidable game of rugby as a forward, so you had to say it with a certain impunity.

Flight Lieutenant Roderick Learoyd
Hampden bomber pilot, 49 Squadron, Royal Air Force

Soon after this raid I was told to go and become PA to Air Chief Marshal Sir Robert Brooke-Popham. I was up in London for a time, for a day or two, and then we went off to Marsham, I think, in East Anglia, to a very big station. And I was accompanying him there and one evening I was in the mess having a drink and Brooke-Popham was called to the telephone and he came back and he said, 'It's for you.' So I went – he hadn't given me a clue – and it was 'Bomber' Harris, who was at that time commander of my Group, 5 Group, and he told me that I'd been awarded the VC.

Well, it's one those things, it's bloody silly, but I didn't believe it and I didn't believe it was Harris. But Brooke-Popham must have been around somewhere because I remember him saying I should take it seriously. I was wrong, it *was* Harris and he *was* telling me I'd got the VC. I didn't know what to say.

Anyhow, I went back into the mess. This must have been early evening, I imagine, because the group captain of the station said, 'I don't know what you want to do, now that you've got this news?' I didn't know anybody there, I was a complete stranger to the place, and he said, 'I'll tell you what, I'll lend you a car' – a Riley, I remember – 'and you can do what you like.' Well, it was too late to do anything really so I just went into Cambridge, I thought I'd go into Cambridge and find a pub or something. I went into one and I remember it was a Scots pub, it had all the tartan decoration. And I was having a beer and I talked to the bloke next to me and I told him, 'I've got a VC.' I couldn't think of anything else to say. And he looked askance and wouldn't believe me and went off. I just came back and went to bed.

Then, of course, next day we went back to London again and that's where all sorts of things happened. I remember being in a nightclub, The Four Hundred, and being put on the stage. They all cheered.

Sergeant James Ward
Royal New Zealand Air Force
75 (NZ) Squadron, Royal Air Force

James Ward, a New Zealander, was second pilot of a Vickers Wellington bomber when, on the night of 7–8 July 1941, he performed the extraordinary deed for which he was awarded the VC: climbing out on to the wing of his burning aircraft – in flight – to smother an engine fire.

'They arrived miraculously home, the plane never to fly again,' the squadron's commanding officer, Wing Commander Cyril Kay, wrote later, 'and as they went off to breakfast and then to bed I went back to the office... to write a citation for Sergeant Ward. All went well until I came to the heading "Award Recommended" but confidently I wrote it in – "Victoria Cross" – and within the space of forty-eight hours it had been approved in turn by the Station Commander, Group Headquarters, Bomber Command, Air Ministry and Buckingham Palace.'*

Born at Wanganui, New Zealand, on 14 June 1919, James Allen Ward had worked as a primary school teacher before joining the Royal New Zealand Air Force in 1940. His account of how he earned his VC, along with the testimony of his pilot, Squadron Leader Widdowson, a Canadian, was recorded for broadcast on 20 August 1941. Ward was killed in action over Hamburg, Germany, less than a month later, on 15 September 1941.

---

* C. E. Kay, *The Restless Sky* (London: Harrap & Co., 1964)

CH 2963

Sergeant James Ward VC, standing in the cockpit of his Vickers Wellington at Feltwell, Norfolk.

Squadron Leader R. P. Widdowson
Canadian pilot, 75 (NZ) Squadron, Royal Air Force

Sergeant Ward was my second pilot on this trip when we'd been taking part in an attack on Münster. It was a beautiful moonlit night and for a change we'd had quite a pleasant time over the target. After we'd dropped our bombs we did another circuit over the town just to watch what was going on and then set course for base. We came to the side of the Zuider Zee and I remember thinking, 'Well, we'll soon be home now.'

Then suddenly we were raked from end to end by fire from an ME 110 which came up from underneath us. The starboard engine was badly damaged, the hydraulic system put out of action and the bomb doors fell open. The wireless and inter-communication sets were made unworkable, the front-gunner was injured in his foot and the cockpit was filled with smoke and fumes. I could see the tracer bullets whizzing past just outside.

Then a fire started in the starboard wing. I could see the glow of it from where I sat at the controls. I shouted to somebody back in the cabin, I don't really know who it was, to tell the rest of the crew to get their parachutes on and stand by to abandon the aircraft. Somebody came up to me and asked if we were over land or over sea and I told him we were just heading for the land. I told the crew to get hold of the fire extinguishers and see if they could put the fire out. They even tried pouring coffee from the Thermos flasks over the burning wing but they found the fire was too far away from the fuselage for the extinguishers to be effective.

When we'd been going down the Dutch coast a few minutes, at about 13,000 feet, I yelled to the second pilot, that's Sergeant Ward, and asked him how the fire was getting on. He said it was still burning but hadn't gained anything after the first flare-up. So I decided to make the sea crossing to the English coast, or at least to try. The sea looked very calm in the moonlight and I remember I thought it would be better to be in the dinghy in the sea than in a German prison camp. Then Sergeant Ward started to get busy.

Sergeant James Ward
New Zealand second pilot, 75 (NZ) Squadron, Royal Air Force

I had a good look at the fire and I thought there was a decent chance of reaching it by getting out through the astrodome and down the side of the fuselage and out on to the wing. Joe, the navigator, said he thought it was crazy. There was a rope there that's usually tied to the dinghy to stop it drifting away if you land on the water, we tied that around my chest and I climbed out through the astrodome and sat on top. I still had my parachute on. I wanted to take it off because I thought it would get in the way, but they wouldn't let me. I sat on the edge of the astrodome for a bit with my legs inside, sort of working out how I was going to do it.

I reached out with one foot and kicked a hole in the fabric so I could get my foot into the framework of the plane. Then I punched another hole in the fabric in front of me so I could get a handhold and after that I made some more holes and went down the side of the fuselage and on to the wing. Joe was holding on to the rope so that I wouldn't drop straight off.

I went out about three or four feet along the wing and the fire was burning up through the wing rather like a big gas jet, blowing back past my shoulder. I had one hand to work with because I was holding on to the cockpit cover [which the crew had been using as a cushion] with the other. I never realised how bulky a cockpit cover could be. The wind kept catching it and several times nearly blew it away and me with it. I kept bunching it up under my arm and then it would blow out again. All the time of course I was lying as flat as I could on the wing. I couldn't get right down flat because of the parachute on my chest.

The wind kept lifting me off the wing and once it slapped me right back against the fuselage but I managed to get a hold again. The slipstream from the engine made things worse, it was like being in a terrific gale but worse than anything I'd known before. I can't explain it but there was no real sense of danger out there. It was just a matter of doing one thing after another and that's about all there was to it.

CH 3223

Photograph of the damage caused to Sergeant James Ward's Wellington on the night of 7/8 July 1941. Cannon shells from an attacking Messerschmitt ME 110 struck the starboard wing (A), causing a fire from a fractured fuel line which threatened to spread to the whole wing. Ward volunteered to tackle the fire by climbing out onto the wing via the astrohatch (B), making hand- and foot-holds in the fuselage and wings (1, 2 and 3) as he moved across to extinguish the burning wing-fabric. His courageous actions earned him a Victoria Cross.

I tried stuffing the cockpit cover down through the hole on the wing on to the pipe where the fire was, but as soon as I pulled my hand away the draught just blew it straight out and finally blew it away altogether. The rear-gunner told me afterwards that he saw it sailing past his turret. I couldn't hold on any longer and after that there was nothing to do but get back again.

I worked my way along the wing and managed to haul myself up on top of the fuselage and got sitting on the edge of the astrodome again. Joe kept the dinghy rope taut all the time and that helped. And by the time I got back I was absolutely done in. I got my left leg into the astrohatch and just sat there looking at my right foot. I couldn't move it. Joe reached out and pulled it in for me and after that I flopped down inside on to the bed and stayed there.

In order to lighten the aircraft we threw out just about everything movable other than valuable things like the bomb-sight and sextant. And though the damaged engine was only developing about a third of its power, we managed to maintain height, about 5,000 feet, I suppose, for a long time and just kept on going. Joe was keeping a plot the whole time; he sort of nipped back in the middle of things, would work out a new position and then go back and help with throwing out more stuff. The wireless operator got the set going again and the rear-gunner stuck to his turret the whole of the time even though he couldn't hear us or see what we were doing.

It took us an hour and a half to cross from the Dutch coast to the English coast. The front-gunner had jettisoned his guns when he was wounded because his turret had been knocked out and wasn't any use at all. He helped fix some other things and then, seeing that there was no more to do, he just sat there and looked at the fire and wondered what was going to happen next.

Then, just when we were within reach of the English coast, the fire on the wing suddenly blazed up again. There was a pool of petrol on the lower surface of the wing and this caught fire. I remember thinking to myself, 'Well, this is pretty hard after having got this far.' However, after this final flare-up, the fire died out altogether, much to our relief I can tell you.

The trouble now was to get down. We pumped the wheels down with the emergency gear. The pilot decided that instead of going to our own base, he'd try to land at another aerodrome nearby, which had a far greater landing space. As we circled before landing he called up control and said, 'We've been badly shot up. I hope we don't make too much of a mess of your flare path when we're landing'. He put the aircraft down beautifully but as we had no brakes we finally ran into the barbed-wire entanglement on the end of the 'drome. Fortunately nobody was hurt, though, and that was the end of the trip.

Squadron Leader R. P. Widdowson
Canadian pilot, 75 (NZ) Squadron, Royal Air Force

It wasn't until after he was safely back in the aircraft again that I heard that he'd actually been out on the wing to try to put the fire out. The more I think of it, the more amazing it seems to me that anyone could have done what he did. Remember that we were flying at about ninety miles an hour at a height of 13,000 feet: in other words, about two and a half miles up in the air. Getting out of the astrohatch is difficult enough when you've got full flying kit on with the aircraft stationary on the ground. As for how he managed to stick on when once he'd got out, I really don't know. He'd got the rope from the dinghy tied round him but that couldn't have been much help. In the end the cockpit cover was torn from his grasp by the rush of wind, but there was now little danger of the fire spreading from the petrol-pipe as there was no fabric left nearby after Sergeant Ward's effort. It eventually burnt itself out and we managed to make a fairly decent landing. Sergeant Ward seemed to take what he'd done as a matter of course, but in my opinion it was a most wonderful show.

Flight Sergeant Rawdon Middleton
Royal Australian Air Force
149 Squadron, Royal Air Force

'Ron' Middleton, as he was known in the air force, was posthumously awarded the Victoria Cross for his actions during a raid on the Fiat works at Turin, Italy, on the night of 28–29 November 1942. Despite terrible injuries inflicted by anti-aircraft fire over the target, Middleton tried to nurse his crippled aircraft home and made it as far as the English coast before ordering his crew to bail out. Five of his crew did so and landed safely before Middleton, reluctant to risk civilian casualties or abandon his aircraft, turned out to sea.

'Flight Sergeant Middleton was determined to attack the target regardless of the consequences and not to allow his crew to fall into enemy hands.' his citation ends. 'While all the crew displayed heroism of a high order, the urge to do so came from Flight Sergeant Middleton, whose fortitude and strength of will made possible the completion of the mission. His devotion to duty in the face of overwhelming odds is unsurpassed in the annals of the Royal Air Force.'

Born at Waverley, New South Wales, on 22 July 1916, Rawdon Hume Middleton had been working as a jackeroo – a trainee stockman – on a sheep station in the outback when the Second World War began. He had then enlisted in the Royal Australian Air Force and, after training in Australia, Canada and England, been posted in 1942 to 149 Squadron, based in Suffolk, as a Short Stirling bomber pilot. The Turin raid was his twenty-ninth operation: one short of a completed tour.

Norman Skinner, Middleton's wireless operator, recorded the following testimony for broadcast on 14 January 1943. Middleton's body was thought lost at that moment but eventually washed up on the coast the following month. Skinner himself was shot down and killed in September 1944 on a sortie over the Netherlands. Middleton's navigator, George Royde, was also killed later in the war.

CHP 1217

Flight Sergeant Rawdon Middleton VC.

Flying Officer Norman Skinner
Stirling bomber wireless operator, 149 Squadron, Royal Air Force

I was the wireless operator in the Stirling crew of which Flight Sergeant Middleton was captain. Even while the action was on, I remember thinking 'I'm watching this, not a part of it'. It was like seeing a film of a burning house. Somehow it never enters your head that you personally won't come out of it alive. I hope this explains why some of the details may not be quite clear. I remember them as if they were in a film I had seen some time ago.

Ron Middleton was an Australian and lived most of his life on his father's sheep station at Bogan Gate in New South Wales. He was twenty-six years old and about the most modest chap I've ever met, and, at the same time, good-looking. He was so efficient that the three gunners of his crew had asked to be allowed to continue to fly with him even though they had completed their tour of operations. They were with us on this trip to Turin.

After dusk, we got the green light from the aerodrome control pilot in his caravan by the runway and Middleton opened the throttles and we took off. Over France, Middleton noticed that our Stirling, H for Harry, was using up a lot of fuel in climbing. We were detailed to go down low over Turin to attack the Fiat works, and that meant that we should have to climb twice to get over the Alps, so we were naturally very careful about the consumption of fuel, and climbed slowly to economise. By the time we reached the Alps we had climbed to 12,000 feet.

There was no moon and we should normally have crossed the Alps several thousand feet higher, but Middleton decided to go on and make his way through the mountains. The front-gunner was told to watch ahead and everybody in the bomber began to look out at the sides of the mountains. We could see patches of snow – white amongst the dark shadows – and there was an anxious moment when the shadows closed in and the front-gunner reported. 'Mountains, straight ahead!' Middleton said, 'We're coming to a dead end,' he opened the bomb doors and the navigator was about to jettison the bombs, so that we could climb to safety, when the front-gunner called out, 'It's there, look to starboard.' Far to the right and below us, we could see the lights of Turin and British flares blazing in the sky above the city. We closed our bomb doors and turned to fly down this pass.

Middleton again asked about the petrol and the flight engineer said that, if we went down low, we might not be able to get back to base. Then Middleton asked if we could make an airfield on the south coast of England. The engineer said, yes, we could. 'Right, we're going down,' Middleton said. Royde, the navigator, went into the bombing well.

As we neared Turin, Middleton skilfully wove his way down through the light flak and the flares. For a moment I wondered if we were going to get entangled in the white silk parachutes from which the flares were hanging. Then we were hit by flak in the wing, which reduced our power of lift, and Middleton called for Flight Sergeant Hyder, his second pilot, to help him with the controls. We heard him say over the intercom, 'We're still OK,' and he began circling again among the flak.

Middleton had just identified the target when a shell burst in the cockpit between him and Hyder and wounded both of them. He said, 'I'm hit.' Then he lost consciousness and the Stirling went into a dive. As we went down, the fuselage and the mainplanes were being hit almost continuously. Hyder got to the controls and brought the bomber out of the dive but we were down to eight hundred feet before we felt her level out. Middleton came to while we were climbing and his first question was whether we were too low to bomb.

We could see the housetops of Turin and tremendous fires. It was a wonderful night for bombers and we dropped our load from just about 1,500 feet and felt the thuds of light flak along the mainplane at the same time. Despite his appalling injuries – his right eye had been destroyed by a shell splinter and the bone above the eye was exposed – Middleton ordered the second pilot back to the rest bunk to have his own wounds dressed. He, too, had been badly hit; but he refused to have a tourniquet put on his wounded leg. 'I want to go back and help Ron,' he said, and he shambled past me, head forward, looking in his determination like a wounded bear. I saw the bloodstains on his green flying suit as he passed the lights on the engineer's panel and I could not imagine how he kept standing.

We thought then of flying to North Africa, to avoid the climb over the Alps, but Middleton was determined to get his crew back to England. To make most of our fuel, we jettisoned as much as we could: the camera, armour plating, oxygen bottles, ammunition, flares, seats, fire extinguishers and even the sextant. Royde, the navigator, prowled around the aircraft with a fireman's axe, chopping off things to jettison. He asked Middleton whether we should drop the guns overboard. Middleton replied, 'Yes, OK, George, carry on. But try not to talk to me, it hurts when I answer.'

We had a four hours' flight ahead of us and the Alps to climb again. Both our pilots were seriously wounded and their windscreen was smashed in so that they were sitting in an icy gale. Sergeant Mackie, the front-gunner, came back and stood by the injured pilots setting the compass and helping them to weave their way through the passes. The time spent in bombing Turin had, we thought, reduced fuel so much that we would be lucky if we reached the sea in order to ditch, so we checked our dinghies. Then the north wind dropped a little and we made better headway. There was still little hope of reaching England safely, however, and our captain must have realised that he could have baled out or crash-landed on the flat plain of France, but he had made up his mind to get his crew back to England, although his wounds were serious.

Over northern France I saw a flash of light above me and realised it was a reflection on the astrodome of searchlights, we were coned by about twelve of them, and more light flak hit the wings. Middleton was an artist at throwing a bomber about and we lost height from six thousand to six hundred feet. He asked again about petrol and, just as we sighted the coast of England, the engineer reported he could guarantee five minutes of fuel but not ten. Middleton asked for his parachute and it was passed to him by the navigator, but I believe now that this was no more than a gesture to reassure us. His voice was very thick and difficult to understand. For a moment I went off the intercom to get a bearing and when I came on again to announce the result I was told that the order had been given to bale out. I went forward, in time to see the second pilot's upturned face disappear, and then I went out.

No one will ever know what was going on in Middleton's mind during those last few moments, but when the engines of a big bomber cut it does not glide easily. So Middleton went out to sea, perhaps thinking he had a better chance of ditching than crash-landing, but evidently he was too far gone to alight safely on the sea. The bodies of the engineer and the front-gunner were found the next day but Flight Sergeant Middleton's body was never recovered. During the return home there were many opportunities for us to have abandoned the aircraft over France and for Middleton to live but he preferred that we, his crew, and the aircraft of which he was captain should not fall into enemy hands. That was the kind of man he was.

Flight Lieutenant William Reid
Royal Air Force Volunteer Reserve
61 Squadron, Royal Air Force

Bill Reid was awarded the Victoria Cross for his actions during an attack on Düsseldorf on the night of 3 November 1943. Though wounded in the head and with his aircraft damaged and windscreen shattered after an attack by an enemy fighter, Reid maintained his course for the target. Then the aircraft was attacked again, being raked from end to end by machine-gun fire which killed his navigator, mortally wounded his wireless operator, wounded Reid for the fourth time and put the intercom and oxygen systems out of action. Still he pressed on to the target, which he and his crew duly bombed before finally turning for home. The return trip was safely accomplished.

His citation ends: 'Wounded in two attacks, without oxygen, suffering severely from cold, his navigator dead, his wireless operator fatally wounded, his aircraft crippled and defenceless, Flight Lieutenant Reid showed superb courage and leadership in penetrating a further 200 miles into enemy territory to attack one of the most strongly defended targets in Germany, every additional mile increasing the hazards of the long and perilous journey home. His tenacity and devotion to duty were beyond praise.'

After recovering from his injuries, Reid flew missions with 617 Squadron until July 1944 when he was forced to bail out over France after bombs dropped from another Lancaster struck and crippled his aircraft. He was captured on the ground and saw out the war in prison camps in Germany and Poland.

Born in Glasgow on 21 December 1921, the son of a blacksmith, Bill Reid had been educated at Coatbridge Secondary School before joining the RAF Volunteer Reserve in 1940 and being trained in the United States as a pilot. After the war he left the RAF, studied agriculture at Glasgow University and worked for twenty years as an agricultural adviser on cattle and sheep feed. Retiring to Crieff, he died in 2001.

Flight Lieutenant William Reid
Lancaster bomber pilot, 61 Squadron and 617 Squadron, Royal Air Force, 1943–44

I was in school actually when the war started and I finished my highers to go to university in 1940. I wanted to join the RAF because my brother was in Blenheims at the time. He went missing in 1940 so my mother felt I should hold on a bit so I did wait and I tried one or two jobs. I then joined the RAF but I was put on about nine months' deferred service, during which time I became a postman at Christmas time and had odd

CHP 794

Flight Lieutenant William Reid VC.

jobs like that. I was actually called into the air force in August 1941. I joined up as aircrew and I happened to pass to get into the pilot training side. In 1943 I was posted to 61 Squadron at Syerston and it was while I was flying with 61 Squadron that I got my VC. That was my tenth trip.

I was attacked just after I'd crossed the Dutch coast. We were flying at 21,000 feet and were attacked with such a burst in my face that I was sure it was flak – ack-ack – that had hit us because I'd had no warnings at all from the gunners. Normally if we were attacked by a fighter they'd say, 'Dive starboard!' 'Dive port!' I lost about 2,000 feet and then they said that it was an ME 110 that had attacked us. I was wounded but I didn't feel as if I was going to drop dead, I didn't see much point in panicking and saying, 'I'm wounded,' and I felt fit enough to drive on.

We flew on and were again attacked about a quarter of an hour later and this time everything went dead. The intercom went dead and we had no oxygen because that was blown off and the compasses were broken and the windscreen was completely shattered. My engineer was wounded in the forearm, which I didn't know at the time but I could see him holding both hands together. The port elevator on the tailplane had been blown away so that I had to hold the stick back in my belly to keep it straight and level and we had to hold full left rudder too. We were down to 17,000 feet by this time: I'd lost another 2,000 feet. So I flew on and then I pointed to the compass, because we couldn't talk to each other, it was too noisy, you couldn't hear, and I pointed back to the cabin where the navigator was, meaning: 'Get me another course.' He came back and shook his hands to say the navigator was lying down, as if he'd been knocked out. I then looked for the Pole Star and the moon.

This particular night we were bombing Düsseldorf but we were heading straight for Cologne, because they were dropping spoof flares there as if we were going to bomb Cologne but in the last twenty minutes we would turn to bomb Düsseldorf. Sure enough, we could see the flares going down, so I turned up to bomb Düsseldorf; and you could see other planes off beside you, which you often did at night, flying more or less in the same direction. I put down the handle for opening the bomb doors, the hydraulics had gone, and I just had to keep it straight and level as far as I could. I just pointed ahead and held it straight and level and then I felt the bombs going. Meantime, the engineer had been giving me oxygen, you carried these oxygen bottles in different places in case you moved the plane above 10,000 feet, and having no oxygen he fed these to me every twenty minutes or half an hour or so. And then I turned back to head for home.

We oscillated a bit then and I suppose I passed out occasionally but I came to again and the bomb-aimer and the engineer kept holding the stick with me. We did go over a lot of areas we should never have flown over and we got flak at us but we didn't get hit again. Eventually we got over what I thought was the North Sea and we came down quicker to get below oxygen height and headed for the English shore.

Then we saw some beacons flashing. It was a small training 'drome so it was no good so we just kept heading on and then we saw in front of us this great big canopy of searchlights. Often this meant you were over a 'drome: if they saw somebody was in trouble, they might lead them in and sweep them towards where they should go. So we could see this big canopy of searchlights but on the way towards that we came upon this great big Drem system [an airfield lighting system for night-time landings] lit up below us. I could see that it was a big runway, so I circled that.

Of course, having no radio I couldn't call up so I flashed my landing lamp for landing. And then, of course, having no hydraulics I had to put down the undercarriage and the flaps, I had to pump it down, and when I pumped it my head started to bleed again and it ran into my eyes. My shoulder was still sore but they were still helping me hold back the stick and we flew round, saw the sodium flares lit up, came down and made a long approach and landed. As we landed the legs collapsed and we went along on our belly for about fifty yards. And it was only then, when I'd switched off everything, that I saw Geoff, my navigator, had slid up beside me. He'd been lying dead back in his cabin and slid forward.

It was an American 'drome, Shipton, in Norfolk, that we'd landed at. We all got out through the dinghy escape hatch and out on to the wing and into this ambulance. They looked at Geoff when they took us into the medical site and he was obviously dead and they put him aside and they started cleaning up my shoulder and my head wound and I had a blood transfusion. We were there that night and then they took us to Norwich Cottage Hospital the next day and I had some more treatment on my shoulder, and two days later the wireless operator died. Then they moved us down, my engineer and I, to Ely RAF hospital in Cambridgeshire.

That happened on 3 November '43 and I was flying again in January '44, when I came back from sick leave. I was posted then to 617 Squadron, which was the dam-busting squadron, but that was after the dam-busting. I then had to make a crew up again and I took with me my bomb-aimer – he was the only one of my original crew who came with me. Then we flew with 617 from then up to 31 July.

On 31 July we were on a daylight trip bombing these V2 bomb storages east of Paris. They were in these tunnels and we were dropping 12,000-pound bombs on the end of a tunnel to try and close it. And just after we dropped our bomb I felt this clump of bombs, a stick of bombs, hitting us from a plane above. I said, 'Stand by to bale out,' because there was no control of the stick, and I think the port outer engine fell away and then we started to turn in. I got my parachute on, the plane was starting to spin down, I was trying to open the side window to slip out of that and then I thought of the dinghy escape hatch on to the roof, so I started to turn the handle above me. And I think the whole nose must have come off then because the next thing all was quiet and I was falling through the air. I felt for my parachute cord and I pulled it, I saw these trees coming up, watched that I kept my legs together as I went into these trees, and I landed right into the top of a tree.

I slid down the tree and I took my Mae West off and I stuffed it under the bushes and then I headed about half a mile into this forest and sat down, took my shell dressing out and wrapped up my hand. I thought I'd look for my escape kit: I could speak enough French to get past and I thought I'd head south and then go to Paris. And as I stood up these three Germans come up with their rifles and bayonets – 'Halten Sie an! Hände hoch!' and whatnot – and that was me taken prisoner.

I was taken to Brussels and interrogated. 'What squadron were you with? Your crew are all dead, you might as well tell us.' I just kept saying name, rank and number and that was it. Once or twice they mentioned the squadron; they probably knew then about 617 Squadron. I never made any acknowledgement. And I remember this fat-looking chap, the officer that was in charge, with his girl listening and writing down anything that he reported. And he turned to her, after I kept repeating my name, rank and number, he pointed to my medal ribbon and he said, 'The same as the Knight's Cross with oak leaves' – or with diamonds or something like this. 'Und so jung' – 'cause I looked young. Twenty-two, I would have been.

Flying Officer John Cruickshank
210 Squadron, Royal Air Force

John Cruickshank, a flying-boat pilot, was awarded the Victoria Cross for his actions on 17 July 1944 while on an anti-submarine patrol in the Atlantic. He attacked and sank a German U-boat, the U-361, and, despite seventy-two separate wounds including pierced lungs inflicted by the submarine's guns, insisted on helping his crew land their damaged aircraft when they made it back to base. 'By pressing home the second attack in his gravely wounded condition and continuing his exertions on the return journey with his strength failing all the time, he seriously prejudiced his chance of survival even if the aircraft safely reached its base,' his citation ends. 'Throughout, he set an example of determination, fortitude and devotion to duty in keeping with the highest traditions of the Service.'

Born in Aberdeen, Scotland, on 20 May 1920 and educated in Edinburgh and Aberdeen, John Alexander Cruickshank had joined the Territorial Army while apprenticed to the Commercial Bank of Scotland and served in the Royal Artillery until 1941 when he transferred to the Royal Air Force. In 1943, after training in Canada and the United States, he was posted to 210 Squadron, a Coastal Command squadron based at Sullom Voe in the Shetland Islands, as pilot of a Consolidated PBY Catalina flying boat. He recovered from his injuries suffered in his attack on the U-361 and left the RAF in 1946 to return to his banking career. At the time of writing he is a living recipient of the Victoria Cross and the last surviving holder of a VC awarded for air action during the Second World War.

Flight Sergeant John Appleton
Australian wireless operator mechanic, 210 Squadron,
Royal Air Force
We went into the ops room, saluted, looked at the map on the wall, noticed that the red ribbon went way up to the north to the Lofoten Islands. It was just another patrol. It seemed to me that it might be a breakout of U-boats from the Norwegian area to get round the north of the UK, down the Atlantic and into the Normandy invasion area. This was 17 July, five or six weeks after D-Day.

So we went up on this trip. It was five hours or so to get there and the sea was dead flat, absolutely dead flat. We flew on this north-easterly course for five hours or so until we got to the patrol area. We did our usual rotation on the hour and I was on the radar, I was sitting there, watching, and I thought I saw a target. It was forty-three nautical miles away when I noticed it. And I watched this target and within a couple of minutes – that's another three miles or so, we used to fly at ninety-five knots – I felt confident that it was a target and that it ought to be worth mentioning. So I reported it to the skipper and he turned the knob on the autopilot and started to home on to it.

It would take twenty minutes to get there, during which time the navigator would have checked his last position and handed it to the wireless operator in case the wireless operator had to send a signal. The people in the blisters would have got ready, switched on their reflector sights and unstrapped their guns, made them ready to be used. Somebody would have gone up to the front turret; as it happened, it was Paddy Harbison, our first engineer. People just generally got ready for some sort of incident. Of course we didn't know what the target was.

When we got within a reasonable distance, Paddy, in the front turret, and the two pilots thought they could see something, a ship of some sort. By this time I was getting very good strong returns so I knew it was a proper target. By the time we got to within five miles, I suppose, we fired the colours of the day from the Very pistol and flashed the Aldis lamp letter of the day. If this ship was one of ours we didn't want it shooting us down and the navy tends to regard any aircraft approaching it as enemy.

This must have confirmed to the ship that we were not on their side. I immediately heard Paddy Harbison and the two pilots on the intercom discussing this. They said, 'It's not a destroyer at all, it's a U-boat.' John Cruickshank then fired the klaxon horn to alert everybody, told everybody over the intercom. By this time John Dickson had gone up forward into his bomb-aiming position, switched on all the bomb-aiming apparatus, checked what he had to check. And we then commenced an attack.

By this time the submarine was well and truly in visual contact and therefore I could stand up and look over John Cruickshank's shoulder. As I could see no more on the radar, it was part of my job actually to observe what I could about the submarine and about the action. And I saw the thing firing at us quite heavily but it wasn't very accurate, the flak was all over the place.

We made this attack and I remember looking straight out of the window as the aircraft banked and turned and I could see out of the pilot's left windows down into the conning tower of the submarine. We did the usual breakaway and I immediately went aft, absolutely certain that I would see the destruction of a U-boat. When I got there I saw a couple of irate crew members and I said, 'What's the matter? What's the matter?' They said, 'Look,' and they pointed to the two wings and there were the six depth charges still there: the depth charges had failed to drop.

I went forward to tell the skipper and they told him on the intercom that the depth charges had failed to release. I heard John Cruickshank say to Dicky, 'What do you think's gone wrong?' and John Dickson say, 'I don't know and I'll check.' John Dickson was a very thorough person, I'm sure he'd have checked very thoroughly. Paddy Harbison had fired his machine guns on the way in but I'm sure quite uselessly: I'd noticed that the U-boat had two pairs of 20-millimetre guns and a 37-millimetre gun, they were all behind gun shields of half-inch-thick steel, and a rifle-sized bullet really was useless on that. Anyway, the skipper said, 'We'd better go in again. Here we go. Everybody ready?'

We made another attack and it was as spot-on as the first. We really went right over the conning tower of the U-boat, no question about that, but I did notice that the flak was considerably thicker this time, far more accurate. It was grouped together instead of being spread all over the sky in front of us: it was aiming straight at us. And we flew straight through this lot and it was quite obvious that we'd been hit.

We had been hit by, I think, a 37-millimetre shell, which is the same sort of shell as a Bofors gun uses, almost the same size as a Bofors. This had obviously exploded quite clearly right in the middle of the forward compartment, the nose compartment. It had killed John Dickson immediately; I could see his body just blown to pieces. Paddy Harbison in the front turret had been hit in the legs. The side effects of the explosion had hit John Cruickshank. A little bit had hit Jack Garnett in the left hand.

I saw that Jack's wound wasn't that bad. I think I bandaged it. But then I looked at the skipper and I saw all his trouser legs were blood-soaked. He hadn't said a word, he was still flying the aircraft; he'd done the breakaway, which meant pulling up and climbing and getting some height to get in a position where he could observe the U-boat and what was happening to it and whether it was sinking or not. Then I realised he was badly wounded so, having opened this first-aid kit, I found a big pair of scissors which were obviously intended for cutting away uniform and cut away the trouser leg in the hope of finding where he'd been hit. And before I got very far with this he went deathly white and collapsed, he nearly fell off his seat. I beckoned to somebody in the navigation department who I think was Ian Fidler and he came and helped me and we steadied John but it was obvious he was badly wounded, you could tell from his pallor and the blood everywhere. At this point Ian Fidler went forward, being a pilot, to help Jack Garnett, who had taken over flying the aircraft.

It was obvious we had to put John Cruickshank on a bunk. He couldn't stay where he was; he was obviously badly wounded. So we carried him through the bulkheads and also over the big mainframe at the rear of the engineer's compartment and put him on the port bunk. He was obviously in terrible shape and I realised he must be in terrible pain. I could see blood starting to soak through even through all his flying gear and pullovers and so on, but he hadn't mentioned any of this at all. He was lapsing between consciousness and unconsciousness. He was obviously in very bad shape.

I thought he was mortally wounded and I wanted to make him as comfortable as possible; we had no facilities for doing any surgery or even to try and extract shrapnel. I started to bandage his legs and I gave him a sip of water. I knew that one had to be careful about giving water to anybody with suspect chest wounds but in the circumstances – having lost that much blood, I could see blood everywhere, soaked into all his clothing – he must have had a dry mouth so I gave him something to sip. I got hold of a shell dressing and soaked it in water and wiped his face with it; I knew how cooling and comforting such an action could be. It was now obvious that he had been wounded from the chest down to his legs although he'd said nothing about wounds at all. And I put whatever I could find to keep him warm. There's usually a couple of blankets lying somewhere and I put them on; other people's Irvine jackets or pullovers, I put those on.

But I thought he must be in terrible pain and inside the first-aid kit there were tubes of morphine. These were very simple devices; they were like a small toothpaste tube about three or four inches long, with a needle built into the end and the whole thing protected by a cap. You unscrewed the cap, put the needle in wherever you could, squeezed the whole of the tube in and then threw the thing away. You were then supposed to write in blood – of which there was copious quantities available – on the forehead the letter 'M' for morphine and, if possible, the time. That was so anybody subsequently treating the patient would know he'd had one lot of morphine, when and how much, and could treat him accordingly. But John Cruickshank was alert enough to see what I was doing and quite firmly said, 'No, no, no, no.' And I think he physically, with his arms, stopped me from attempting to inject him with the morphine. Well, that was his wish. I didn't think it was the right decision but that was his wish, so I put the cap back on the tube and put it back in the bag. I could guess that he realised that morphine would have affected his ability to do almost anything. It would have knocked him out presumably and he didn't want to be knocked out.

I was more concerned with his comfort and I was determined to stay with him, because there's nothing worse than coming round from one of these lapses into unconsciousness and finding nobody there, just a draughty battered-about aircraft, fire-damaged at that. So I stayed with him there but, I must admit, after going back and forth up front to see how the other two pilots were handling things and how the navigation was going. I thought we were going OK because Ian Fidler had worked out a rough course to get home.

After a while I'd made Cruickshank as comfortable as I thought I could, I'd wiped his face, given him water and so on, and he said, 'How's Dicky?' which was the name we all used for John Dickson. I was completely stumped by this. I thought, 'How do you answer this?' to a man who, I thought, was mortally wounded anyway. I did think he was so badly wounded he wouldn't make it. All I was concerned about was him being comfortable and I didn't want to ruin this by blurting out, 'Well, he's dead.' But before I could say anything he just guessed that Dicky was dead from my look and my hesitation in responding to his question. They were close mates: they were different sort of people, altogether different, but they'd flown together almost every trip since February 1943 and they were the two commissioned people on board. And so John Cruickshank realised that Dickson was dead and he said, 'Well, Jack's the skipper.' I said, 'Don't worry, Jack's fine and everything's perfectly all right and Ian's navigating. No problem.' All I wanted to do was make the skipper relax. There was nothing I thought he could do.

We got over base at three-thirty in the morning. I said to the skipper, 'We're over base,' and his immediate reaction was, 'Help me up, help me up.' I said, 'No, skipper, all's well. We've got Jack Garnett and Ian Fidler up front.' But Cruickshank was quite determined that they couldn't do it by themselves. He said, 'You must help me up,' so I got some help from somebody in carrying the skipper up forward, through those bulkhead doors. Width-wise they barely let your elbows through and when your arms are carrying a lifeless man – and John Cruickshank was six foot three, a big man himself – it was very difficult. Not so much difficult for ourselves, but we thought, 'How agonising for a person badly wounded.' Also I was aware that veins and arteries may have stopped bleeding, may have congealed and healed up a bit, mainly because they were blocked by a piece of shrapnel. To move a person and then move the piece of shrapnel could start the bleeding all over again and he'd lost enough blood as it was, we didn't want him to lose any more. But eventually we got him up forward.

I don't know to what extent he actually took over control because there were limitations to what he could do, but I'm sure he might have just been doing override action, with Jack Garnett flying, and also putting in advice. He'd have been doing, say, a quarter of the flying. He could have used expressions like, 'Lower, lower. Not so low. Take it easy.' He could have worked the throttles, for instance. 'Too much power, not enough power' – all this sort of thing. I don't know the details of what they did.

It still wasn't light enough to land so we waited, I think, about forty minutes or so circling the base. And I looked down from the blister in the half-light and I could see all sorts of activity: all these people on the water in their boats and tenders and dinghies and so on. I could see that everybody was there: the station commander; the squadron commander; station engineer; the medical people were probably in three or four boats, so that no matter where we actually landed we could have medical people within seconds on to us. And eventually we landed, fortunately the water was calm, and we aimed for this so-called Heinkel Gap which was a piece of beach at the end of the landing area which was designated an emergency beaching spot, the idea being to run the thing up on to the sand.

The dinghies came alongside and I could see the medical people hovering over the sliding hatches above the two pilots and they were particularly attending to the right-hand seat where I knew Cruickshank was sitting. And while this was happening I realised that the camera needed to be salvaged: the camera is located on a bracket and takes pictures automatically once the depth charge release sequence is started. So I went and retrieved the camera and looked after it and eventually I said to someone, 'Would you please get this back to base, back to the ops room?' Eventually I persuaded one of the motorboats to take it back.

The camera was taken ashore and it had this picture. It was taken automatically and you can see from the line of the picture that we were dead across the conning tower, it's slap bang in the middle of the picture, and you can quite clearly see the depth charge splashes where they landed each side of the submarine. The camera had been taking pictures from the very beginning of the first attack and I understand that nobody had bothered to switch the camera off – nobody had thought about it, frankly – and that frame was the very last frame on the roll of film. We were lucky to have it. If we'd been a second or two later, we'd have missed

C 4590

The remarkable photograph taken from Flying Officer John Cruickshank's Consolidated Catalina during his second attack on the German submarine U-361 west of the Lofoten Islands. The splashes from the first of his depth charges can be seen astern of the submarine. Machine-gun fire from a gun housed in one of the Catalina's 'blisters' can be seen hitting the sea to the top left of the picture. The submarine was later confirmed sunk and Cruickshank's accurate attack, and his gallantry in assisting the second pilot to fly the damaged aircraft back to base, despite his severe wounds, earned him the Victoria Cross.

it. Subsequently I found out that Paddy Harbison in the front had noticed, as we broke away, a violent explosion, which we suspect was one of the submarine's own torpedoes going off because the explosive content of a torpedo was more than that of a depth charge.

I got ashore. Everybody was hanging around at the pierhead and there was an aircrew truck or some vehicle there to take us back, 'cause six or seven of the crew weren't even hurt in any way at all and all they wanted to do was get back and get cleaned up and get some breakfast and sleep. I was about to get in the same vehicle and a medical flight sergeant said to me, 'Where do you think you're going?' I said, 'Well, back to the mess, get cleaned up, have some breakfast.' He said, 'Look at yourself. Get into the ambulance.' So I looked in a driving mirror and I could see I'd been hit: my face was covered in caked blood. I suppose I must have been rather a frightening sight for Cruickshank every time he looked up at me to see this gory bloodstained person treating him; if I'd known, I'd have done something to wash the blood away. Anyway, I got in and they took me to the station sick quarters. Then I was in a military hospital in Lerwick for about a fortnight.

It took me a while before I was able to go up and see John Cruickshank in the so-called officers' ward. We were on the ground floor, he was on the first floor, but after a few days they said, 'Yes, you can go up and see him.' By this time I was able to get up and look after myself even though my head was all tied up with bandages and I went up and saw the skipper and we briefly spoke and chatted. Word trickled through eventually that he had a large number of shrapnel wounds. I never saw any medical report, it was all confidential, and John never spoke about it, but I would imagine he might have had two or three major wounds, I'm sure. There was certainly something serious in his thigh, which I'd tried to bandage up, and he was certainly hit with something quite substantial in the chest, which could include near misses to the lungs, heart and other organs. I don't know the precise detail of how he was wounded but I know that an enormous amount of blood was lost.

After I came back from leave I was called to the operations room and I went in and the intelligence officer said, 'The Air Ministry want to have a chat with you.' I thought, 'God, the Air Ministry? What do they want with me?' They gave me a red phone, a red scrambler phone, and I thought, 'This is getting really important': I'd never used a scrambler phone before. When I was told to, I pressed a red button and presumably it was all scrambled and somebody came on the phone at the other end and they asked me all about the action and I told them.

A few days later, on the PA system at the airfield, they announced that John Cruickshank had been awarded the VC. There was an account in all the newspapers – all the newspapers except I think *The Times* – which was something like what I'd told the Air Ministry people. But the Air Ministry's press release was considerably toned down. They didn't reveal the background to our being there; they certainly made no reference to radar at all; they just gave the impression that we'd stumbled upon this U-boat. Sadly, this press release has been the sole piece of information some authors have used since then to write the account of John Cruickshank's action, which doesn't do justice to what John Cruickshank did.

Flight Sergeant George Thompson
9 Squadron, Royal Air Force

The son of a farmer, George Thompson was born at Trinity Gask, Perthshire, Scotland, on 23 October 1920 and had been educated at Kinross High School before being apprenticed, aged fourteen, to a local grocer. He joined the Local Defence Volunteers when war broke out and the Royal Air Force in 1941. After serving as groundcrew on various bases in the Middle East he volunteered for aircrew. 'I'm browned off,' he wrote in a letter home in 1943, explaining why he wanted the transfer. 'It's not that I want to do any of that heroic stuff, but this job isn't very exciting.'* Joining Bomber Command as a wireless operator, he was awarded a posthumous Victoria Cross for his actions on 1 January 1945 when, with his Lancaster bomber badly damaged and ablaze after being attacked over Germany, he fought to save the lives of two of the aircraft's gunners.

Flying Officer Harold Denton
New Zealand Lancaster bomber pilot, 9 Squadron, Royal Air Force

It was a beautiful morning, cold but clear, and I couldn't suppress a certain feeling of exhilaration as U for Uncle, that's my Lancaster, purred along with the French coast contoured far beneath us. I rather liked daylight trips. You felt more, as it were, free as the air. The weather still remained good as I altered course. I just glanced round to see other Lancasters at our prearranged rendezvous and continued on our way for Germany. Really, one just sits and thinks or hums a light tune as the aircraft slips through the sky.

Through the haze and loosely billowed clouds I could see France beneath and occasionally rivers stretched like twisted, silvery ribbons across the flat country. The time over the target had been set just before noon, and, glancing at my watch, I found we had been flying for something like three hours when I saw the faithful Spitfires escorting us. They are wonderful planes as they streak through the clouds and just remind me of excited children round their mother when they are near us. I could see the River Rhine quite plainly. Although we knew we were somewhere close to this area, spasmodic bursts of flak welcomed us. Our target was the Dortmund-Ems Canal and it was such a clear morning, so much so that I could see the clear stretch of water minutes before we were timed to attack. You see, we were the last of a fairly long run. I spoke to the crew. Everything was OK, we went in, the bomb-aimer said, 'Bombs going.' Then it came.

---

* *The Sunday Express*, 30 April 1961

CH 14685

Flight Sergeant George Thompson VC.

I remember that moment. There was a terrific blast that shook the aircraft violently and completely filled it with smoke. A few seconds later the air cleared and I saw that the nose and canopy had been shattered. I knew we'd been hit by a burst of flak. I remember seeing the blackened figure of the bomb-aimer struggling up from the nose, clutching his burst parachute. The intercom had been smashed so I couldn't speak to the crew. Glancing out at the engines I saw that the starboard inner was on fire. I did the only possible thing, to feather the engine and use the automatic extinguishers. The fire went out immediately. I opened out to full throttle with the other three engines and realised that I had to reach [the recently liberated] France or Holland as soon as possible. With the trimming tabs damaged and the aircraft tail heavy, we lost height steadily. The thought rushed through my mind how lucky I had been. For almost an hour we limped through the sky with the bomb doors swinging open and both turrets ablaze.

Meantime, little did I know that Tommy [Thompson], with supreme endurance, had dragged, barehanded, to a place of safety, the unconscious mid-upper gunner in the face of fierce flames and exploding ammunition. He quelled the flames and then rushed to the rear-gunner and pulled him from his position.

I gasped and then my heart pounded as I saw three Focke-Wulf 190s coming towards us, I thought the end had come, but to my amazement and relief they passed us about two hundred yards to port. I can only conclude that they had no ammunition left. As we neared Arnhem more flak was hurled up at us, mingled with tracer bullets. I had to make several more steep dives and alterations of course but I think we had been hit in another engine for the port inner was on fire. Actually, when I managed to extinguish the fire, this served to balance the aircraft a little better. However, it was a pretty grim situation for we were losing height at a rate of 500 feet a minute. We had dropped from 10,000 feet to 2,000, which meant we had only four minutes' flying time to go.

Swiftly I glanced round for a suitable landing ground. At the same moment, much to my relief, a flight of Spitfires had spotted our plight. I saw a small paddock in which I might have been able to crash-land and was just going in when the Spits swooped in front to warn us. I glanced up to see some high-tension cables just ahead. The old aircraft was wobbling badly by now and I must land somewhere. A chance came just a little further on. It was two square paddocks, side by side, with clumps of trees one side and at the opposite end to which I was approaching. Nearby was a little Dutch village. It was a chance, but I had to take it. For a moment I thought that one wheel was still down as a result of damage over the target. It *was* down, but fortunately folded up as we landed. It was a pancake landing and we slithered along and hit a bank, toppled over it with two engines torn away, then finally came to rest against another bank across the second field. For a tense moment I waited for the aircraft to catch fire or explode but again relief came to me as petrol oozed away into the soft ground.

Next thing was to struggle out of the smashed aircraft and in doing so I met a figure burned beyond recognition. It was not until he spoke that I recognised George Thompson. I found out the crew had been at crash positions and that no one had been injured in the landing. Staggering, Thompson said to me, 'Jolly good landing, skipper.'

Even now I can't understand the supreme endurance and the immense strength that enabled George to do what he did. To lift anything at all heavy in the confined space of a perfectly sound aircraft is extremely difficult. To drag a man from his burning turret, with a gale blowing in the aircraft, to put out flames with bare hands and to part-drag and part-lift this grown man over and past the many holes in the fuselage was superhuman. But to do the same thing for the rear-gunner and afterwards help with the extinguishers was what George Thompson did. I never dreamed that there'd been such a fight for life in the aircraft.

Evidently our Spitfire escort had notified a nearby station of our position and within twenty minutes Canadian doctors and an ambulance were on the scene. I had taken Tommy to a nearby farmhouse. He was in a pitiful condition, weak and helpless. I gave him a shot of morphia and dressed his wounds with anti-burn ointment. He was later transferred to a hospital in Holland. I spent four days in the hospital and frequently visited Thompson. He would not be thinking of his pain but asking how the rest of the crew were getting along. I have never seen such bravery. He died three weeks later.

ITALY, 1943–44

In 1943, having secured victory in North Africa, Allied forces began landing in Axis-occupied southern Europe with the aims of diverting enemy troops from the Eastern Front, knocking Italy out of the war and securing better control of the Mediterranean. Allied troops invaded Sicily in July and in September began landing on Italy's toe. The Italian government, having already ejected Mussolini, surrendered days later but formidable German forces were already in place. Fighting defensively in a series of well-selected and well-prepared positions, the Germans were to ensure the Allies' northward advance would be slow and bloody. Rome would fall only in June 1944 and much of northern Italy was still in German hands when the war came to an end. In all, twenty Victoria Crosses were awarded for actions on Italian soil, to nine British soldiers, four Indian soldiers, three Canadians, two Gurkhas, a South African and a Dane.

Company Sergeant Major Peter Wright
3rd Battalion, Coldstream Guards

Peter Wright was awarded the Victoria Cross for his 'superb disregard of the enemy's fire, his magnificent leadership and his outstanding heroism' during an attack against well-entrenched enemy positions on a steep wooded hill near Salerno on 25 September 1943. During the action, with his officers wounded or killed, Wright took charge of the company and single-handedly silenced three enemy machine-gun nests, then consolidated the position, brought up ammunition and organised his men to repel a counter-attack. Recommended initially for the Distinguished Conduct Medal, Wright received that decoration in 1944 from King George VI. However, the King felt that Wright's deed deserved a Victoria Cross and, following his personal intervention, the facts were reviewed and the VC was awarded.

Born at Mettingham, Suffolk, on 10 August 1916, the son of a farmer and one of fourteen children, Peter Harold Wright had joined the army in 1936. Nicknamed 'Misty' in his regiment, he served in India, Egypt and North Africa, being wounded at Tobruk, and after the war returned to Suffolk and farmed. He died in 1990.

Company Sergeant Major Peter Wright
3rd Battalion, Coldstream Guards
Our objective was Point 270. We moved down the road and then got on top of a hill and beyond the valley was the hill that the Germans were holding. We were given our orders, that on the morning of 25 September we would, on a two-company front, attack and hold this point. Well, we moved off in single file with No 1 Company leading, I was behind the company headquarters, and we moved down the valley and through grapevines under cover. There was a lot of scrub, very dry. As we moved down everything seemed quiet, we thought this would be a piece of cake. Anyway, we hadn't got far up the hill when hell let loose: machine guns, mortar fire and so on.

Lieutenant Christopher Bulteel
3rd Battalion, Coldstream Guards

I followed No 1 Company and Sergeant Major Wright. You must hear a Spandau one of these days to hear what sound it makes: it sounds like a newspaper being torn up. The rate of fire is so great that you find it very difficult to distinguish an individual shot, and this was going on from something like a dozen Spandaus all the time without stopping and the noise was quite indescribable. I was going up through the wood and I remember thinking how curious it was that autumn had come so quickly and that the leaves were falling so fast. Later I remembered that these were evergreen trees and there was no wind: those leaves were being knocked off the trees by enemy machine-gun fire and they were coming down so fast that it seemed like an autumn's day. That was the kind of fire we were going through.

Company Sergeant Major Peter Wright
3rd Battalion, Coldstream Guards

We started suffering casualties, the hill caught alight and I went forward to see what was happening, to see if I could give any assistance.

First I came across casualties. Then I came to the company commander. He'd been wounded from the tip of his toes to the top of his head by mortar fire. His orders to me were, 'Find all the officers. Tell them I'm wounded and to carry on.' Well, I moved through to try and find the officers.

I saw different casualties and stretcher-bearers were attending to them; I saw some were dead. And the first officer I came across was one of the platoon commanders: he was dead. I was looking for the other one and going along the hill to the far end, there was a lot of terraces, and on these terraces they were getting a lot of machine-gun fire. So I got further up the hill and saw these machine-gun posts that were holding up, more or less, the advance. I then went back to a small section and took as many grenades as I could and said, 'We've got to wipe out these three machine-gun posts. Keep firing in that direction and I'll go up a bit and then try and bounce these grenades over these terraces and wipe them out.'

How I done it, I couldn't tell you now. I suppose I was younger and doing the job that I was trained to do. Anyhow, we managed to silence these three machine-gun posts and then things seemed to get better.

I moved up the hill, only about thirty men seemed to be on the top, and I then found the only officer that I thought would be alive and well: Lieutenant Buxton. He was very badly wounded as well, and, well, this being a frontal position and I hadn't an officer, I got as many more men up as I could, two of the platoons, and said, 'Keep your heads down. If the Germans counter-attack, give them everything you've got.' Then I went back down the hill, pulled one or two people out who could have got burned through the fire. I then managed to settle down a bit, sent a message back to the commanding officer that we had captured our objective and were consolidating.

Guardsman Philip Charles Gourd
3rd Battalion, Coldstream Guards

I was behind a clump of trees, but I could see, when 'Misty' Wright said he would go and silence the machine guns. There were three machine guns and he asked for covering fire. So the Germans were taking cover in these three separate little trenches and he ran along tossing grenades into all three and he destroyed not one but three machine-gun nests, for which he got the VC.

Now, when Peter Archer did a depiction – he went out after the war, went to the site and did a picture – he put lots of smoke and lots of gunfire and he showed the Germans leaning out, collapsed, over the edge of their trenches. Well, it wasn't quite like that. The way he did it made it look more spectacular, more dramatic, but what happened was they just fell down into the bottom of their trenches; they weren't on view, like he did them, at all. But I suppose if you're doing a depiction you've got to make it a little bit dramatic.

Fusilier Frank Jefferson
2nd Battalion, Lancashire Fusiliers

Frank Jefferson was awarded the Victoria Cross, as his citation states, for his display of 'supreme gallantry and disregard of personal risk' during an attack on the Gustav Line, near Monte Cassino on 16 May 1944. When the enemy counter-attacked with armoured Sturmgeschütz assault guns, he went forward 'entirely on his own initiative' and under heavy fire and, with his PIAT anti-tank gun, fired on the leading assault gun, destroying it and killing its crew. He then reloaded and advanced on a second, which retreated before he could get within range. 'Fusilier Jefferson's gallant act not merely saved the lives of his Company and caused many casualties to the Germans,' his citation concludes, 'but also broke up the enemy counter-attack.'

Born in Ulverston, Lancashire, on 18 August 1921, Francis Arthur Jefferson survived the war and in 1950 went to live in the United States. Returning to Britain in the 1970s, he died in 1982.

Fusilier Frank Jefferson
2nd Battalion, Lancashire Fusiliers
I joined the army in 1942 and went to Africa in May 1943 with reinforcements for the Lancashire Fusiliers. I arrived too late for the African campaign and the first real action I saw was in Sicily with the Eighth Army. Soon after that we really got down to business, after landing at Taranto on the Adriatic coast of Italy. I was in Italy for the next eleven months during which time I took part in the fighting at Termoli, the Sangro crossing and the famous battle of Monastery Hill.

After a short rest period our division was brought in for the big push against the Gustav Line. During the first attack our company's objective was two small farmhouses which were being used by the Germans as strong machine-gun posts. The tanks were ordered to go in first and we were to follow on behind, on foot and under heavy fire from mortars, machine

NA 15430

Fusilier Frank Jefferson VC in front of the German Sturmgeschütz assault gun – referred to as a tank in his own account and his VC citation – which he had knocked out with a PIAT in May 1944.

guns and 88-millimetre shells, but due to an anti-tank obstruction our tanks had great difficulty in covering the ground. This, however, didn't stop them from engaging the enemy's heavy tanks. But with our tank support unable to advance we had to push forward on foot in the face of heavy German fire, which had already knocked out several of our tanks.

My company was one of the leading companies and, after a bit of a do, we took our objective, silencing the machine guns and taking many prisoners. After making certain that no Germans were left, we started to dig in. But before we'd finished this, the Germans launched a counter-attack with tanks and infantry to try and recapture the position.

The two farmhouses were about a hundred yards apart and as the German tanks came in from two directions they gave us everything they had. We had one platoon in each house and the other platoon was soon in a bad way, they had been shot up very badly and were falling back, so then our position drew all the enemy fire. We took what cover we could and, by the time the leading German tank was about fifty yards away, I thought it was about time that something was done about it. And as I had the only PIAT in the platoon, I knew it was up to me to do it.

So, getting to my feet, I went forward with my PIAT and when the tank was about twenty yards away I fired one shot, which hit it just below the turret. The recoil of the PIAT knocked me flat on my back but when I got up again I saw the tank was done for. It was burning fiercely and I could hear the crackling of bullets exploding inside.

I went back to my No 2 and reloaded my PIAT and then I saw the remaining German tanks turn tail and retire, after seeing their leader in flames. Soon after this, our tanks succeeded in overcoming the obstacles and we reformed and continued our push forward.

Corporal James Watts
2nd Battalion, Lancashire Fusiliers
I had to go to the command post where the colonel was and, whilst I was making me way back, there was a fusilier sitting down on a bit of a hill

and there was a German tank that had been knocked out. I said, 'What's happened here then?' And one of the lads says, 'He's just knocked that tank out.' And I said, 'Oh, well done,' and just pushed on to deliver me message and I stayed in the command post for about half an hour. Whilst there, I heard the colonel and my company commander, Major Delaney, and they were discussing something. I was trying not to be nosy, shut me ears but I couldn't help it, and years later it dawned on me what they were talking about. They were compiling the citation for the man who'd knocked the tank out, and he got the VC: Fusilier Jefferson.

Rifleman Thaman Gurung
1st Battalion, 5th Royal Gurkha Rifles

Born in West Nepal in October 1924, Thaman Gurung was the youngest ever Gurkha VC. He was posthumously awarded the medal for his actions on 10 November 1944 at Monte San Bartolo while acting as a scout to a fighting patrol. Alone, he repeatedly engaged enemy positions pinning down his patrol and finally, to cover its withdrawal, stood in full view of the enemy – 'although he well knew that his action meant almost certain death,' as his citation states – and emptied two full Bren gun magazines before he was killed.

Captain Anthony Harvey
1st Battalion, 5th Royal Gurkha Rifles
In October/November of '44 we had been in a rest situation as a division and we had come forward as a division. We'd turned right, due east from Florence, and gone through a little village and had to go over the spine of the country. Wasn't terribly high. I had taken over A Company and because it was a lovely sunny day I had gone forward with a patrol. Normally one sent a strong fighting patrol or a platoon patrol or even sometimes a half company, and I had sent this patrol forward and I went

IND 4697

Drawn portrait of Rifleman Thaman Gurung VC.

with them because I'd been out of action and I thought it would be good to get back into the swing of things.

The leading scouts had gone along the spine of this particular mountain, it wasn't terribly high but it was very high compared with the roads underneath, and the leading scout, whose name was Thaman, came upon two Germans in a sentry post. Luckily for him they were both asleep. He charged with his kukri. He didn't have to use it, and they both surrendered. There must have been some communication signal as the rear of that German position was somehow alerted to the fact that their sentries had been captured and, within a very short time, mortar fire of some intensity was coming down on the position.

I was with the rear section of that platoon and the German prisoners had come through us and I'd sent them back to my Gurkha second-in-command, who was about four hundred yards behind us. We couldn't move forward and a message came from the leading section commander that we, the other section, was to retire. We were taking shelter in a fold in the ground because the fire, both small arms and mortar, was so intense that it was dangerous to be moving about. However, there was a sudden lull in the firing and I, with my runner, ran for it.

What we didn't know until afterwards was that Rifleman Thaman had gone to the top of the hill and had seen the rear positions of the Germans and had engaged them with grenades. He had then fired his tommy gun until his ammunition ran out and it was this that I believe enabled us to withdraw without being killed. He then grabbed the light machine gun, the Bren gun, from one of his chums and said to them, 'Run for it, I'll keep the Germans' heads down,' and he did this with the light machine gun and the magazines that they always carried until he was shot through the throat. He died, but the rest of us got away.

There is no doubt that he saved our lives. And long after the action a court of inquiry was set up and all the witnesses were sworn in and made to tell what they knew about it, as a result of which an application for the award of the VC was made and was granted. And so Thaman was granted a posthumous VC.

Although I had the greatest respect for the Germans and still have, on the occasion of Thaman's action they booby-trapped the dead bodies so that when our patrol went out at night to recover them they also were blown up. And that did make both the British and the Gurkhas very, very angry indeed. We couldn't do much about it because we didn't get into contact immediately, but it did make us very angry indeed that Thaman's body particularly had been booby-trapped.

North-West Europe, 1944–45

On D-Day, 6 June 1944, Allied forces began landing in massive strength on the coast of Normandy in northern France, a prelude to pressing their advance on Nazi Germany. German resistance was fierce and weeks of bloody fighting passed before Normandy was taken. The Allies pushed on towards Belgium and the Netherlands.

In September, in an ambitious attempt to make quicker progress, Operation Market Garden saw 30,000 airborne troops – American, British and Polish – sent into the Netherlands to capture a series of strategic bridges. All but one was seized, the exception being the bridge at Arnhem where two-thirds of the British 1st Airborne Division were killed, wounded or captured. Fighting in Belgium and the Netherlands continued well into 1945 but by the spring Allied forces were over the Rhine and into Germany, continuing to meet resistance almost to the end.

Stanley Hollis, a company sergeant major of the Green Howards, received the first Victoria Cross of the Second Front within hours of the first landings on D-Day. Four more were earned in Normandy before the fighting there was over and five at Arnhem, including a posthumous award to a Royal Air Force pilot of Transport Command. A further seven VCs were earned before the Rhine was finally crossed in March 1945 and a final four on the far side of the Rhine.

Corporal Sidney Bates
1st Battalion, Royal Norfolk Regiment

The son of a rag-and-bone merchant from Camberwell, London, Sidney 'Basher' Bates was born on 14 June 1921. When war broke out he was working as a carpenter's labourer. He joined the Royal Norfolk Regiment in 1940 and was posthumously awarded the Victoria Cross for his actions near Sourdeval, in Normandy, France, on 6 August 1944 during an enemy attack on his position by troops of the 10th SS Panzer Division.

Captain Ian Dye
1st Battalion, Royal Norfolk Regiment
We'd been bussed round to a place called Sourdeval and the battalion had debussed to take over from the Monmouths, the battalion we were relieving. And we were settling in and the Monmouths were just getting ready to go, we'd got into their holes, when the most enormous barrage came down on us which made any movement out impossible. So we then had a situation where Norfolks and Monmouths occupied the same company positions, totalling about one hundred men per company. This barrage was a prelude to a major German armoured assault to break out of an encirclement we were imposing, and it was where one of our men won a Victoria Cross, a man called Corporal Bates, and I witnessed it from where we were. It was amazing, really.

Because the German attack was preceded by two or three Tiger tanks, the Germans came forward in column, the panzer grenadiers riding on the backs of tanks. And when they got to within, say, two hundred yards,

Corporal Sidney Bates VC.

HU 2054

the tanks in echelon came out behind them so you had a solid row of a dozen or fourteen tanks with panzer grenadiers between them running with their rifles, and the tanks were firing an 88, a hell of a bloody weapon, and machine guns. And the difficulty always in these circumstances – particularly when you're getting shelled as well – is to get the soldiers' heads up. A good section commander can do this. Corporal Bates was a section commander.

The panzer grenadiers got to within about a hundred and fifty yards, I suppose, and Bates said to his section, 'You stay here. I'm going to sort this fucking lot out.' And, with that, he left the trench, carrying a Bren gun with the sling over his shoulder, and he ran forward about thirty yards firing at these grenadiers. I could see it from where I was, from the flank, and it was so amazing to see a single soldier. Then he was hit and he went down, and he actually changed the magazine, got up and went forward again another forty yards and he was hit again. He stayed down, a minute possibly, and then he got up, still firing, and staggered another fifteen yards and then he went down and he didn't move again.

And the company, seeing this – you could hear them shouting, 'Go on, Basher!' – they got their heads up and they started firing in spite of all the amount of firing coming at them. And you could see the German grenadiers falter and stop and then they went to ground, which is always a good sign, and we kept firing at them and they got up and started to fall back. They got behind their tanks, which the tanks didn't like very much, and then we brought anti-tank weapons in and we called our own artillery down on top of ourselves because it was so close, and it was round one to us without any doubt. And all of us who witnessed this had no doubt at all that, if Bates had not done what he did, within a short time the panzer grenadiers would have been amongst us and that would have been a very tricky situation. So that's the story of Bates's VC, which was wonderful.

This attack was late in the afternoon and firing went on until the early evening. Then eventually our stretcher-bearers got out. Bates was only fifteen yards from a German soldier.

Lance Corporal Ernest Seaman
Stretcher-bearer, 1st Battalion, Royal Norfolk Regiment
Basher, he killed seventeen Germans firing a Bren gun from the hip. Very thin, very athletic. I was involved picking him up. He had a bullet-hole through the throat and through his legs but he was still alive, but they tell me he died two days after he got back.

Captain David Jamieson
7th Battalion, Royal Norfolk Regiment

David Jamieson was awarded the Victoria Cross for his actions on 8 August 1944 near Grimbosq, in Normandy, when, after establishing a bridgehead over the River Orne, he led and organised his company in resisting a series of enemy counter-attacks over a thirty-six-hour period.

As his citation concludes, despite wounds to his arm and eye, 'Captain Jamieson continued in command, arranging for artillery support over his wireless and going out into the open on each occasion to encourage his men. By the evening the Germans had withdrawn, leaving a ring of dead and burnt-out tanks round his position.

'Throughout this thirty-six hours of bitter and close fighting, and despite the pain of his wounds, Captain Jamieson showed superb qualities of leadership and great personal bravery. There were times when the position appeared hopeless, but on each occasion it was restored by his coolness and determination. He personally was largely responsible for the holding of this important bridgehead over the River Orne and the repulse of seven German counter-attacks with great loss to the enemy.'

The son of a chairman of Vickers Armstrong, David Auldjo Jamieson was born on 1 October 1920 and educated at Eton. Having joined the Territorial Army, he was mobilised on the outbreak of war. He remained in the army until 1948 and then began a successful career with the Australian Agricultural Company. He died in 2001.

Captain David Jamieson
7th Battalion, Royal Norfolk Regiment

I was born in London, in my father's house in Westminster, in October 1920. I left school in Easter 1939 and I met some young friends during the summer who took me to the drill hall at Dersingham for the Territorial Army and there I met a recruiting sergeant who asked me had I military experience. I said I'd been in the corps at my public school and he said, 'Right, you're for a commission. Definitely officer material.' So I went to attend the drills and soon after I was commissioned a second lieutenant into what was then the 5th Battalion of the Royal Norfolk Regiment.

The battalion split in 1939 so we became the 7th Battalion and we were sent to Talavera Barracks at Aldershot, ready to embark for France, at the end of 1939. But my colonel, Colonel Debenham, marched me in and said, 'Jamieson, I think you're too immature to lead a platoon in war. You must go on a Young Officer's course and be trained.' I was horrified, but there we are. Eighteen years old, that's what happens. So I went to an officer-training course at York, a place called Strensall, and after doing that – usual procedure – went back to the barracks.

I didn't go into action much before we got to the River Orne in August 1944. I was then second-in-command of D Company, then old Freddie Crocker was wounded so I took over D Company and we moved off. We were somewhere near Villers-Bocage, more or less a defensive position, a lot of night patrolling went on. Then we jumped on to these tanks, I'm six foot six and it's extremely difficult to keep your feet out of the tracks, but anyway we sat for hours on these tanks, trundling steadily towards the Germans, without any opposition much until we reached the River Orne. And that's the only battle I ever took part in, the battle that then ensued.

We arrived on the banks of the River Orne, about a mile back, and the colonel said that I and Jim Walcott, another company commander, were to take down a reconnaissance patrol to see whether it was possible to get over the river there and particularly whether tanks could. So we crept along, we crept along. It's rather lovely, the River Orne south of Caen. It's

Captain David Jamieson VC.

HU 2004

called 'Little Switzerland': the hills fall quite steeply down to the valley and they're very deeply wooded. So we got quite close and there we could see the Germans digging in just the other side. We could see their cigarette smoke; we could hear the clang of their things.

We went back and said, 'We don't think we ought to try and cross here, there are troops opposite,' and so on. But we were in a brigade with both North and South Staffordshire battalions and one of them found a crossing place nearer Caen.

I was rather unfortunate, I thought, because I was told to lead the battalion at night through a wood down to the new crossing place that had been found. The other battalions would go first and make a bridgehead and we'd follow and go through them and lead out in front. 'Oh,' said the colonel. 'It's all right, they've taped the whole thing. You just follow the tape.' Well, there wasn't any bloody tape. I was in charge of seven hundred men, all carrying enormous loads, through a wood, and we got lost, really, so it was a terrible struggle and eventually I found a way through but of course we were getting mortared. Anyway, eventually I found a good place, we went over and then I met the colonel of the South Staffordshires who was just on the far bank. His men had gone beyond, not very far. I think they were a hundred yards over.

So off we went and went through them and by dawn we'd dug in, I think, and had some sort of position. The effect of all this had been to allow the engineers to build a lightish bridge on the ruins of an old bridge, the first possible place you could put a bridge south of Caen, and the carriers had brought the anti-tank guns over: I'd got three six-pounders. Then a tank came over called an AVRE, that was a thing that blew enormous petards, and, as all the surrounding buildings were impossible to fit anti-tank guns into, I blew all the buildings up with my AVRE. Then I got Sergeant Courtman, who was in charge of the three guns, to site them in the ruins. We had one platoon with him and two platoons a little further back in an orchard. Eventually they sent a troop of Churchill tanks over.

I don't know how many times we were attacked. The first time we had great success, it all worked. We saw the German tanks with their binoculars, looking and looking. Out they came, out of the wood, straight across our front, and Sergeant Courtman knocked out all three just like that. Next thing that happened, they attacked a bit further over. And in that battle they came round behind and they shot two of my Churchills, so I only had one Churchill left.

Meanwhile, all the British generals rang up – because it's a lovely valley, they could sit safely on the other side and watch all this, you see – and said, 'You're commanding the divisional artillery now.' Then I got the whole corps medium artillery. Of course, some of my men were killed: we really landed some of it on us. God knows how many guns I was trying to control. A hell of a job. All I could do was give them six-figure map references, so I did that.

The next day, another attack came in. And I tried to signal to the final tank to keep back, because we were under great fire and the German tanks were coming in on to our position, and I leapt out of my little hole and I rushed up – in those days, you go to the back of the tank and you pick up a phone and you're meant to talk to him – but he didn't answer, I couldn't get him. So there wasn't much else to do: the hatch was open at the top and, being very long-legged, I climbed up the back of the tank and leant over and banged and said, 'Hey, get the hell out of here!' Well, at that moment the tank was blown up. The force of the exploding 88-millimetre shell just threw me off and I was covered in blood and God knows what and of course the tank brewed up and that of course was my last tank gone. I returned to my hole, feeling very sorry for myself. We had a good chap, a first-aid man, and he cleaned all the blood away. All I'd got was one eye completely gone and my arm was bleeding a lot, but not seriously, mostly from little bits of tank. Well, I didn't feel so bad anyway so we went on.

Meanwhile, essentially, I should think some old general said, 'Well, that chap's rather out on his own. We'd better send some more troops.'

And he sent a battalion up to take over what I had, on the evening of the second day, and, thank God, I was evacuated. We marched out, we got out, and they put me in a carrier and I was taken back to the first-aid post. And that was that. I think we'd crossed the river on the morning of the seventh and then I was evacuated on the evening of the eighth. We'd lasted through the seventh and the eighth and then out I came.

I was evacuated to the forward aid post and then I just fainted and I don't know what happened. But Freddie Crocker, my company commander, a great old friend, he said, 'What's happened to that fellow Jamieson?' and he followed up and found I'd gone to a big hospital with large tents, a tented hospital, and I was still unconscious. I think for about forty-eight hours I just lay comatose. But Freddie was very good. Of course I was covered in blood still and I remember him saying he had such a row with the people, told them to clean me up and get me done. A good friend, Freddie.

Major Frederick Crocker
7th Battalion, Royal Norfolk Regiment

I was back in the safe area, a mile or so back, with the B Echelon troops. But as soon as things quietened and I heard what was going on, I went forward to see what was going on and I went down to the Orne. I found our doctor had had a pretty hectic time and then I went to look for Jamieson, he'd been wounded in the arm and the eye, and I went back myself to look for him. And I had a very difficult time doing so.

I got to a forward dressing station, a tented place, and I walked in there. There was nothing much happening; I saw two RAMC officers in uniform having a chat. And I went round and went into the first tent and I found David Jamieson on a stretcher. He hadn't even got his boots off. He was asleep, there was a tin of cold tea by his bedside, he'd had no attention whatsoever. And I went up to these two officers who looked at me rather scornfully because I was a very scruffy-looking soldier, I was muddied and in denim dress, but I was quite indignant at what had happened, or what hadn't happened, to David Jamieson. And in fact I waited while they dressed him and bathed him, put him in a pair of one of the officers' own pyjamas and saw him on the way back.

David was a splendid chap. He'd been commissioned right from the beginning and he really hadn't had a chance to do anything really active, this was his first time. And I think he must have felt, not deliberately but at the back of his mind, that I'd come into the battalion after him and had taken command and that whatever happened he wasn't going to fail in the job. And he did a magnificent job. And so did a Sergeant Courtman who was in that action: as his men were knocked out, he was moving from one anti-tank gun to another and he was quite brilliant.

Captain David Jamieson
7th Battalion, Royal Norfolk Regiment
I was then evacuated – wonderful system – put in a Dakota and they sent me back to hospital. Worcester, I think it was. Quite rightly, the chap in charge of the hospital said, 'God, there's nothing much wrong with you. Get out of here, you're taking up space.' So I went back home on leave.

Then I went to a disastrously unhappy place, it was an officer's collection camp in Ulster, a series of Nissen huts, and we all sat there, waiting, wondering what was going to happen. There was nothing there except drink; and one Nissen hut had a cinema where they put on rather old films so I used to do that. And I came out of this cinema and the only chap who I really knew there came up and he said, 'Do you know a fellow called Jamieson in your regiment?' I said, 'Well, I can't think of another one, no.' He said, 'This is a very odd thing. A fellow called Jamieson got a VC in your regiment.' So that's what happened, I got it that way.

Flight Lieutenant David Lord DFC
271 Squadron, Royal Air Force

The son of a soldier, David Samuel Anthony Lord was born on 18 October 1913 in Cork, Ireland, and brought up in India. After considering a career as a Roman Catholic priest, he joined the RAF in 1936. As a pilot he flew on the North-West Frontier, in the Middle East and over Burma, being awarded the Distinguished Flying Cross in 1943, before joining 271 Squadron at Down Ampney, Gloucestershire, which had the task of dropping parachute troops and supplies and towing gliders. He died on 19 September 1944 in the action for which he was awarded the Victoria Cross, while trying to drop much-needed supplies to the British 1st Airborne Division during its desperate fight at Arnhem in the Netherlands. Flying low in the face of intense anti-aircraft fire, his aircraft had been hit twice and had one engine on fire when he found two containers were still in the aircraft. Lord began a second dropping run, despite the risk of his starboard wing collapsing, then ordered his crew to bale out. Seconds later, and with Lord still at the controls, the wing collapsed and the aircraft crashed.

Flight Lieutenant Douglas Ivor MacDonell
Dakota navigator, 271 Squadron, Royal Air Force

I was navigator to David Lord who was a highly experienced Dakota pilot. He'd been out in India with 31 Squadron supplying Orde Wingate and the Chindits with supplies over the Hump and up in the jungles and so on. An excellent pilot, quite a fearless character. The co-pilot was a navigator actually but we sometimes flew navigators as co-pilot; a marvellous map-reader, he'd been on a low-level Boston squadron, attack bombers, going over France and in the desert and he could map-read at any height and particularly lower down. Ballantyne was newly commissioned but he was an ex-Coastal Command wireless operator. Altogether we had a lot of experience and, with my own limited experience, we were a pretty good crew.

I was courting a girl I'd met when I was in Peterborough way back when I was in elementary flying school and she and I decided to get married on 16 September. We made all the arrangements, everyone was perfectly happy about the arrangements, and then about 12 September, I think it was, the CO called me in and said, 'I understand you're getting married this weekend, Mac.' I said, 'Yes.' He said, 'Well, you'd better get the hell out of here, quickly, because they're just about to seal this camp. There's a big op coming off and we don't know where it is or what it is, and it's best if you don't know anything about it. Obviously if you've been briefed with a target name or anything it's too big a risk to take. But now that you know nothing about it, away you go.' So away I went on leave.

I found out on the Sunday, the day after we got married, when we were on honeymoon, that the drop had taken place at Arnhem. I went back to my unit, it was only a six-day leave, on the Friday and went into my hut, the hut I shared with Lord and Ballantyne and co, to find them all missing: the blankets were piled up, their kit was piled up on their beds. It was a terrible shock. It just spelled everything out so starkly. I can't really describe it. By all accounts – asking a few questions around – they'd been seen to crash. They said there was no chance of any survivors except one guy who baled out.

Harry King was the chap who got out when Lord's aircraft went in and one parachute was seen; Harry was the guy who went in my place as navigator on that occasion. And he was able to give a first-hand account and as a result David Lord got the only Victoria Cross ever awarded to a Transport Command pilot in the whole history of the Command. Lord had taken this burning Dakota in not just one run but a second run in order to get his supplies hopefully to the right people on the ground and Harry King was able to confirm all this; if he'd not survived we'd have never heard of David Lord again. He himself had been hurled out of the aircraft as it started spinning towards the ground. He'd clipped his parachute on – wise lad – because it was pretty damned clear that they were going to have to bale out anyway. I think he was four hundred feet when he actually got out, which is nothing.

Lance Corporal Eric Harden
Royal Army Medical Corps
Attached 45 (Royal Marine) Commando

Born on 23 February 1912 in Northfleet, Kent, Henry Eric Harden was a sergeant of the local division of the St John Ambulance Brigade when he was conscripted in 1942 into the Royal Artillery. Later he transferred to the Royal Army Medical Corps and volunteered for service with the commandos. He was serving as a troop medical orderly when, on 23 January 1945, at Brachterbeek, Holland, he performed the act for which he was posthumously awarded the Victoria Cross, when he tried to save the lives of three wounded men.

Marine Frederick Leonard Harris
A Troop, 45 Commando, Royal Marines
In January we were in actual fact supposed to be going to the Far East but they decided, in their wisdom, that they didn't want to send us to the Far East, they were going to send us back to Europe. I think they were getting a little bit worried that progress wasn't as good as it ought to have been, particularly with things like the Ardennes in the air, so they sent us back. We went to Tilbury and got on the train ferry to Ostend in Belgium, we had two nights in what was a German barracks in Ostend, and then we got on this train up to a place in Holland.

We dug in on the edge of the Maas. It was all iced over and Jerry used to send a patrol out occasionally across the ice. We had trip flares out in front of us and every now again a trip flare would come up and light the Jerries up and we used to have a little pop at them. You had to be very careful because all your weapons froze, particularly the automatic weapons: if you didn't

Lance Corporal Eric Harden VC.

HU 2015

keep cocking your Bren gun and making the movement go, for instance, you'd soon seize up.

6 Commando moved along first and they took Maasbracht fairly easily. 45 came through 6 Commando and we went into Brachterbeek – there was just a little bit of sniping, the Jerries had moved back out – and we were then told to follow them down towards Linne, a fairly biggish town. And we were going down this road from Brachterbeek, where there was a railway station at the bottom, you could see it as plain as you like, when all of a sudden there was hell let loose. There was a windmill on the left-hand side and there was fire coming from there and coming from the station.

So, of course, we all went to ground. The road was fairly high and there was a bank down the side, and me and me mate Don dropped down on the bank and propped the Bren up on the road and put a few bursts down towards the station. Whether it had any effect or not, we don't know. Old Lieutenant Thomas, he said, 'Try and get into the cottages on the other side of the road.' I said to Don, 'We'll have that second cottage,' and I grabbed the Bren up. The idea when you hit a doorway is to put your boot up and kick the door in, but Dutch doors are about that thick. Course, I just bounced off this flipping door. Don smashed the window and dived inside and I tried to get meself into the recess of this door, and old Jerry had spotted me and he fired his Spandau from the station and it took off all the corners of all the brickwork round the door and shot off all the corners of me leather jerkin and parachute jacket, and it shot the pocket of me parachute blouse off and two 36 hand grenades dropped on to the ground. It was a bit hairy, like. Anyway, Don had managed to get inside and he came and unbolted the door and I was indoors but me Bren was still laying out on the road. I got one of these old besom brooms, twig brooms, and I was scrabbling this Bren gun towards me. If I'd have gone out for it, this Jerry would have got me, he kept shooting bursts up the road, but I finally got it. I went into one of the back rooms and put the Bren on a table and knocked out one of the windows and put a few bursts into the windmill. It was obviously a strongpoint.

We didn't know this but they were copping it behind us. The rest of the troop had spread out across the fields. Immediately behind these cottages were two or three of these potato clamps and some of the guys had taken cover there. There was also a little barn and some of the lads had got in there, the troop commander's HQ was in there: Sergeant Major Wiggy Bennett, he was in there; Lance Corporal Harden was in there; Dickie Mason, Johnny Havill, the little two-inch mortar group, they was in there. And then there was some shouts coming from the right flank, from the road, voices calling out 'Help!' and that sort of thing. We understood then that there were guys out there who had been wounded. And Lance Corporal Harden, he rushed out.

Marine Derrick Cakebread
A Troop, 45 Commando, Royal Marines
When everything opened up, I went back to a lone cottage and up into the attic, to a little window there, and I put me sights up to about a thousand yards. There was a windmill and I guessed that's where the firing was coming from and I started shooting all over the place. And the old sergeant major said, 'No, don't shoot there, we've got wounded down there and there's going to be medic.' That's when the doc went out, dressed them, said they'd got to come back or they'd die out there. He said he'd got to bring them back 'cause it was freezing out there.

Marine Frederick Leonard Harris
A Troop, 45 Commando, Royal Marines
He must have gone about two hundred yards across the open land and he brought Wheeler back first. He dressed his wounds and brought him back on his shoulders and dropped him into this barn area. Then he went out to dress the other two guys' wounds, that was Marine Wale and Lieutenant Cory, and he dressed their wounds and then came back again and said that they were stretcher jobs and he wanted a couple of guys to help him. So Johnny Havill and Dickie Mason, they kind of volunteered and went out with him with a stretcher.

They got Wale back but on the way back Wale took another shot and he died of his wounds later. Then they went out again after Lieutenant Cory. Apparently Lieutenant Cory had told them to leave him, not to sacrifice their lives, but they brought him back in. And they'd carried him quite a bit, about fifty or sixty yards, Johnny was at the front, Doc Harden was at the back and Dickie Mason was helping, when suddenly the stretcher went down at the back and Lance Corporal Harden had been shot through the head. They laid him out and had a look to see what had happened but there was no hope and, with that, they gradually pushed Lieutenant Cory across the icy ground and got him in.

Corporal Edward Chapman BEM
3rd Battalion, Monmouthshire Regiment

Edward Thomas Chapman was awarded the Victoria Cross for his actions in 1945, near the Dortmund-Ems Canal, Germany, while a section commander during an advance on Osnabrück. His citation reads:

On 2nd April 1945, a Company of the Monmouthshire Regiment crossed the Dortmund-Ems canal and was ordered to assault the ridge of the Teutoberger Wald, which dominates the surrounding country. This ridge is steep, thickly wooded and is ideal defensive country. It was, moreover, defended by a battalion of German officer cadets and their instructors, all of them picked men and fanatical Nazis. Corporal Chapman was advancing with his section in single file along a narrow track, when the enemy suddenly opened fire with machine guns at short range, inflicting heavy casualties and causing some confusion.

Corporal Chapman immediately ordered his section to take cover and, seizing the Bren gun, he advanced alone, firing the gun from his hip, and mowed down the enemy at point-blank

Corporal Edward Chapman VC, BEM.

HU 2048

range, forcing them to retire in disorder. At this point, however, his Company was ordered to withdraw but Corporal Chapman and his section were still left in their advanced position, as the order could not be got forward to them. The enemy then began to close up to Corporal Chapman and his isolated section and, under cover of intense machine-gun fire, they made determined charges with the bayonet. Corporal Chapman again rose with his Bren gun to meet the assaults and on each occasion halted their advance. He had now nearly run out of ammunition.

Shouting to his section for more bandoliers, he dropped into a fold in the ground and covered those bringing up the ammunition by lying on his back and firing the Bren gun over his shoulder. A party of Germans made every effort to eliminate him with grenades, but with reloaded magazine he closed with them and once again drove the enemy back with considerable casualties.

During the withdrawal of his Company, the Company Commander had been severely wounded and left lying in the open a short distance from Corporal Chapman. Satisfied that his section was now secure, at any rate for the moment, he went out alone under withering fire and carried his Company Commander for 50 yards to comparative safety. On the way a sniper hit the officer again, wounding Corporal Chapman in the hip and, when he reached our lines, it was discovered that the officer had been killed.

In spite of his wound, Corporal Chapman refused to be evacuated and went back to his Company until the position was fully restored two hours later.

Throughout the action Corporal Chapman displayed outstanding gallantry and superb courage. Single-handed he repulsed the attacks of well-led, determined troops and gave his battalion time to reorganise on a vital piece of ground overlooking the only bridge across the canal. His magnificent bravery played a very large part in the capture of this vital ridge and in the successful development of subsequent operations.

The son of a Welsh coalminer, Chapman was born at Pen Y Graig, Pontlottyn, Glamorgan, on 13 January 1920. After the war he worked for an engineering firm and as a porter on Pontlottyn station, before becoming a nylon-spinner with ICI Fibres at Pontypool where he worked for the next twenty-five years. He also became a noted exhibitor of Welsh Mountain Ponies and in 1953, for his service with the Territorial Army, was awarded the British Empire Medal. He died in February 2002.

Corporal Edward Chapman
3rd Battalion, Monmouthshire Regiment

I was very poor at school and I left at fourteen and went underground. It wasn't a mine as such, it was in the hillside, a tunnel, and they took the coal from each side of the tunnel. I was just pulling the coal out from the face on a kind of sledge from where the colliers were taking the coal out. When I got to the age of sixteen I went underground in the colliery; they wouldn't take you under sixteen years old. Soon as I became twenty, I was called up. I think I was the only one from that colliery that was called up. Then word came that they wanted the colliers back and I could have gone back but I never bothered: I'd enjoyed myself underground but I thought I could enjoy myself in the army. I was called up into the Monmouthshire Regiment, the TA sent for me at Newport, and I went straight into the 2nd Battalion.

In 1944, I was wounded in France, about three miles short of Falaise, and I was six weeks in hospital. I was hit in the foot. We were marching up to the scene of action, we had to move to attack a road, but when we got to the road the buggers had pulled back. But of course we were under observation. The battalion was going in single file – left-hand side and right-hand side of the road – in sections, ten men on the left, ten men on the right a little bit further back, but we were under observation and the Germans mortared or shelled us on the road. When the shelling came down we got off the road, each side was orchard and quite a bit of wood, and three or four men got killed and I got a blast and had six weeks in Bayeux under canvas. They had a big hospital under canvas there. When they sent me back, supposedly to the 2nd Mons in the 53rd Division, I ended up with the 11th Armoured Division with the 3rd Mons.

On 2 April 1945 the battalion moved up through woods and climbed up on to this hill and when we got up on to the hill we fanned out. The Germans were on the far slope, sort of overlooking a canal, and we were sort of round them then. But of course the Germans in that time had seen what was going on, they could see us, and the buggers had got round the back of us and so up they come. Or the best they could. They were only youngsters, mind; they were only youngsters themselves. But they were ferocious.

I was a section leader and I had about nine men with me. 1 had one man, he was about twenty; the others were eighteen-year-olds, could have been bloody seventeen. My Bren gunner, Roy Nash, he was about nineteen. The rest of my men with me, I had about seven or eight besides Roy Nash, I hadn't had them long, they had come in ones and twos to make up my section, and Roy Nash was the only one I could put the Bren gun to. He had been with me for about twelve months and he was a good 'un and he was the only one who was any good with a Bren gun. The boys I had, they had no bloody idea. They was rookies, real rookies.

When we'd started the advance – thickly wooded, trees about nine to ten or twelve-foot high, perhaps, fir trees, roughly four-foot apart – we hadn't gone ten or fifteen yards and the bloody Bren gunner got a bullet through his hand. He shouted, 'Corporal! Corporal!' The other seven or eight looked at me and I called Roy, I could see he was in trouble, I went back and I could see he had a bloody bullet in his hand. I didn't have nobody there then who I could give my bloody Bren gun to; the others, they didn't know what a bloody Bren gun was, hardly. So I had to go back and get all his bloody gear, the [ammunition] belts, and gave a couple out here and there, I had to be quick about it, and we advanced. The men I had, they were seventeen-year-old babies, bloody babies, you know. They wasn't men, like; they had boys' feelings. At about eighteen boys are starting to widen out but they're still boys. I was twenty-four; they were seventeen, see. They shouldn't have been there. They wouldn't do nothing without me telling them.

So I took the Bren gun off him, see, and I went forward with the Bren gun. And we went forward roughly fifteen hundred yards until we came to opposition. By this time most of my battalion was on my right and I was near enough on the left flank and we had to get down now because we were held up by the Germans with the fire coming towards us. They were bloody zipping between the trees and everything. And in a matter of seven or eight minutes a platoon commander came up. We were only in single file, there were people behind us, so of course when my men stopped and I stopped the officer come up and said, 'What's the reason for stopping?' And I was telling him that we could see them moving back and forth in front of us, like, and as I was saying that he took a bloody bullet. I forget where, but he was down anyway.

He was alive then. I had to get right up to him and I could see he was still alive and I was wondering what the hell I was going to do with this bloody man. He wasn't a company commander, he was a platoon commander, he'd come forward from the people behind me, and he was dying, see. So what I done then, I called to the men, 'Close up towards me!' and I picked him up. He was a twelve-stoner, I was only a ten-stoner, but I screwed my way under him and up on my knees and I had him on my back. How the hell I had the strength to pick him up is unbelievable. And I went back about fifteen or twenty yards, I expect, and I met the backing-up people and then they took him over on a stretcher, but he was dead. Before I met these men I'd had to cross a track they used to take timber years ago, and the Germans, they'd covered the bloody track, and he took a bullet on the way back while I was carrying him. One went through my belt and one went perhaps a quarter of an inch into my skin and I think the force of that knocked me down and him on the side of the track. I was exposed but the men coming up weren't very far away so they took over, and then I rejoined my men. I'd pulled my section back – I couldn't leave them there, they were bloody babies – back to more or less where we'd started.

The citation, see, was not my work at all. You know whose work it was? My section. Eighteen-year-olds. Except for my Bren gunner, Roy Nash. When we got down the hillside they asked about this officer who'd been carried back, they wanted to know now the fighting was over. Well, of course, the men said, 'Corporal Chapman took him back.' Then they had them up one by one to the battalion orderly room, asking them all questions about this, and from that I got the VC.

There's a little bit I can add to the citation, to make it a little bit more clear:

A company of the Monmouthshire Regiment crossed the Dortmund-Ems canal and was ordered to assault the ridge of the Teutoberger Wald, which dominates the surrounding country. This ridge is steep, thickly wooded and is ideal defensive country. It was, moreover, defended by a battalion of German officer cadets and their instructors, all of them picked and fanatical Nazis.

Very good men, they were. Good fighters, they were bloody good fighters. All youngsters.

Corporal Chapman was advancing in his section in single file along a narrow track...

It wasn't single file, see. We had advanced so far up to a certain point when the fire started in front of us and then we had to spread out, seven or eight yards between us.

...when the enemy suddenly opened fire with machine guns at short range, inflicting heavy casualties and causing some confusion.

Short range: you can imagine that because we couldn't see them and they couldn't see us because of the trees.

Corporal Chapman immediately ordered his section to take cover and, seizing the Bren gun, he advanced alone, firing the gun from his hip, and mowed down the enemy at point-blank range, forcing them to retire in disorder.

I already had the Bren gun. Whoever wrote that had made little mistakes. My men have done all that: the men were taken away, to brigade, I should imagine. These are my men's words, not mine.

At this point, however, his Company was ordered to withdraw but Corporal Chapman and his section were still left in their advanced position, as the order could not be got forward to them.

That's right. That's quite right.

The enemy then began to close up to Corporal Chapman and his isolated section and, under cover of intense machine-gun fire, they made determined charges with the bayonet. Corporal Chapman again rose with his Bren gun to meet the assaults and on each occasion halted their advance.

I got up a couple times. But when they say I got up, it was only bloody knees up. You can imagine: you see two hundred or a hundred men in front of you, you don't bloody stand up. And if you'd got a tree you'd lie there behind it and as soon as you see something you'd fire, even at a bloody leaf falling.

He had now nearly run out of ammunition. Shouting to his section for more bandoliers, he dropped into a fold in the ground and covered those bringing up the ammunition by lying on his back and firing the Bren gun over his shoulder.

That's right.

A party of Germans made every effort to eliminate him with grenades...

That's right. But the grenades never reached us. The trees and the leaves were that thick the Germans couldn't get too close to us to throw grenades. Their grenades were lighter than ours, we had a 36 grenade but the German grenade was a lighter grenade, but even so they couldn't come within thirty or forty yards of us to throw the damned grenades. Most of the grenades was hitting the bloody trees and I never lost one of my men.

...but with reloaded magazine he closed with them and once again drove the enemy back with considerable casualties.

Aye.

During the withdrawal of his Company, the Company Commander had been severely wounded and left lying in the open a short distance from Corporal Chapman.

No, he wasn't the company commander; he was a platoon commander, a lieutenant. He came up to me to see what was holding me, 'cause when they could see me down they wouldn't come forward. He came up and had to ask me what was the hold-up.

Satisfied that his section was now secure, at any rate for the moment, he went out alone under withering fire and carried his Company Commander for 50 yards to comparative safety.

It wasn't fifty yards. This is what the men said. See, they were taken away and each one had his story.

On the way a sniper hit the officer again, wounding Corporal Chapman in the hip...

Aye. Through the belt. That's the only wound I had.

...and, when he reached our lines, it was discovered that the officer had been killed.

Killed, aye. He was killed before he reached the lines, man. He was dead, I think.

In spite of his wound Corporal Chapman refused to be evacuated and went back to his Company until the position was fully restored two hours later.

Aye. Youngsters...

Throughout the action, Corporal Chapman displayed outstanding gallantry and superb courage. Single-handed he repulsed the attacks of well-led, determined troops and gave his battalion time to reorganise on a vital piece of ground overlooking the only bridge across the canal. His magnificent bravery played a very large part in the capture of this vital ridge and in the successful development of subsequent operations.

See, this is all right to read, but there was a whole battalion there. You could write this for every bloody man who was up there. They picked on me because it worked that way but there was hundreds of blokes there who got nothing. I think it's been highlighted because I took the officer; I think that's what highlighted it. And I *had* to take him back. He was alive when I picked him up but I think he was shot the second time, on me.

Private Thomas Griffiths
2nd Battalion, Monmouthshire Regiment
Edward Chapman VC: he was a lovely, delightful little gentleman, he wouldn't say boo to a goose, but he had something about him. Apparently he destroyed a lot of the enemy, probably about twenty or thirty.

Captain Ian Liddell
5th Battalion, Coldstream Guards

Ian Oswald Liddell earned the Victoria Cross on 3 April 1945 when, under fire, he de-fused enemy bombs on a bridge over the River Ems, near Lingen, Germany. He was killed in action three weeks later.

Born on 19 October 1919 in Shanghai, China, where his father was in business, Liddell had joined the army on the outbreak of the war and was commissioned into the Coldstream Guards in November 1940. He served for a time under Colonel James Coates as one of a secret bodyguard of hand-picked men detailed to protect the Royal Family in the event of an invasion. In command of a platoon, Liddell was said to have been responsible for guarding Princesses Elizabeth and Margaret.

Captain Alan Brooke Pemberton
5th Battalion, Coldstream Guards
We didn't cross the Rhine ourselves until a bridgehead had been gained on the other side and then we went over. There were various moments on the way up that live in my memory. One was the crossing of the Ems River at Lingen, when the company commander of No 3 Company won the VC. He won the VC by going across a bridge on his own with a pair

Captain Ian Liddell VC, second from left.

BU 3162

of wire-cutters and he cut the wires connected to the bombs [on and] under the bridge, which enabled the rest of the company to get over, and he was awarded a VC. Ian Liddell was his name. I knew him very well. He was second-in-command of the company when I joined it and then he was promoted to take over command of No 3 Company and I was promoted to be second-in-command of No 1 Company, so I replaced him. Very self-effacing, a very amusing man. Enjoyed life; great raconteur; played the piano brilliantly; great fun to have around. But a modest sort of man. Not an obvious person who you'd expect to win a VC.

Lieutenant Robert Laurie
5th Battalion, Coldstream Guards

I'd joined the company at the end of the Wesel bridgehead battle, which had been a very nasty battle. I took over a platoon from a great friend of mine who had just been killed. The platoon of course weren't very pleased to see a new officer and I thought, 'Dear oh dear, this is going to be very difficult,' until Ian turned up and he just flattened out all the problems. He was absolutely brilliant. He just had this incredible knack of leadership. He always managed to make people happy. And of course he was a brilliant musician: in those days I was very fond of jazz music and when I discovered he could play a trumpet as well as Louis Armstrong, I thought, 'Well, you're all right.'

We were told that this bridge was still standing so the first thing was, Ian said, 'Well, we'd better go and have a look,' and we all climbed into the company jeep, I think the driver was called Mason, and we drove off with a German map. And we went round a corner and Ian screamed, 'Stop, Mason!' The map was incorrect and we bloody near drove on to that bridge. So we jammed on the brakes and hit reverse and out again. Well, that was profoundly shaking, so we got out of the jeep and went across country and down a bank and there was a little house, a cottage. We went in through the back of this, it was unoccupied, and did our recce with field glasses from the windows. Ian said, 'Well, there's only one way to do this. We'll get all the support we can from the 1st Battalion gunners and then two platoons can advance across those water-mills and get down and fire on the riverbank. And I'll go over and cut the wires.'

Well, Peter Hunt from the 1st Battalion tried to dissuade him, Lump [Windsor-Clive] and I quite openly questioned whether it was a very sensible idea, but obviously he wasn't going to take any notice, he was going to do it and that was it. And he'd given us our orders: I was going to go over the left-hand side and Lump was to go to the right-hand side; Lump's platoon was going to go over first and mine second. Third platoon was under the CSM in reserve. There were only us three officers left in the company.

Ian then said, 'There's only one slight snag. I haven't got any wire-cutters.' Nobody seemed to know if there were any company wire-cutters, or, if there were, where they were. But after a good deal of humming and hawing, Lump said, 'I've got some wire-cutters but I'm very fond of them because they were my father's in the first war. But you can have them.' Ian said, 'Thank you very much.'

And then the whole circus started. We started the battle. Covering fire and the Typhoon rockets came over, all hell was let loose, so much so that you couldn't think, really. And Ian, as he promised, climbed over the roadblock at the end.

I had a full view of him. I noticed that he'd dropped his precious tommy gun getting over the barricade. Then he ran like a lamp-lighter and cut the wires at the enemy end, then he cut the wires on our end, climbed back up on to the roadblock, and then off we went. Mine was the second platoon over, Lump was already going through the position on the left, and Ian was standing at the end, unarmed because he'd dropped his tommy gun. I saw a German soldier coming out of a trench, I didn't know whether he was armed or what his intentions were, but he was behind Ian and Ian was between me and him, so I said, 'Ian, look behind you!' He saw this chap coming out so he flung the wire-cutters at him and hit him, and both the soldier and the wire-cutters disappeared below ground. That's how they got lost. It was so typical of Ian.

Captain Alan Brooke Pemberton
5th Battalion, Coldstream Guards

It was all planned and carried out very spontaneously without much delay. He just said, 'I'm going to do this, I want as much fire support as possible,' and got some tanks up and got the company in positions to fire, and he just went. He had to climb over a barricade to get on to the bridge – it was almost unbelievable – with Germans sitting just on the other side. They were keeping their heads down, 'cause all hell was being directed at them from the tanks and other people. Even so, it was almost unbelievable. It was, I think, as good a VC as you could get.

Lieutenant Robert Laurie
5th Battalion, Coldstream Guards

Well, after the thing was over, Colonel Roddy [Hill] sent for us all. We were in a German dugout and Colonel Roddy was in tears. That rather impressed me. He thanked us all and sent us back to our platoons. Then we heard that Ian was obviously going to get a very good medal and Lump and I had to write our accounts and then the war recommenced.

Then we had the awful, ghastly business of Rothenburg. It was wooded and we were told to dig in. We were going to take over 2 Company the following morning and Philip Rashleigh had just joined as a replacement for John Northcott. And because Philip was brand new, same as we had been, he was looked after by Ian, who went forward into his platoon position to see if he'd got dug in all right, and Ian was in a slit trench with Philip when a sniper got them both. I was always told that the bullet ricocheted off Philip's spine and killed Ian.

Both Ian and Philip Rashleigh had a peculiarity: they both wore brown boots. My platoon was in reserve, Lump was up on the right, and suddenly I saw a party coming through the woods carrying a body obviously and to my horror I saw brown boots. I thought, 'Oh dear, poor old Philip hasn't lasted long.' And then along comes another one with more brown boots and I realised the worst.

Ian never recovered consciousness. They always say he died of wounds; I'd say 'killed in action' was more accurate. He was as good as dead when they brought him out.

THE WAR IN THE FAR EAST

The surprise Japanese attack on Pearl Harbor on 7 December 1941 was followed immediately by attacks on British possessions across the Far East. Hong Kong, Singapore and Malaya quickly fell; Japanese troops pushed into Burma and soon forced the British Army to make a fighting withdrawal to the Indian frontier.

By 1943, British and Indian forces in Burma were beginning to counter-attack. Progress was slow. Allied strategy gave priority to defeating Nazi Germany, which meant resources for the war against Japan were limited, while the Japanese were a formidable enemy, highly motivated and frequently prepared to fight to the death. The challenges of the monsoon climate and hilly and jungle-covered terrain were extreme. Nevertheless, in 1944, under Lieutenant General William Slim's direction, 14th Army, including Brigadier Orde Wingate's Chindits, a long-range penetration force that had first crossed into Japanese-held territory in 1943, began to recover lost ground and hold Japanese attacks as well as taking a serious toll of the enemy.

Bitter fighting in the Arakan, north-west Burma, in early 1944 was followed in the spring by the epic defensive battles of Imphal and

Kohima in the Assam hills in north-east India, where British and Indian troops outfought a major Japanese offensive. The fighting in these battles was intense: in Assam, many thousands of Japanese were killed and not much more than a hundred were taken prisoner. As 1944 wore on, the Japanese, over-stretched and under-supplied, began to pull back. They were pursued and harried by 14th Army, which continued to encounter stiff opposition well into 1945.

The fighting in Burma saw twenty-nine Victoria Crosses awarded to British, Gurkha and Indian soldiers, including four to Wingate's Chindits. Elsewhere in the Far East, five VCs were awarded for actions in Malaya and Hong Kong and at sea during the early Japanese attacks of 1941–42. Against Japanese forces advancing through or holding out on islands across the south-west Pacific, Australians received two Victoria Crosses in Borneo, seven in New Guinea and two in the Solomon Islands, where a Fijian soldier was also awarded the medal. The final VC actions of the war were a daring X-craft raid on Singapore Harbour and an air attack off the Japanese mainland.

Lieutenant Alec Horwood DCM
1st/6th Queen's Royal Regiment (West Surrey)
Attached 1st Battalion, Northamptonshire Regiment

Alec George 'John' Horwood was born in south Deptford, London, on 6 January 1914 and before the war had worked as a clerk in a London jam factory. Mobilised in 1939, he served in the ranks in France and was awarded the Distinguished Conduct Medal for a gallant escape after being captured during the evacuation from Dunkirk. Commissioned in late 1940, he earned a posthumous Victoria Cross for an attack on a Japanese position at Kyauchaw, in northern Burma, in January 1944.

Indian troops lining up to attack Japanese positions in the Arakan, 1944.

IND 3457

Captain Terence Rupert Molloy
1st Battalion, Northamptonshire Regiment

The task the battalion had to undertake was the capture of an isolated Japanese bunker position on the Yu River, a distance of about three miles from where we were. This bunker position had been reported by another unit some months before. It was on a track leading from the Chindwin River and it was considered it might be a staging post for the Japanese build-up for their possible attack on Imphal.

The programme of the attack on the position was that there would be a bombardment first from Liberator bombers – they'd taken a photograph of the actual location, they knew exactly where the position was, so they were going to do some precision bombing before our attack went in. Well, we waited and waited. As far as we were concerned, we were all keyed up and ready, but it took days before the Liberators decided that the cloud cover was sufficiently open for them to mount this attack. Then the day was chosen and we moved up.

We were only three miles from the position. But three miles, even going up a path, represented at least three hours' walking and everything had to be carried on the men of course. And we moved up in single file up this track towards the Japanese position and spent the night in the jungle a mile from it – we weren't allowed any closer. And there we waited for the dawn when the Liberators would do their attack. This they did, we could hear the bombs dropping and so on, and we stayed the night there after this bombing took place.

We all thought, 'Oh, well, that must have put paid to the Japanese position,' but in the night we could hear automatic fire coming from the Japanese position. Presumably they thought somebody was attacking them, probably some tree or branch falling down had put the wind up them. So we knew that by no means were they finished off by the bombing and that we'd still have a task ahead of us. The attack went in and 1 Company led the way and got held up by the Japanese bunkers. Then a second company went the same way and got held up.

John Horwood, he was actually the mortar platoon commander, he'd been up directing the fire of the mortars, and he was a very brave and a very determined man. He could see the Japanese were in front of him and after the failure of the attack he decided that he himself would lead one. There were some Gurkhas attached to us, a small platoon, and he managed to gather some of them up and lead an attack. It was rather a hopeless thing, I suppose, but he was extremely brave, a gallant chap: he'd already won a DCM at Dunkirk during the evacuation there. A very strong character, a very determined manner. He saw no reason why we should all be hanging back as we might have been, he was determined to have a go himself.

Lieutenant John Edgar Alexander Hopkins
1st Battalion, Northamptonshire Regiment
We had John Horwood as we called him – Lieutenant A. G. Horwood – up with us. He was the mortar officer and he was acting as the forward observation officer for his mortars and firing them from wherever he was. I kept losing men mostly from these wretched grenade attacks, occasionally bursts of rifle fire, all we could do was try to keep the Japanese quiet with Bren gun fire, and then John Horwood in the afternoon said, 'Look, I'm sure these chaps would run if we got at them. We ought to attack them.' I said, 'Well, I've only got twelve men left.' He said, 'Well, that's no good, I'll go and see the CO and see what I can do,' and he went back. He came back a bit later and he said, 'I've borrowed a platoon of Gurkhas,' and these Gurkhas came up and started getting organised to put in this attack, fixing bayonets, and out came their kukris suspended from their wrists.

So in went this attack with John Horwood leading it. I was giving covering fire from over on one flank with a Bren gunner and then the next thing I saw was John Horwood standing on a tree stump, directing this attack. And then there was obviously a burst of fire from somewhere on the right and John fell and then the attack fizzled out.

Then a perfectly remarkable thing happened. A fellow called Jarvis, Private Jarvis, who was a stretcher-bearer, always known as 'Boy' Jarvis because he'd come to the battalion on Boy's Service a few years back, came up and said, 'Where's Mr Horwood?' I pointed out this tree stump and I said, 'The left-hand side of that tree stump. That's where he fell but I'm sure he'd be dead.' He said, 'Oh. All right.' Next thing, there was a great burst of firing and grenades and things and I looked up and towards where this was happening. And there was 'Boy' Jarvis, standing there, taking off his equipment beside this tree stump and putting John's body into a blanket, and picking up his equipment and heaving the blanket over his shoulder and walking back as calmly as you like, and absolutely nothing hit him and why not I cannot imagine. It was the calmest thing I ever saw.

The outcome of this was that John Horwood was awarded the Victoria Cross and 'Boy' Jarvis, I put him in for a Military Medal, which he gained and which he certainly should have had. To see this lad standing there taking absolutely no notice of the enemy was really quite something.

Naik Nand Singh
1st/11th Sikh Regiment

Born in Patiala State, Punjab, India, on 24 September 1914, Nand Singh was awarded the Victoria Cross for his actions on 11–12 March 1944 during an attack to recapture a position gained by the Japanese overlooking the important Maungdaw-Buthidaung Road in the Arakan, Burma.

Under heavy machine-gun and rifle fire he led his section up a steep knife-edged ridge and, though wounded, captured three enemy trenches with the bayonet. 'Naik Nand Singh personally killed seven of the enemy,' his citation ends, 'and owing to his determination, outstanding dash and magnificent courage, the important position was won back from the enemy.'

IND 3975

Naik Nand Singh VC.

After Independence, Nand Singh remained in the Indian army. He was killed in action in December 1947 while fighting Pakistani forces in Kashmir. The following account was recorded in 1944 by Nand Singh's divisional commander.

Major General Sir Frank Messervy
Commander, 7th Indian Infantry Division

This is the story of the act which gained for Naik Nand Singh of the 1st/11th Sikh Regiment a very well-earned Victoria Cross.

His regiment had, in a most successful attack, secured the heights of both sides of the road from Maungdaw to Buthidaung. This defile was the gateway to Buthidaung and was the last good position available to the Japs guarding the town. That night the Japs managed to infiltrate round the flank of the battalion position and dig themselves in on a spur commanding the road. This spur was only a hundred feet or so high but like so many hills in the Arakan was an absolute knife-edge with precipitous slopes covered in thick impassable bamboo jungle. There was only one way up, along the narrow path that led to the top. Single file was the only possible formation for the attack.

As dawn broke and the Jap position was spotted from the battalion headquarters, urgent action had to be taken. The spur had to be cleared before a tank column accompanied by a Gurkha battalion passed through into Buthidaung. The column was due in about an hour's time. The company of which Nand Singh was a section commander was given the task. Nand Singh's section was to lead the attack and his objective was three enemy trenches at the top of the spur. Once these were captured the rest of the company could get a footing and be able to get on with some fire support. But to get these first positions no fire support was possible. Determination, dash and high courage on the part of the leading section were the only means of getting there.

With a tremendous shout of, '*Sat Sri Akal!*' the famous Sikh battle cry, Naik Singh led the attack. As the enemy positions were approached, the narrow track was swept with automatic fire and bombarded with hand grenades. Every man in his section was knocked out but by some miracle he himself, alone, was seen to reach the first trench, though apparently hit. He disappeared from view but emerged after a time and crawled towards the next trench from which a shower of grenades landed all round him, one bursting within a few feet of his head. He crawled on, hurled his own grenades and entered the enemy trench. Again he disappeared from view but soon staggered out and went straight at the next trench into which he jumped and at last his head appeared and victoriously announced that the position was captured and the enemy garrison killed. His company followed up without delay and with this foothold on the top in our hands was able to clear the remaining positions. Thirty-seven Japs were killed. Only three managed to make their escape.

Nand Singh had been hit by a bullet in the thigh before reaching the first trench and also had a large number of fragments of grenades all over his body. But he's a tough hardy peasant of a Punjabi with ten years' army service and he was back again at duty in his battalion within six weeks. Such is the stuff of which our Indian battalions are made.

Lieutenant George Cairns
Somerset Light Infantry (Prince Albert's)
Attached 1st Battalion, South Staffordshire Regiment

George Albert Cairns was born on 12 December 1913 and, when war broke out, was working in a bank. Married in 1941, he joined the army the following year. In March 1944 Cairns was operating behind the lines in Japanese-occupied Burma with Major-General Orde Wingate's Second Chindit Expedition when, during an attack on an enemy hilltop, he performed the deed for which he would receive a posthumous Victoria Cross.

As the citation explains, 'he was attacked by a Japanese officer, who, with his sword, hacked off Lieutenant Cairns' left arm. Lieutenant Cairns killed this Officer; picked up the sword and continued to lead his men in the attack and slashing left and right with the captured sword killed and wounded several Japanese before he himself fell to the ground.'

After the original recommendation for his VC was lost in the air crash that killed Orde Wingate on 24 March 1944, Cairns' young widow and King George VI both played roles in marshalling the necessary evidence that led to it being finally awarded in 1949. It was the last-announced VC of the Second World War.

Lieutenant Harry Williams
Animal transport officer, 77th Brigade

We set off for the railway line which runs between Mandalay and Myitkyina in the north. The purpose behind this was to put a block on that railway and deny the use of it to the Japanese for provisions. To get to this railway we had to cross a range of hills – it was very hilly – sometimes quite precipitous slopes, mules falling down, loads coming off. Anyway, we arrived ultimately at a little village called Henu, which was the railway station of a larger village called Mawlu, and it was there that Brigadier Calvert, reconnoitring ahead, had decided to place this block, which became known as White City, on the railway.

There were seven little hillocks that overlooked the railway and when dawn broke we found we were actually overlooked, from what became known as Bare Hill, by a Japanese position. God knows how they had decided to establish one there. And so, almost immediately from the first day, we were under pretty heavy fire from Bare Hill.

A charge was led by Calvert, of South Staffords principally and in which I was involved, to take this hill; there were some 3rd/6th Gurkhas there as well. He called upon the Staffords to leave their positions and charge up this hill and exhorted them to show everybody, the Gurkhas included, how the thing should be done. I remember him saying, 'Staffords to the right and Gurkhas to the left!'

It might have been unwise, really, because if the attack on the Japanese positions had not been successful the block itself may have been under some threat, because some of the people taking part in that charge were, for example, mortar platoon personnel, some machine-gunners, animal transport as well. So it was a polyglot lot of specialist people who really should not have been involved quite so gratuitously in that attack. Anyway, it was successful, so that's all in the past now.

The men fixed their bayonets and it was, really, almost a traditional charge up the hill. I suppose there'd be about fifty or sixty Staffords. All I can remember is dashing among some open ground and climbing a low hill and just shooting at everything that I could see. So far as we know, all the Japanese on that hill were killed. I'm afraid that I killed one or two: it was real hand-to-hand stuff. The Japanese were extraordinarily resilient soldiers.

It was during that operation that we gained our VC, a chap called Cairns, George Cairns, who was a great friend of mine. He was the mortar platoon officer but he joined in the attack that was launched up this hill. A Japanese officer had hacked off his arm but despite that he still managed to kill his assailant and was urging his men forward when he literally died. But his example was tremendous. And I remember Calvert standing over George Cairns. Although I didn't hear, apparently George said to him, 'Have we done all right, sir?'

Much later he was awarded the last awarded VC of the war. The citation, which went out with Wingate, was initially lost 'cause Wingate was killed when he was flying out of Burma some weeks later. But when, in fact, George VI knew of this – this was after the war – he caused inquires to be made and George Cairns was posthumously awarded the VC.

Lance Corporal John Harman
4th Battalion, Queen's Own Royal West Kent Regiment

John Harman was awarded the Victoria Cross for his actions on 8–9 April 1944 during the Battle of Kohima, in north-east India, when British and Indian troops held and repelled the Japanese advance into India.

The son of a millionaire businessman, a famous financier who bought Lundy Island in the Bristol Channel in 1925, John Pennington Harman was born in Beckenham, Kent, on 20 July 1914 and educated at Bedales. After school he travelled round the world, working as a lumberjack in New Zealand and on a sheep station in Australia, before returning in 1940 and spending another year farming on Lundy. He then joined the army and went almost immediately with the Royal Fusiliers to India, where he transferred to the Royal West Kents.

Major Donald Easten
4th Battalion, Royal West Kent Regiment

Orders came: 'Back to Kohima.' I was commanding the leading company that went up, D Company, and as we got to a crossroads at Kohima, up in the mountains, we were fired on. I said, 'Right, de-bus,' and we got out of our vehicles and we ran up the hill into the position, which at that time was held and had been largely dug by a battalion of the Assam Rifles, who I don't think had ever been in action before. But they had done a very good job, they'd burrowed all over this hill position and dug lots of trenches and made overhead cover and so on in parts of them. We were the first company in and I was told to hold the position while the other companies came through, and then I was made reserve company.

I thought, 'That's very pleasant, we can just sit here in reserve,' but I think within half an hour I had to send a platoon to reinforce one of the other companies because they were being attacked. The next day I launched an attack with one platoon on a position the Japanese had got

Lance Corporal John Harman VC.

HU 2021

IND 4886

The grave of Lance Corporal John Harman VC in the military cemetery at Kohima, not long after the battle.

into the night before. And so it went on, like that, for fourteen or sixteen days. I think if the battalion had not got in there the place would have been overrun in a very short time with only this very inexperienced battalion of Assam Rifles, who weren't exactly a warrior race in any case. There were also, probably, about a hundred convalescent British soldiers of various regiments who had been caught up there too and they were formed into platoons and sections and helped reinforce us, really, because they hadn't got any commanders to look after them. And it was at that time that Lance Corporal Harman of my company won the Victoria Cross, posthumously.

One night, Japanese infiltrated between my company and C Company who were next to me and when we woke up in the morning they were in a machine-gun post in between the two companies and making it extremely difficult. For one thing, movement was almost impossible in daytime with these people there. And while I was discussing with my sergeant major how we were going to tackle this, Lance Corporal Harman, without saying anything to either of us, ran forward.

He got under the line of fire of the Japanese machine gun, he pulled a grenade out of his belt, pulled the pin out, counted 'One, two,' and put it through the slit of the bunker and then dived in after it and came out with the machine gun and said, 'There are two dead Japanese in there.' Well, that was the first thing he did, which was pretty amazingly brave.

And then, that night, the Japanese attacked C Company very heavily and they pushed C Company out of their forward trenches and got into them themselves and were firing almost point-blank at us. And again, as reserve company, I was called to try and restore the situation. And once again this chap Harman said to his section – I was with him – 'Right, give me covering fire,' and he fixed his bayonet and he charged this short distance down the hill, firing as he went, and he shot, I suppose, two or three Japanese, bayoneted one and the rest fled. And as he came back up the hill, this was in a ravine, they opened up from the other side and they hit him. He made it back to me, I was fairly close to him, of course, and he died in my arms actually. I was shouting for the stretcher-bearers and they came up but by the time they got to us he was dead.

After the battle, after the siege was over, I told my commanding officer what had happened and he said, 'There's only one thing you can do and that's to recommend him for the Victoria Cross,' which I did and it was awarded.

Lance Corporal Ivan Daunt
4th Battalion, Royal West Kent Regiment

We were better armed, I think, than the Japs but the difference is they'd come forward where you'd hesitate. Take Harman, Lance Corporal Harman: he played them at their own game. When they came at you, Harman couldn't stand that, so he got out of his trench and went after them. But he paid the price.

At Kohima we were very close because of the perimeter, mostly two men in a trench: you always had one chap with you all the time. You were never on your own, we used to dig our own trenches and stick together. But Harman said, 'I've been out there, I've done a recce on me own. You're better on your own. I killed a couple of Japs asleep.' Another time, he said, 'I'm in trouble, Major Winstanley's reprimanded me. He said, "Where was you?" I said, "I went out to the toilet," but I didn't, I went out on me own. I went round listening and to see.'

And he said, 'I'll tell you something, if you're short of rice, I can take you to a place where the Japs have stored sacks of rice. If one of you would like to come with me, I'll go back.' Well, I didn't go, but he went back himself and he brought us back quite a bag of rice and I cooked the rice for the lads. Blimey, they all lapped it up. That was another occasion with old Harman.

See, it takes you time to weigh up a person, don't it? One mate, a friend who was with him all the time, said, 'I can't stop him. If he wanders off, I can't stop him. I ain't going to go and I can't stop him. And of course his father's a millionaire.' We said, 'What?' – we were sitting around having a talk – and he said, 'His father's a millionaire. Owns Lundy Island.' So it all came out then.

But he was different. They soon made him a lance corporal but from what I know about the man he didn't want to be, he wanted to be himself. I found out that he'd been almost round the world on his own: had the money, see. He sounded somebody who was a bit bored of life. It's a job to explain, really. Nobody was like him, really. If you had two or three thousand men, you wouldn't find another one. He'd pick up a bit of grass and he'd say, 'Now, this bit of grass…' and he'd give a lecture and you'd be fascinated.

Very brave man. When you think about it, he had everything going for him. But it wasn't enough. It had to be, didn't it? It had to be.

Major Donald Easten
4th Battalion, Royal West Kent Regiment

I knew him fairly well. He was a public schoolboy, his father was a very rich man, owned Lundy Island, but Harman never wanted to be an officer. With his education and so on he could have gone for officer training but he always refused. He was brilliant as a company sniper: in the Arakan he would spend hours out in no-man's-land between us and the Japanese trying to pick off some Jap who stuck his head up somewhere. I don't think he ever did, actually, but every day he was happy to go out and spend hours hidden, hoping to shoot somebody.

And he was a loner. He wasn't stand-offish, but he was a man who really preferred to go his own way. Very much an individualist. If he could have won the war on his own, he would have done. I think he was that sort of chap. I liked him as a man and I admired his independent spirit, really.

He did an amazing thing, which I only heard of many years later. A British plane crashed on the cliff of Lundy Island when he was there, the tail end of the plane was sticking out across a steep cliff and in it was the rear-gunner. And Harman got the pilot out, who was unhurt apparently, and then he crawled down this plane and got the air-gunner out, who, unfortunately, had been killed, but he got him out with this thing teetering on a very, very high cliff over the rocks. He was the sort of chap who liked doing things like that, a very brave man.*

He was a bit of a visionary, I think. He had strange views on life. He told me once – we were lying under a bank being shelled – 'Sir, while you're with me, you're absolutely safe, because I met an old man in Spain who told me that I was going to live till I was seventy.' I said to him, 'That's fine for you, Harman. But the old man of Spain didn't say this to me, he said it to you.' He had these strange ideas, but, by golly, he was a good chap. He was with me then because I had to go off to visit a company of Rajputs [an Indian army unit] who were quite a long way away from us and it meant going across country where there might have been Japanese about, and I took him with me because he was the sort of chap you knew would be a good man to have if anything happened. He was a very good shot; he always kept his weapons absolutely in perfect order and so on.

He was about the scruffiest soldier you ever saw in your life to look at. He was a very big man and half his uniform didn't fit him. In Burma, all the uniform we had, of course, was a green battle-dress type of top and trousers made of drill and it rotted and wore out pretty quickly, so it was always being replaced, and Harman was a big chap and it always seemed that his shirt was too small for him or his trousers too big or something. He never, ever seemed to get the sort of uniform that fitted too properly. He was fairly tall and very solid. Very broad. Huge shoulders.

The only time his family cropped up was when we couldn't get any boots to fit him. His boots were worn out and I think we had to put him

---

* According to a press report of 1944, the crew of the aircraft, which had crashed in fog, were in fact killed and Harman, without ropes or assistance, climbed down a sheer cliff which had been thought impossible to descend and recovered the dead men's identity discs and papers before burying the bodies and climbing up again. *The News of the World*, 25 June 1944.

into rubber shoes or something until we could get a pair of boots his size. And he must have written home about this as a joke, he thought it was rather funny that the British Army hadn't got a pair boots to fit him, and his father took it up directly with Churchill. So a signal came whistling back, 'Why hasn't this chap got any boots?' That was the time that I discovered that his father was this rather rich influential man. Harman was most upset about that. He apologised and said he'd never write and tell his father anything like that again, he didn't want to get any of us into trouble.

One time, when we were in the Arakan, the rations were good but they were pretty dreary and dull: an enormous amount of bully beef and biscuits. And cattle from the village behind us used to come through our lines every morning and go and graze in no-man's-land between us and the Japanese and then go back in the evening to their village. And Harman came to me one day and said, 'Sir, that is beef, *fresh beef*, and it goes through here every day and it goes back every evening. If I shot one of those, the company could live on it for a week.' So I said, 'Well, that's a point,' and I got on to battalion headquarters on the field telephone and put this to the adjutant who nearly had a fit and said, 'There'd be an international incident if you shot one of these cattle. The Indians would come into the war against us or something.' So I said to Harman, 'I'm sorry, can't do it,' but I also said, 'Of course, if one broke its leg or something like that you would have to put it out of its agony.' He said, 'I quite understand.' And half an hour later I heard a burst of tommy gun fire and within a few minutes Harman appeared in my company trench, saying, 'Extraordinary coincidence, sir. But one of those cows has just broken its leg in the cookhouse area.' I said, 'What an extraordinary thing, Harman.' And we lived on fresh beef for a week. That was the sort of chap he was.

Private Thomas Jackson
4th Battalion, Royal West Kent Regiment
He was a genuine bloke. If he knew there was a sticky job coming and there was two of you, he'd be with you. He wouldn't say, 'You go and I'll

wait here for you,' sort of thing, he was with you. When you spoke to him, he never had a coarse word. Boys talk about birds, the feminine type, but he was more intellectual, Jack, to speak to; he'd talk about other things; he had a nice sort of way. I don't know of anybody in our company or in his platoon that had a bad word for Jack, he were that kind of person. He'd fill in with you and lead you. He weren't no fool.

When he killed the cattle, he asked me about my tommy gun and I told him to go and get lost. He said, 'Let me borrow it, and two or three rounds.' I says, 'Get lost, Jack. I'm the only one with a tommy gun in the company so you couldn't pretend where you got it from. What are you going to do?' He said, 'I'll tell you when I come back.' Next thing, I see him disappearing with a shovel, a GS [General Service] shovel, the old spade, and when he came back he was saturated: he'd been sweating, digging in the heat. Then he disappeared and then a little while later I heard, 'Rat-tat-tat-tat!' Then I heard no more for a long, long while. After a while, back comes Jack, beaming all over his face. I said, 'How many did you kill, Jack?' I was thinking of enemy, like. 'Only one,' he says. He'd coerced this head of cattle over towards him, shot it – but before he done it, he'd dug two holes – and when he killed it, he gutted it and cut the meat out and threw the offal and all the rubbish in one hole and hung the bits of meat over bamboo which he'd got in the other hole. So back he comes with the tommy gun. 'You don't need to check it,' he says, 'I've cleaned it.' Knowing Jack, I knew he had, see, so I laughed. And various people of various ranks had a bit of steak.

Great bloke and I mean that. You speak to anybody you might meet out of the company, there won't be one bad word about Jack. He were that kind of person.

Captain John Randle
2nd Battalion, Royal Norfolk Regiment

Captain John 'Jack' Randle was posthumously awarded the Victoria Cross for his actions while clearing Japanese positions on GPT Ridge, Kohima, north-east India, between 4 and 6 May 1944.

Although wounded in the knee by grenade splinters, he first took command of his company when its commander was hit, organised the capture of the company's objective and helped bring in wounded men. He then carried out a vital reconnaissance of the next objective, a formidable chain of enemy bunkers dominated by what became known as 'Norfolk Bunker'. Next day he led the attack on it, during the course of which he was killed.

Born in India on 22 December 1917, John Neil Randle had been educated at Marlborough College and Oxford. He had secured a position with the Bombay Trading Company and was due to sail for Burma when the war broke out and he was mobilised instead. He had been in India for two years with his battalion when, in April 1944, it was sent to take part in the desperate fighting at Kohima.

Randle's brother-in-law, Flying Officer Leslie Manser, a bomber pilot of 50 Squadron, RAF, was posthumously awarded a Victoria Cross following a raid on Cologne in May 1942 when he remained at the controls of his doomed and burning aircraft long enough to allow his crew to escape by parachute.

Captain Samuel Hornor
2nd Battalion, Royal Norfolk Regiment
The word went round, 'Dig in,' so we dug in on the top of GPT Ridge. We dug in there, established our position. Everybody then had to get casualties back, the doctor set up his RAP a little further back and he was very, very busy, as were the stretcher-bearers. There were all sorts of people wounded all over the place. Jack Randle was wounded in the leg quite

IND 3698

The shell-torn slopes of the battlefield at Kohima, 1944.

HU 2000

Captain John Randle VC.

nastily, he was limping about and he'd got it bandaged up, but he wasn't going to be evacuated, especially as his company commander was knocked out. And people came back and a plan was made because it was quite clear that on the left front there was a bunker, a big one. It had been overrun but they couldn't hold it because all these bunkers were covered by each other. They were very clever, the Japs. They'd put a chain of bunkers and each one would cover the next one, so if you captured one you'd get shot to pieces by the next one.

So Colonel Scott reckoned this big bunker, which came to be called 'Norfolk Bunker', was an important key to the position and it must be attacked at last light and held. David Glasse and the carrier platoon were detailed to take that job and I remember so clearly David giving me his watch and saying, 'Take that and write to Louise, won't you, and see that she gets this.' I said, 'We're going to see you again shortly, David.' He said, 'I doubt it, I doubt it.' He just knew he was going to get killed. And off they went, they overran it, David Glasse got killed and they couldn't hold it because they were shot off it again by other bunkers below. So there we were.

On 5 May there was deliberation, quite a lot of discussion, as to what to do next. You could see this wretched Norfolk Bunker and it was quite clear that the whole position hung on it. It looked like a sort of mound, brushwood on the top; about four or five men were in it with a small narrow slit that covered all the ground in front of it. Down to the left was a smaller one and it was critical to get that as well because it was covering Norfolk Bunker. There was a short O group, the company commanders were all briefed as to what the next step was, which was for B Company to attack and at all costs try to demolish Norfolk Bunker. From then on, we could do a further advance, perhaps.

Jack was just given his orders, not in any very great detail. One of his platoon commanders was in fact Sergeant Major Fitt because officers, you see, were dwindling all the time and platoons hadn't got platoon officers any more. And at last light on the fifth, as it was getting dark,

Jack Randle went out. His leg wasn't improving things but he managed it all right. He went out with Fitt and I forget how many others, the other platoon commanders, very few of them. They had to crawl very carefully so that they could get a good view of Norfolk Bunker and also a view of a bunker a bit further back, which was covering it. Jack Randle detailed Fitt to pay special attention to that, for his platoon to attack that bunker, which was critical to the whole thing. At the same time he would deal with the attack on Norfolk Bunker. It was a very vital, very brilliantly done reconnaissance, just as all reconnaissance should be before a battle. We were all waiting for the sixth and hoping against hope that the attack would succeed. Jack got his company out very quietly in the dark to form up. Every Bren gun that we'd got, practically, was organised to cover them.

Company Sergeant Major Bert Fitt
2nd Battalion, Royal Norfolk Regiment
The plan was to attack Norfolk Bunker from the front. My platoon was the spearhead, through the centre; 12 Platoon was to the right. There were only two platoons, really, to go forward. It was an out-and-out frontal attack because we were going in at dawn, at first light, and we thought at the time that was the most obvious way in which we were going to take it, because we'd got to climb up a hill to take it. It was sloping, fairly steep, open ground, the trees had all been shelled and all their branches had been knocked off. There was very little cover, very little cover.

We laid up on the start line and Captain Randle came up and he laid beside me and he said, 'I've seen all the horrible things that's happened to me in my past'. He meant all his past history, anything that he'd done wrong. I said, 'So have I, and I'm just about fed up with laying here.' We were getting shot at, right, left and centre.

We moved forward, we got about halfway, and when we got to the bottom of the hill Captain Randle had already been hit. Then he was hit again, in the upper part of his body, and I shouted to him to go down and leave it to me, 'cause you could see that he had already lost blood. He said, 'No. You take that left-hand bunker, I'll take this right-hand one.'

I thought that when he ran towards the bunker he was determined that we would get that position. And on top of that I think he had an idea that he would not come out of that attack: what he'd said about him seeing all his past and what-have-you, that sort of thing. He was a good man and a good leader, a very good leader. I didn't see his wounds but he was hit at least twice before we ever got to the bottom of the hill, and he staggered twice. And when he staggered, that told me that he had been hit fairly heavily.

Now, they were two light machine-gun posts and they were carving up the company terrible. We'd been under fire all the while, they'd spotted us and I'd already lost my leading section commander, Corporal Barrett. He can't have been more than four yards from me when he was killed from the bunker that I was going to have a go at. I went straight in and got this bunker, I managed to get a grenade in and I knocked this bunker out altogether, I pushed it in through the slit. And I immediately spun right, because I thought I could have got to where Captain Randle was and got on top of that bunker before anything happened, but unfortunately, as I turned right, I saw Captain Randle at the bunker entrance.

He had a grenade he was going to release into the bunker and he had his weapon with him and I just stood there, I couldn't have done a thing to save him. If he could have held out for about three minutes I would have got on top of the bunker and knocked it out without getting hurt. But unfortunately he'd been hit again, at point-blank range, and as he was going down he threw his grenade into the bunker and he sealed the slit where the gun was firing from with his own body, so that nobody could shoot from it. But he had in actual fact got the occupants, killed them. That's exactly as it happened. He sealed the bunker with his own body. I saw all this as I was running across. The distance between the bunker that he sealed and the one I attacked was no more than twenty yards, couldn't have been more than that.

I say I could have done it. As things were, I would have certainly made an attempt to do it, I would have got it if I possibly could. I mean, I didn't want to see him go down; I didn't want to see *Captain Randle* go down. I had a lot of respect for him as a company commander and I knew very well that we hadn't got no officers left.

Afterwards I told Colonel Scott verbally what had happened and I said that Captain Randle should be awarded some form of decoration – I couldn't say a VC, you can't do that – in recognition of what he'd done. Colonel Scott said, 'I'll see that's in hand.' That was the finish of it as far as I was concerned.

Captain Samuel Hornor
2nd Battalion, Royal Norfolk Regiment

He was a great chap was Jack Randle. He was very sort of harum-scarum. I remember, at Fairford, Jack was the sort of chap who wouldn't get up in time for some sort of silly parade so he'd quickly throw on his uniform and on occasion his pyjama trousers appeared at the bottom of it – that sort of thing. He was a very, very good chap. He was training to be a lawyer. He was a great friend of Leonard Cheshire's at Oxford just before the war. Then Jack at some stage got married to Mavis and later on Leonard Cheshire went on to do great things and he got a VC, Jack got a VC and his brother-in-law, Mavis's brother, got a VC, another posthumous one. Incredible: three VCs all linked together.

You could say that on that occasion that he shouldn't have been leading from the front but that was the sort of chap he was, he led from the front. We thought it was absolutely marvellous: 'Jack, he tried to take the bloody thing himself.' The citation covered the patrol the previous evening, which was of vital importance. Without that patrol, that reconnaissance, the attack couldn't really have even started, it would have been blasted before it had even started, so it was for the patrol and reconnaissance the previous morning and the actual attack itself. The first time we went back to Kohima after the war, the general said, 'I think I'd like you, Sam, to stand in front of Jack Randle's grave and read out the citation to everybody.' A difficult thing to do, but I did it.

Havildar Umrao Singh
33rd Mountain Battery, Royal Indian Artillery

Umrao Singh was awarded the Victoria Cross for his actions on the night of 15–16 December 1944 when the advance of the 81st West African Division down the Kaladan Valley, Burma, ran into strong Japanese opposition. At that moment he was in command of a small detachment of howitzers.

Under attack from at least two companies of Japanese infantry and though wounded by grenade fragments, he held off four assaults by firing a Bren gun and by efficiently directing the fire of his fellow soldiers. When his ammunition ran out and most of his men were killed or wounded and with his howitzer in danger of being overrun, he then seized a gun bearer – a heavy iron rod similar to a crowbar – and, as his citation states, 'calling once again on all who remained, he closed with the enemy in furious hand-to-hand fighting and was seen to strike down three Japanese in a desperate effort to save his gun, until he was overwhelmed and knocked senseless. Six hours later, when a counter-attack restored the position, he was found in an exhausted state beside his gun and almost unrecognisable with seven severe wounds, and ten dead Japanese round him.'

Born in Punjab in 1920, Umrao Singh survived the war and served in the Indian Army from Independence until 1965 when he returned to farm a two-acre smallholding inherited from his father. Years later he was still living in a small mud-brick house and working this land but refused to sell his medal, saying to do so would dishonour the men who had fallen beside him when he had earned it. The last Indian holder of the VC, he died in 2005. The following is a translation of an account he gave to the journalist and broadcaster, Sir Mark Tully.

Havildar Umrao Singh
33rd Mountain Battery, Royal Indian Artillery

I had volunteered to try and clear a hill which the Japanese were occupying. It was near the sea in the Arakan. We went down a path which I had made and unfortunately the Japanese had discovered that we had made this path so we ran into a party of Japanese in very thick bamboo. You couldn't even tell whether there was anyone there or not, all the main troops who were accompanying me ran away or were killed, but my troop remained with me and we started firing on the Japanese until eventually we ran out of ammunition for our howitzers.

I told the troop to withdraw. They said they wouldn't withdraw without me, so I withdrew with them. Then I thought to myself, 'Well, a gunner never leaves his gun,' so I went back in again and started firing at them with my Bren gun which was all I had and this went on for about five hours, occasionally firing when someone came within five yards of me, until eventually I ran out of ammunition. So then I picked up a hammer [the gun-bearer] from my howitzer and I attacked the Japanese with this and I managed to kill quite a few of them.

Eventually some aeroplanes flew overhead and this frightened the Japanese and so they ran away. I then collapsed because I had several wounds. When I was eventually rescued I was told that thirty to thirty-five dead Japanese had lain in the area where this little fight had taken place. Of course I didn't kill them all. Many of them were also killed by my colleagues in my troop.

Eventually, after hospital, I was sent back to a training camp and it was announced that I had been awarded the VC and I didn't have the first idea what on earth it was. I thought that perhaps it meant that I was going to get a Viceroy's Commission. I was taken to the commandant and he told me, 'You have become a *bahadur*,' which means a brave man, a hero, and then I understood that I was being rewarded for bravery. But then I thought to myself, 'I don't really know what bravery is. I was told that I'd joined the artillery to fight, and I fought, that was my job.'

When I went to London to receive my VC I was absolutely amazed. I had a wonderful moustache in those days and a lot of women came up and started kissing me on my moustache and I didn't know what on earth was happening. I went and looked in a mirror and I saw that I was covered in this lipstick, so I washed it off quickly. At first I was a bit afraid of London but then I got to like it very much.

Lieutenant George Knowland
Royal Norfolk Regiment, attached No 1 Commando

George Knowland was posthumously awarded the Victoria Cross for his actions inland from the Kangaw beachhead, Burma, on 31 January 1945, when in command of a forward platoon of twenty-four men occupying an important hilltop position that came under heavy and repeated enemy attack from three hundred Japanese soldiers.

'In spite of the ferocity of the attack, he moved about from trench to trench distributing ammunition, and firing his rifle and throwing grenades at the enemy, often from completely exposed positions,' his citation reads. Later, with the enemy less than ten yards away, he took over a Bren gun when the crew was wounded and stood in the open firing from the hip to cover the men's safe treatment and recovery. When a further attack came he fired a two-inch mortar from the hip, killing six Japanese with his first bomb, then used his rifle.

'Being hard pressed and with the enemy closing in on him from only 10 yards away, he had no time to re-charge his magazine,' his citation concludes. 'Snatching up the Tommy gun of a casualty, he sprayed the enemy and was mortally wounded stemming this assault, though not before he had killed and wounded many. Such was the inspiration of his magnificent heroism, that, though fourteen out of twenty-four of his platoon became casualties at an early stage, and six of his positions were overrun by the enemy, his men held on through twelve hours of continuous and fierce fighting until reinforcements arrived. If this Northern end of the hill had fallen, the rest of the position would have been endangered, the beach-head dominated by the enemy, and other units farther inland cut off from their source of supplies.'

Born in Catford on 16 August 1922, George Arthur Knowland had been brought up in Croydon, spending time in an orphanage after the death of his mother, and joined the Royal Norfolk Regiment as a private in 1940. After volunteering for service with the commandos, he had seen service with No 3 Commando in Sicily and Italy before being commissioned in January 1944 and posted to the Far East to join No 1 Commando.

Private Victor Ralph
No 1 Commando

The Japs were pulling out down through the Arakan. There was a road inland which went over the mountains and our generals decided that a key point there, to cut this road, was at Kangaw. It was impossible for one reason or another to go overland to Kangaw so we had to make another landing. We went out for quite a long time in our landing craft, sailing in line astern, until we landed in a mangrove swamp quite close to Hill 170.

We, No 1 Commando, were first ashore on that occasion. We negotiated the mangrove swamp, which wasn't particularly easy, it was very hard on the back and on the legs, but we did get through eventually to the paddy fields and we could see the hill in front of us, three of four hundred yards of paddy field, maybe a little more, in between us which again was fairly swamped. It wasn't terrifically difficult to get through but the Japs of course were opening up on us and we dived and ducked and weaved and so forth. But we took the hill fairly comfortably.

Having taken the hill, various patrols went out on a routine basis. 44 Commando took a hill close by us and were told not to dig in because they weren't going to stay there very long but that night they were shelled very, very heavily and they lost a lot of men, and they rejoined us on Hill 170. But during the next ten days or so the Japanese shelled us day after day, quite a number of shells, but nothing spectacular till the time came that we were to be relieved the next morning. One of the Indian divisions was coming in to take our position and we were going to go back. And lo and behold, on that morning, the shells were much thicker than they had been, an awful lot was laid down, and quite suddenly the Japanese put in their main attack to dislodge us from Hill 170, which was the key feature.

It was virtually hand-to-hand fighting all day. It was 4 Troop that took the brunt of the first attacks and, as we did lose a lot of people one way or t'other, various sections of the Commando, 3 Troop and various other troops, came to help out; troops of No 5 Commando and troops of 42 Commando came at different times. We were all involved, sections of the whole brigade, all day long. It really was a terrific battle. A little bit like Rorke's Drift; something like that, I would say, except that the Japanese had modern weapons just as we had. It was quite an overgrown hill, which was one of the problems, of course. You couldn't see individuals approaching until they were virtually on top of you.

One of our officers of 4 Troop, Lieutenant Knowland, I don't know if he was just mad or very, very brave, he fought with all sorts of weapons. It was very, very hectic but he was walking about actually in the open with a two-inch mortar, which he was firing from the hip, with a Bren gun, with a tommy gun, with a rifle. Anything he could lay his hands on he was using and he took out an awful lot of Japanese. Eventually he was killed and he received the VC posthumously. He was a very recent member of our unit, we really knew nothing about him, he was virtually a stranger to us, but he was a good, keen, young lieutenant. He was from the Royal Norfolk Regiment and I think he had served in Europe. He was a Londoner. Croydon, he came from. I'm told he was an orphan.

Captain Dominic Neill
3rd Battalion, 2nd King Edward VII's Own Gurkha Rifles
I never saw his full citation but the story came back to us that he had repelled, virtually single-handed, at least three counter-attacks on his troop position and on occasion was seen firing a two-inch mortar from the hip at the enemy to repel them, which was quite an effort. The kick of a two-inch could have so easily broken his hipbone if he'd had the base-plate on his hip, but obviously he must have held it in such a way that he got away with his trick. He was clearly a very, very brave young man and thoroughly deserved his Victoria Cross. It was just sad that it had to be posthumous.

Lieutenant Ian Fraser DSC
Royal Navy

Leading Seaman James Magennis
Royal Navy

Crew members of the same X-craft submarine, Lieutenant Ian Fraser and Leading Seaman James Magennis were each awarded the Victoria Cross for their roles in laying explosive charges under the hull of a 10,000-ton Japanese cruiser, *Takao*, moored in the Strait of Johor, Singapore, on 31 July 1945.

Born in Ealing on 18 December 1920, Ian Edward Fraser was educated at the Royal Grammar School, High Wycombe, and joined the Royal Navy in 1939 after two years on merchant ships. In 1943 he was awarded the Distinguished Service Cross for 'bravery and skill in successful submarine patrols'. In 1944 he volunteered for service with X-craft.

'The courage and determination of Lieutenant Fraser are beyond all praise,' his citation concludes. 'Any man not possessed of his relentless

A 30568

Stripped to the waist and framed in gauges and controls, a crew member sits at his action station in an X-craft midget submarine of the Royal Navy's Pacific fleet.

A 26940 A

Leading Seaman James Magennis VC (left) and Lieutenant Ian Fraser VC DSC. Fraser was the commanding officer and Leading Seaman Magennis the diver in an X-craft submarine that attacked a Japanese cruiser, the *Takao*, in the Johor Strait, Singapore, in 1945.

determination to achieve his object in full, regardless of all consequences, would have dropped his side charge alongside the target instead of persisting until he had forced his submarine right under the cruiser. The approach and withdrawal entailed a passage of 80 miles through water which had been mined by both the enemy and ourselves, past hydrophone positions, over loops and controlled minefields, and through an anti-submarine boom.'

James Joseph Magennis had been born in Belfast on 27 October 1919. Enlisting in the Royal Navy as a boy seaman in 1935, he had been posted to submarines in 1942 and volunteered for X-craft and midget submarines the following year, being trained as a diver. He was awarded his VC for 'very great courage and devotion to duty and complete disregard for his own safety' when fixing limpet mines to the hull of the *Takao* and later releasing an explosive charge that had become stuck from the side of the X-craft.

'A lesser man would have been content to place a few limpets and then to return to the craft,' his citation explains. 'Magennis, however, persisted until he had placed his full outfit before returning to the craft in an exhausted condition. Shortly after withdrawing Lieutenant Fraser endeavoured to jettison his limpet carriers, but one of these would not release itself and fall clear of the craft. Despite his exhaustion, his oxygen leak and the fact that there was every probability of his being sighted, Magennis at once volunteered to leave the craft and free the carrier rather than allow a less experienced diver to undertake the job. After seven minutes of nerve-racking work he succeeded in releasing the carrier.'

The only Ulsterman to earn the Victoria Cross during the Second World War, Magennis left the navy in 1949. In 1952 he was forced to sell his VC for £75; it was then purchased again by an anonymous donor and returned to him on the condition that he did not sell it again in his lifetime. Magennis worked in a circus for a time before training as an electrician and settled eventually in Yorkshire. He died in 1986.

Fraser left the navy in 1947 and set up a commercial diving business. He died in 2008.

Lieutenant Ian Fraser
Commander, XE-3 (Royal Navy X-Craft submarine)

In 1944 I was made first lieutenant of a submarine called *H44*, which was one of these old 1914–18 War type of submarines. We were based in Londonderry doing Asdic-running: a very unexciting period of my life. Then a signal came from the Admiralty one day asking for volunteers for special and hazardous service. I had a sub lieutenant with me, the third hand, and we both volunteered; I wanted to get away from this ping-running and do something more exciting. And as a result of that we both found ourselves sent to HMS *Varbel*, the shore base at Rothsea for the 12th Submarine Flotilla, which was the submarine flotilla that dealt with all the special projects like midget submarines, human torpedoes and all the different types of underwater craft.

I was quite surprised when I saw my first midget submarine. They weren't like human torpedoes where you put on a diving suit and sat astride; they were proper submarines. They were about fifty-seven feet long, about thirteen feet from top to bottom and the actual hull width was about six feet. You could stay at sea for up to three weeks if you had your own food; you had a Gardner diesel engine; you had a range of about a thousand miles on the surface, two periscopes: a proper submarine.

The war in Europe was coming to an end and they decided that there was nothing further there that X-craft could do. So we six X-craft were all hoisted on board a depot ship called HMS *Bonaventure*, which was a converted Clan Liner, she had a very heavy lifting derrick fore and aft, and we were taken in her to Australia. There we went to the Barrier Reef and started doing some working-up exercises on getting underneath ships and cutting submarine telephone cables and various things like that. Eventually we went to a place called Labuan, in Borneo, and I was delegated an operation to go into Singapore harbour to attack and stick limpet mines under a Japanese battle cruiser called the *Takao*.

We set sail in July 1945 being towed by a submarine called the *Stygian* and we were towed from Borneo to the entrance of the Singapore Straits – a tow of about six hundred miles – and there we did the crew change: the passage crew got off and my operational crew and I got on. We then slipped the tow and we made the passage up the Straits of Singapore until we came to the island of Singapore itself.

Now this cruiser that we'd been detailed to attack was lying at the old Admiralty dockyard which was on the north side of Singapore Island and it meant going some twelve miles up a narrow channel, which is called the Johor Strait. So we went through the boom at the entrance to the harbour, the gate of which was open, at about nine o'clock in the morning on 31 July 1945 and navigated our way up this channel – I suppose it was about half a mile or a mile wide – until we saw the *Takao*.

It was heavily camouflaged, lying very close inshore on the north end of Singapore Island with its stern towards the island and its bows pointing up towards Burma. And once I'd sighted it I let all my crew have a look through the periscope, the other three chappies of the crew. One of them was a New Zealander, 'Kiwi' Smith, I had an engine-room artificer called Charlie Reed and my diver was Leading Seaman Magennis. I thought it was quite an exciting thing to see and I thought that they'd like to see it and I let them all have a look at the *Takao* through the periscope before we started the attack.

Eventually we got close enough and we started to attack it, we ran in and went underneath it. You go under very slowly, as slow as you can possibly go. There's a porthole in the top of the submarine which you can look through and it's bright daylight and then you suddenly see it getting darker and darker and darker and you suddenly see the plates of the hull with the weeds hanging down and the rivet holes, the rivets, all that sort of thing. Then you stop the submarine, give it a little bit astern, and stop dead. And we settled on the bottom, opened the door and put the diver out.

When Magennis got out he found that the bottom of the ship was heavily encrusted with barnacles – it had been there a long time. He took the limpet mines out but he had to scrape the bottom of the ship with his diving knife to get a bit of clear plate for him to attach the magnets and he had quite a considerable job to do it. It took him about forty minutes to put six limpet mines on. He then came back into the submarine, we flooded down, and we couldn't get out, because the tide had gone out. We were in a very narrow hole under this thing, there was hardly any room, and the tide had gone out a foot or so and the ship had sunk down and we just couldn't move.

I was a bit frantic then – I really did feel frightened then. And it took me about twenty minutes of going ahead, full astern, blowing tanks, filling tanks, just trying to nudge a hole in the seabed so we could climb out, and eventually we did, we came out and went up a bank and on to the seabed proper. And there we found that one of the side charges hadn't come off and it was stuck – once the limpet mines had been placed you just release the side charges because you don't want to be towing those back with you, it made you lop-sided. So Magennis had to go out again in his diving suit and lever this thing off, which he did, about fifty yards away from this cruiser in about thirty feet of water, very clear water. If they had looked there, looking down, the enemy must have been able to see a black shape out there; and to make matters worse his diving suit was leaking so he was sending a stream of bubbles up to the surface all the time. But eventually he released the charge and got in again and we made our way back out of the Johor Strait. The gate was still open and we got out through the gate and out to sea and eventually we were picked up by the larger submarine and towed back to Singapore.

When I got back to Labuan a couple of days later I went up with Captain Fell, the captain of the *Bonaventure*, and had a look at aerial photographs that had been taken over the spot. The old *Takao* was still there, albeit sitting on the bottom, presumably, but you couldn't really tell, she hadn't blown into smithereens. And Captain Fell said, 'Well, we've got to do something about this. You'll have to go back again and have another go at it.' Well, that really did upset me: having done one what I thought was a considerably successful attack, to have to go back again. But nevertheless we said 'OK' and we fixed to go back seven or eight days later. And I always remember sitting on the deck of *Bonaventure* watching a film – we'd got vittled up with new stores and everything ready to go – and the film was stopped and the captain came out and told us that they'd dropped an atomic bomb and the operation had been put off for a while. And then of course they dropped the second one and the Japanese capitulated so we didn't have to go back to Singapore. I was very grateful for that.

Eventually I was awarded the Victoria Cross, with Magennis, and we were both ordered to be flown back to the UK to get our Victoria Crosses at Buckingham Palace. And it was suggested that I should go to Singapore on the way and find out what had happened to the *Takao*, which I did and I spent fourteen days there. I was taken on board by Japanese officers – one of them had been educated at Oxford, spoke with a very refined Oxford accent – and they showed me over the ship. All the charges had gone off and the whole of the ship had sunk and sat on the seabed about six feet deeper than it was before we started the attack. I went right down to the bottom and they were opening all sorts of hatches. As a matter of fact I was a bit frightened. I thought, 'God, knowing the Japanese mentality, they're going to chuck me down one of these holes and lock me in'. But that didn't actually happen.

Lieutenant Hampton Gray DSC
Royal Canadian Naval Volunteer Reserve
1841 Squadron, Fleet Air Arm

The final act of the Second World War for which a VC would be awarded was performed by Lieutenant Robert Hampton 'Hammy'

Gray, a Canadian fighter pilot in the Fleet Air Arm. He was post-humously awarded the VC for leading an aerial attack on an enemy destroyer in Onagawa Bay, Japan, in the Thoku region of Honshu, the largest of the Japanese islands, on 9 August 1945. The attack took place less than a week before the Japanese surrender.

Born at Trail, British Columbia, on 2 November 1917, Hampton Gray had been educated at the Universities of Alberta and British Columbia and joined the Royal Canadian Naval Volunteer Reserve in 1940. The following year he joined the Fleet Air Arm as a pilot. After two years' service in Africa he was posted as a Corsair pilot to 1841 Squadron, based on the aircraft carrier HMS *Formidable*, and in August 1944 took part in several attempted attacks on the German battleship *Tirpitz*. In April 1945 he went with *Formidable* to the Pacific to join the war against Japan.

Lieutenant Commander Richard Lovelace Bigg-Wither
Commanding officer, 1841 Squadron, Fleet Air Arm, Royal Navy

We got up to the Sakishima Gunto islands and we relieved the *Illustrious*, which had broken down. Our job was to neutralise the airfields on these two or three islands. There were about four airfields on them and that was the time when the Americans were landing in Okinawa and we were detailed off to neutralise these airfields so the Japs couldn't stage-in aircraft and refuel them there and use them to attack the American fleet at Okinawa. We used to do two-day operations, bombing the runways and the fighters strafing the aircraft on the ground and anti-aircraft guns and that kind of thing, all ground-attack work, which was rather danger-ous because the Japs shot down quite a number of our people.

I remember the night that the *Illustrious* left, one of the squadrons from *Indomitable* had finished their tour of duty and were being relieved and were going home and they had a big party on board. And halfway through this party, after many drinks, the CO of this squadron, a chap called Tommy Harrington, took me aside and he said, 'Biggy, if you want to live, never do more than one run on any target up here. If you do two, they'll get a bead on you and that'll be the end of you.' And I took that advice. But the CO of my other Corsair squadron on board, 1842, Lieutenant Commander 'Judy' Garland, he was shot down the very next day doing exactly that, doing two runs on the same target.

Well, we did two days' operations and then we withdrew about a hundred miles to refuel. And while we were doing that, an American task force came in and did exactly the same job, so that these airfields were continuously attacked every day for about six weeks. We attacked radio stations and small craft in the water, some of which were said to be suicide motor-torpedo boats. Anyhow, we went on day after day after day and it was a very tiring thing because we didn't have any spare pilots. I had twenty Corsairs in the Pacific and no spare pilots. So we were all flying something like seven to eight hours a day, doing an operation into targets, strafing and so forth, and the next one would be a combat air patrol over the fleet in case we were attacked. And of course we were attacked and had two kamikazes land on board us. We also had combat air patrols over the islands at about 20,000 feet, more or less out of range of the anti-aircraft guns. The object of that was to prevent any enemy aircraft landing or taking off during the times when the airfields were not actually being attacked. So from dawn to dusk – we used to take off before dawn, somewhere around 5.30am, and go on to about seven in the evening – we were continuously flying, keeping watch over these islands to see that they weren't using them.

Well, we heard about it [the first atom bomb] the following day, 7 August. At that time we were in the refuelling area and we were to start attacking again on the eighth. I must say I wondered why we were being asked to continue attacking after this enormous bomb had been dropped and it seemed pretty clear to everybody that the Japs couldn't withstand that for very long. So I was most surprised, really, when we did those last two days of operations and in a way I rather resented it, because in those two days I not only lost my senior pilot, Hammy Gray, but two other pilots, one Canadian and one British. I just thought it was unnecessary to go on.

I had a good friend on the staff and I asked him about it, I said, 'Do you think we really ought to be going and risking people's lives after this has happened?' and he said, 'Well, the Americans want us to do it, so we've got to do it.' But he said we were given instructions from the captain to take it easy, not do anything dangerous in these last days, and strafe from a greater height and so forth. But my dear friend Hammy Gray saw these destroyers and destroyer escorts in this little harbour.

I'd already been off with my attacking force that day, we'd done quite a bit of damage to the airfield, and he got there and couldn't find anything worth attacking so he decided to go back and get these destroyers. And on his first run he was hit. He flew right over the destroyer and dropped his bomb at very low level, skipped it into the side of the vessel, and flew over the ship and then turned right over and went straight in.

Sub Lieutenant Albert Hughes
Corsair pilot, 1841 Squadron, Fleet Air Arm, Royal Navy
At the last minute before take-off, our leader, Gray, was given a verbal message: 'Warships in this bay, Onagawa. High priority.' It was a routine flight out at 10,000 feet, eight aircraft in two units of four and four. We looked at the airfield and he decided that it had already been attacked earlier that day anyway, and we had seen the shipping in the bay so we decided to go for the shipping.

We were flying over hills and then we had to fly more or less down the contour of the hills and then level out to what would be effectively a fairly low-level diving attack, not a steep dive at all, all eight aircraft going down this one direction. When I went over, firing at the ship and lifted to go over it, there was only one plane in front of me, couldn't see any others, and suddenly his wing exploded and he hit the sea instantly. That was it. The man who was my number one became the leader for the rest of us, we formed up and went back and we made more attacks, and we sank two destroyers and put a bomb into a third.

Gray had a reputation because he'd attacked the *Tirpitz*, he'd already won the DSC and he was due for another one and he had this very characteristic determination to go straight into it. It's all you can do in that situation. In combat flying, dog-fighting, skill counts; but as soon as that same squadron goes down to attack well-defended ground targets the loss rate goes up by a factor of three and it's the leaders who suffer because now skill isn't counting. If you're flying straight at guns, it doesn't matter what you do: you're a sitting target.

The Korean War

THE KOREAN WAR

In June 1950, communist troops of the Democratic People's Republic of Korea invaded South Korea, its pro-Western southern neighbour. United Nations forces were sent to halt the attack and successfully drove the invaders back, then crossed into North Korea, whereupon China intervened on the communists' side. In late 1950 a massive Chinese force pushed back the UN and South Korean forces and then continued to advance into South Korea. Heavy fighting continued until the summer of 1951 when peace negotiations began and the war descended into trench warfare across the mountains and hills. Conditions were akin to the Western Front during the First World War and continued this way through 1952 into 1953. But in July of that year an armistice was reached, which remains in force today.

By the spring of 1951, the British force was 12,000-strong: the next largest proportion of UN troops after those provided by the United States. During the conflict, many British units saw heavy fighting and four Victoria Crosses were awarded. One of these was awarded posthumously to Lieutenant Philip Curtis for his actions in

April 1951 when the Chinese launched a sudden series of massed attacks against the British lines.

Lieutenant Philip Curtis
Duke of Cornwall's Light Infantry
Attached 1st Battalion, Gloucestershire Regiment

Born in Devonport on 7 July 1926, Philip Kenneth Edward Curtis had, as a boy, been an air raid precaution messenger during the German air attacks on Plymouth. Joining the army in 1944, he had been discharged in 1948 and then recalled in 1950 for the new war in Korea. He was posthumously awarded the Victoria Cross for his actions when ordered to counter-attack an enemy-held bunker during the fierce Chinese assault across the Imjin River on 22–23 April 1951.

Sergeant Frank Cottam
A Company, 1st Battalion, Gloucestershire Regiment

Ever since 1801, when the Glosters earned the right to wear cap badges at the back and the front, having fought back to back against the French, they'd formed this habit of getting themselves surrounded and fighting back to back. This was the regiment I was posted to, from Japan, in 1951. And in April of '51 the platoon I was with, 2 Platoon of A Company, were sitting on top of a very flat-topped, steep-sided hill, which, because of its shape and size, we used to know as Castle Hill or Castle Site.

A Company was the most forward company and my platoon was the most forward platoon of A Company. We were overlooking the Imjin River and lying astride the route traditionally taken by invaders coming out of Asia and heading down the Korean peninsula towards the ancient capital of Seoul. And at about ten o'clock, ten-thirty maybe, on the night of Sunday 22 April, the Chinese swarmed over the Imjin River at the start of an offensive designed to sweep all before it and capture Seoul within about forty-eight hours.

When the Chinese first started to cross, the ambush patrol held them up for about half an hour or so and then had to pull back because they were running out of ammunition. My platoon was the next to get hit, sometime shortly before midnight. We held them all that night. However, sometime just after first light they managed to get a lodgement in a bunker at one end of the platoon position, just outside of the platoon perimeter.

I had wanted to fill this bunker in when we had first took over from the Americans, 'cause I could see it could be a potential problem, but I was told to leave it alone because General Ridgway was coming up sometime to look over the battlefront from there. Why the hell he couldn't look over it from one of our foxholes or even stand up on top of the hill, as we did most for the time, I don't know. But the bunker had to be left there and so I'd strung a barbed wire fence, what we called a double-apron face, across the top of the hill between our right-hand section and the bunker.

When the Chinese got in there we cleared them out once with a couple of bombs from a rocket-launcher but within about half an hour or so they were back in. And then the reserve platoon commander, a fellow called Curtis, Lieutenant Curtis, came forward with some of his lads to help us clear them out again and in the process he won the VC but lost his life.

Curtis got hit in the backside from shots from the bunker and he went down. It wasn't a serious wound, it wasn't life-threatening, and his lads wanted him to stay down while the medics patched him up. But he lost his rag completely and he got up and he charged the bunker on his own.

Corporal Cyril Papworth
Medical orderly, Royal Army Medical Corps, attached to
1st Battalion, Gloucestershire Regiment
Lieutenant Curtis had been hit and I was sent for. But in the meantime, between the time the message had arrived and I had got rid of the

backlog of casualties, Lieutenant Curtis had pushed off the men around him and gone forward again. He managed to throw his grenades into the bunker and the Chinese fired their machine guns at the same time, he was mortally wounded and the gun and the Chinese were destroyed in the bunker.

Sergeant Frank Cottam
A Company, 1st Battalion, Gloucestershire Regiment
Corporal Papworth came forward with a stretcher. He threw the stretcher over the wire, went through a gap that I'd left in the middle of the wire, went up to Curtis's body, got it on a stretcher and dragged him round the wire and back; he was dead by this time, of course. Now that was one of the most brave things I think I've ever seen. He was wearing a red cross but he had no way of knowing whether the Chinese would recognise it, whether they would honour it if they recognised it or whether they would just open up on him. In my book he's a fellow that should have had the VC; he actually got a Military Medal but what he did I thought was extremely brave.

Reflections

Courage is a complex quality. While the holdings of the Imperial War Museum's Sound Archive can illustrate the diversity of deeds and circumstances that can lead to the award of a Victoria Cross, they also provide a glimpse of some of the characteristics of men who have earned it. On occasions the key features are leadership, duty, teamwork or cool professionalism; on others they are independence and spontaneity. Sometimes men have been motivated by a simple and selfless urge to save others' lives. Aggression, frustration and anger have been factors. Stamina, skill and physical strength can be important. It is also apparent that when courage is witnessed and recognised with the award of a medal, then chance, too, may have played a vital role.

Captain Dominic Neill
3rd Battalion, 2nd King Edward VII's Own Gurkha Rifles,
recounting an attack on a Japanese hilltop position in the Arakan,
Burma, September 1944
Leaving the reserve section guarding our rear and flanks I told the fire sections to advance in open order towards the Jap bunkers on the summit. We advanced in groups, bound by bound, alert the whole time

to the possibility of enemy subterfuge. We passed more of our dead comrades' bodies and then finally reached the bunker strongpoints with their substantial overhead log covering. We searched every position. No Japs anywhere.

I then took Havildar Subakar and a few riflemen to search our men's bodies for identification. We checked the identity discs of each easily identifiable shaven-headed corpse of our Gurkha dead. I searched everywhere for the body of Steve,* expecting to recognise him easily from his thick dark brown wavy head of hair, but wherever I looked there were only shaven heads to be seen among the ranks of our dead. Perhaps Steve had only been wounded and had been taken away alive, when the Japs withdrew, to be used as a live dummy for bayonet training? And then I came across the corpse of one of our men that was lying only two arms' lengths from the firing slits of one of the forward bunkers; this corpse seemed rather larger than the others: could this be Steve? I looked more closely and found that this particular corpse was lying very slightly on its right side and then I saw a yellow lead pencil sticking out from the corpse's top left battledress pocket. A yellow pencil was Steve's hallmark: he always carried them so.

He died two arms' lengths away from that Jap bunker. No one apart from the small party of C Company who went with him to help B Company saw exactly what he did: those Gurkhas cannot tell us his story because they all died too on that ill-starred morning. But for my money, and from my intimate knowledge of Steve as a friend and my familiarity gained by experience of the Japanese soldier as an indomitable fighting man, I would say that Steve's actions on the morning of 8 September 1944 were the stuff of which VCs are made.

---

* Thirty-year-old Major Joseph Eric Stephenson, 2nd King Edward VII's Own Gurkha Rifles, a pre-war professional footballer with Leeds United and England.

Why did Steve do what he did when he went to see if he could help B Company? Why did he, perhaps, attack that bunker single-handed? Why does any good man do what he does in war?

Corporal Charles Turnbull
8th Battalion, Durham Light Infantry, 1944–45

All that anybody was pleased about was when he came through something and survived, not about winning medals. I don't think anybody ever set himself out to win a medal. It was just that he was the type who could adapt to the situation and get on with the job and it would just be a case where the army authorities thought that recognition had to be given to somebody. The company commander or the platoon commander would make the recommendation and the allocation would be taken up and it had to be allocated.

Private George Iceton
6th Battalion, Durham Light Infantry, 1939–43

There's always a feeling that to get an award you've got to be in the right place at the right time; you've got to be *seen* by the right people at the right time. There's a difficulty with senior ranks, very senior ranks. Very often they're the senior ones and they can't put themselves forward. Colonel Jeffreys,* I've said many times, I think he should have been a VC, but he happened to be the senior man at the time and there was nobody senior there to put him forward. It seems a great shame to me that that is the situation. I suppose it's a matter of pride on the part of the senior person there: if he's the senior man there he doesn't like putting himself forward for an award. But Colonel Jeffreys, for me, was a VC if ever there was one, because he saved a lot of lives at Arras.

---

* Lieutenant Colonel Peter Jeffreys DSO (1909–2003), 6th Battalion, Durham Light Infantry, 1939–1944

Lieutenant James Leslie Lovegrove
South Lancashire Regiment, 1917–18
If you won a big battle, immediately the whole division was awarded medals. I recommended the bravest man – I was given the option – and my captain said, 'Dirtiest man on parade,' and gave it to somebody else.

Private Walter Ernest ('Josh') Grover
2nd Battalion, Sussex Regiment, 1916–18
Medals were given and medals were not given. We were lying in front of this German trench, waiting to get in, and I noticed two men coming over carrying a box of rifle ammunition. One was shot down and still this other chap dragged this box along till another man came and helped him. He was shot down and still this chap hung on to this box and dragged it in. Nobody saw him; only me, I suspect. Should have had a medal. But you see, that was the unfairness of it all.

Major Alfred Percy Bulteel Irwin
8th Battalion, East Surrey Regiment, 1914–1918
During the Somme attack on 1 July 1916 we reached the German third reserve line to the left of Montauban. We were so lamentably few that there was very little we could do that night. I posted the men as well as I could but we were not attacked – we were heavily shelled but we were not attacked – so we got away with it, and the next day we were relieved. We'd come down from something like eight hundred to something under two hundred in that attack and it seemed to me a dreadful waste of life. Of course it was just his plain duty that he did but Captain Gimson was completely unperturbed by the very heavy machine-gun fire and he and his stretcher-bearers were at it the whole morning, bringing in chaps that were lying out in the open.* And I was so impressed by his *calmness*, he

---

* Captain E. C. ('Jimmy') Gimson DSO, Royal Army Medical Corps, Regimental Medical Officer, 8th Battalion, East Surrey Regiment

was taking no notice of the battle at all, he was just getting on with his job, and I thought this was surely enough for a VC. And I think he would have got it if the divisional commander had not already forwarded a VC recommendation for one other medical officer in the brigade. Also, General Maxse, who was commanding our division, came up next day and found me writing out recommendations and in particular Gimson's recommendation for a VC and told me it wasn't sufficiently journalistic and rewrote it, and I think that's why Jimmy didn't get it.

Private James Edward Coglan
6th Battalion, Durham Light Infantry, 1939–1944

A lot of people who weren't responsible for their actions have won medals. They're not responsible for their actions 'cause they've been that keyed up they don't care if they get killed. They've won VCs and done a lot of good because they've been keyed up, they just didn't care, and have gone for it.

Fusilier Trevor Edwards
Royal Welch Fusiliers, 1940–45

I remember Joey, the other machine-gunner, he lost his bottle with a sniper. He ran out with a machine gun, a Bren gun, and instead of putting the bipod down pulled the bipod up and put it on his thigh and started to hit the trees, like, trying to shoot this sniper down. But he was out in the open and when he got back they were going to put him on a charge. 'You're in a battle, there's discipline,' this officer said. 'Bloody fool, I've got a good mind to put you on a charge.' But he was risking his own life. That's why people get medals, I think. They don't know they're doing these things but they get the VC or the DCM or things like that. Spur of the moment, you see. They might be a timid sort of chap, frightened sort of chap, but it gets on a man's mind so much when he's pinned down for so long, can't get out, that his cool goes and he runs out and he'll start shooting and whatever. And when he comes out of it all they give him a medal.

Gunner Fergus Anckorn
188 Field Regiment, Royal Artillery, captured at Singapore, 1942

I think sometimes when you get the VC it's not because you're brave, it's because it's the end and you're going to do what you can, take as many with you. I say that because on three occasions I've said, 'It's all over,' and at that moment complete calm comes over you.

We'd landed at Singapore when it had seven days to live. We really only had time to get our guns off the boats to allow about five days of action, then our war was over. Our gun had been hit and I was sent down to get another one down in the town of Singapore – I was a gun driver – and on the way back I was spotted by Japanese 27-bombers who bombed me out of existence. I just about lost my right hand in that, I was hit everywhere, and I jumped out of the lorry and in mid-air I was shot. I ended up in a post office where a surgeon was operating. Then I woke up again in Singapore hospital, the Alexandria Hospital.

It was then that the Japanese came in and killed everybody in their beds. They killed over two hundred. In my ward there were seventy-one of us and four survivors; needless to say, I was one of the survivors. I kept going in and out of consciousness, I saw them coming in and killing everybody, and I said out loud to myself, 'It's over. This is the end. I'll never be twenty-five.' Then I must have passed out again and they bypassed me.

I couldn't have run out of that hospital if I'd wanted to and when you can't move and you're just stuck there like that and they're coming to kill you, you say, 'It's over.' Utter calm just comes over you. All those people being bayoneted, I never heard one person make a sound. Not a sound. Not even the Japs. No one made a sound. I think they must have been like me: 'It's over. Let's wait for it.' And I think the same thing happens when you get a VC. You're in a cave and you've got ten Germans coming in to kill you and you think, 'Well, I can't get out, I'll kill as many as I can,' and suddenly you find you've killed them all and you get the VC. Very few people, I imagine, would charge forward at something with the purpose of trying to get a medal.

Company Sergeant Major Peter Wright
3rd Battalion, Coldstream Guards, won the Victoria Cross in 1943

If my wife was here, she would say, 'He went bloody mad. He's still mad.' I suppose when you see your officers and men fighting, dead, wounded, you forget everything and, you know, get at 'em. And when you've reached the rank of a company sergeant major in the Coldstream Guards or the Brigade of Guards you're expected to do your duty.

Guardsman Philip Charles Gourd
3rd Battalion, Coldstream Guards, 1942–45

Peter Wright was a Suffolk man with a nice friendly Suffolk drawl. Most unassuming. He was lovely chap; he was great. It's funny, those who do such great deeds are so unassuming, aren't they? The noisy ones are not so liable to do such things. But he really was something.

Second Lieutenant Tom Adlam
7th Battalion, Bedfordshire Regiment, won the Victoria Cross in 1916

You did a job out there. I never realised that there was anything unusual about it. There was a job to be done and you just got on and did it. I was more frightened going up to the trenches, sitting, waiting to start; I was very frightened then, very frightened indeed. But when we got going you've got a group of men with you, you're in charge of those, and we were all taught we had to be an example to our men and if you went forward they'd go with you, you see. And you sort of lost your sense of fear, I think, thinking about the other people.

I'm a man of a rather nervous disposition, really. I remember once when I was in Ireland I had to go to a new mess and I wandered around the parade ground for half an hour before I could go in because I was nervous of meeting other people. That way I'm very nervous. I'm rather shy, I suppose. I don't know; must be a kink somewhere.

Lieutenant Philip Neame
15th Field Company, Royal Engineers, won the Victoria Cross in 1914
I think it's largely a matter of character: whether the fellow's got the guts to face up to certain forms of danger. That's what it comes to.

Private Arthur Simpson
1/6th (City of London) Battalion, London Regiment, 1916–1918
There was a bloke laying out in no-man's-land, well and truly wounded, and this bloke went out and he tried to bring him in and he couldn't get him in. He came back and went out again and got him in on a shovel: he couldn't drag him or lift him so he dragged him in on a shovel. We told our erks, our officers, that he did this and that, but nothing ever came of it. Now to my mind if ever a bloke was entitled to a bloody decoration he was, but there was no officer or anybody saw it so therefore it was never reported, was it?

Three times he went out to get that bloke in. He said to me, 'Look at that poor sod out there. I'll get him in.' 'You silly bugger,' I said. 'You won't stand a bloody earthly.' Anyway, he crawled out and he tried to pull him a bit and he couldn't get him and he came in again, he got hold of a shovel and he sort of got it under him and dragged him in, pulled him in, on the shovel. That, to my mind, was more worthy of a gong than a bloke that's all full of beans, goes and does this and takes this and does that, see?

I mean, sometimes some of these blokes might have had an extra tot of bloody rum or something and they turn round and think to themselves, 'Christ, I'll fight anybody now,' and go over the bloody top, see, and do something and somebody sees him do it.

A bloke that goes out cool, calm and collected like that – he knew what was happening, he knew he was taking a chance – not like once but three times and he drags this bloke in, to my mind that sort of thing's real bravery. Admitted, it wasn't too far out; but there it was, he went over the top and stood a chance of catching a parcel every time, didn't he? I mean, I wouldn't have done it, I'd have thought twice about it. But that's how it goes. I should imagine there's lots of things like that in wars, all wars, lots of incidents happen like that that are worthy of gongs that have gone by and been passed up. Still, there you are. People have got different ideas of things.

Captain W. J. Brockman
15th Battalion, Lancashire Fusiliers, 1916–18

There are some people, incredible people, who, I think, *like* it. There are some people, I'm sure, who have no fear at all. I've met them. They're an absolute menace to everybody else. There was a chap we had, commanded a battalion in our brigade, a fellow called Marshall, who was the bravest of the brave.* He finally got himself killed in the end; got a VC and everything you can think of. There were those types.

Private Fred Dixon
Surrey Yeomanry, 1914–17, and Queen's Royal West Surrey Regiment, 1917–1918

I think if you look at the dictionary definition of courage it just refers to it as 'bravery' or 'boldness' and cowardice is 'faintheartedness'. But it isn't

---

* Lieutenant Colonel Neville Marshall VC MC, Irish Guards, attached 16th Battalion, Lancashire Fusiliers. See pages 84–89.

as simple as that; it's very complex. I do not regard fear to be dishonourable, I think that the feeling of fear is built into most animals and is part of the mechanics of self-preservation. And any man who said that he didn't feel afraid at any time in the front line is either a liar or an imbecile. Those are my feelings about it.

A natural reaction to fear is action, either in flight or aggression. Now, the man in the trench, he can't run away and he can't indulge in a one-man offensive against the enemy. I'm inclined to think that many cases of shellshock were caused by the infantryman having to sit down and take everything which came his way without being able to do anything about it. I also think that a stretcher-bearer was better off, he could busy himself actively with the wounded, and a signals linesman could become actively engaged with mending telephone lines which were broken. Bravery in that case is shown when a man is fearful yet continues to carry out his obligations.

But bravery to my mind should never be confused with rashness. I remember, as an instance, when we were holding the Scherpenberg [a hill position at Ypres on the Western Front] against the Germans who were on Kemmel, several 'five-nines' dropped on the hill and a signaller from one of the companies wanted a nose-cap, so, in daylight, he went looking for one. Of course, he was seen by one of the German observation posts on Kemmel and a shell came over and killed him. Now that wasn't bravery, that was sheer foolhardiness. There were intelligence men whose job it was to look for nose-caps: a matter of detective work, to send them back to people behind the lines, forensic work. Now, if one of the intelligence men had gone out under the conditions that were then existing he'd have been a brave man; he wouldn't normally have gone out under those conditions, knowing what he knew, but his duty called him and he would go. The man that was killed *would* have been a brave man *if* he'd recognised the danger.

I think fear becomes cowardice when, for some reason or other, one withdraws oneself from one's moral obligations, but it can be accounted for. I wouldn't like to assess cowardice in anybody because this is affected by poor health, lack of sleep, physical wretchedness and one's mental and emotional equipment. I remember once I had toothache badly, I went to the MO and asked him if he could have me sent to the Casualty Clearing Station to have it out and it was at the time of an advance and he wouldn't do it. But I had no rest and when I went back in the line I was as jittery as a chicken.

And I wouldn't like to assess bravery. I remember on one occasion I was told by the signal officer to find the signal office of the 11th Queens, on our left, on the other side of the Scherpenberg. There was no moon, I remember, and the darkness was absolutely total. I found the dugout and I had to run a line from that point, from the other side of the Scherpenberg to our own office, across the face of a hill that I'd never seen in daylight – it was at night-time – and it was machine-gunned and it was shelled. Now, a friend of mine has told me since that he was profoundly glad that he hadn't been picked for the job because he didn't rate my chances of survival very high. Well, I didn't feel that way about it, because here was action: I ran out one reel of wire from the 11th Queens' headquarters and then I had no more; I had to continue my way across the face of the hill to our own dugout to get some more, go back again in the dark, find the end of the wire, join up and take it back to our own office. The signal officer was so pleased with the success of my mission that he gave me similar jobs to do! But he evidently thought it was worth something. He kept saying, 'I'll put you in for some stripes tonight.' I didn't want the damned things. What I would like to draw out is the fact that what I considered a routine job, my friend looked upon as a matter of bravery.

What was the reason for the difference in our outlook? I think I know the reason for that. He was forming an opinion from inside a dugout, comparatively safe. Now, it requires a good deal of moral courage to come from the safety of a dugout into a trench when the latter's being shelled.

But once you're in the trench it requires a considerable amount of moral courage to get up on the top, unless assisted by the urge for action. Now, once on the top, where there is no safety, conditions do not appear so dangerous, even though one knows that things are dangerous. Having achieved the ultimate in danger by a series of comparatively safe situations, there's nothing more you can do about it.

To sum up, I would say that there are areas of black and white in the picture of courage and cowardice but there are *very* large areas of grey. Only the definite tones are distinguishable and the remainder are influenced by such things as health, viewpoint, situation, education, emotional and mental make-up and background of the person concerned. And also those of the onlooker, which are very important.

Private David Edwards
Support Company, 2nd Battalion, Monmouthshire Regiment, 1943–47
I knew him [VC recipient Corporal Edward Chapman*] for years afterwards. In the army I knew him in a casual way, you know. He knew me as Dave, I knew him as Ted; he was with C Company and we would be attached to the company. He was a quiet-spoken fella. He liked fishing and he liked horses and he kept ponies as a young chap.

People imagine VCs to be Rambos. But on one occasion a reporter said to him, in my presence, 'You're a sort of Rambo, Mr Chapman?' 'No,' he said, 'I'm not. I am *absolutely* not.' I remember that. And he wasn't, his manner was quiet; but he was a chap who called a spade a spade.

Post-war, when we'd get together, he was very interested always in what had gone on over there and he studied the background to things and he came over with us quite a few times when we went back to revisit places. When we'd be preparing to go, we'd pick him up at his house and

---

* Corporal Edward Thomas Chapman VC, see pages 278–288

his wife would say to him, 'Ted?' 'Yes, Rhoda?' 'Come here, Ted.' And he'd go over to her and she'd get a comb and she'd comb his hair down, she'd put a parting in it, and we used to stand there and he'd be looking to us and he'd be looking up at the ceiling and he'd stand there while she parted and combed his hair. That's not the image you get either.

Glossary

ACI – Army Council Instruction

Ack-ack – slang for anti-aircraft fire

ADC – Aide de Camp, a personal assistant to an officer of high rank

AVRE – Armoured Vehicle Royal Engineers, a modified tank developed during the Second World War primarily for breaking down enemy fortifications

BEF – British Expeditionary Force

Bren gun – a British light machine gun of the Second World War

Brevet – a warrant authorising an officer to hold a higher rank temporarily

CMB – Coastal Motor Boat

CO – Commanding Officer

CRE – Chief Royal Engineer, the senior Royal Engineer in a British Army division

DCM – Distinguished Conduct Medal. A British Army gallantry medal for Warrant Officers, NCOs and soldiers, second only to the Victoria Cross. Now discontinued

DFC – Distinguished Flying Cross. A Royal Air Force gallantry award instituted in 1918 for commissioned officers

DSC – Distinguished Service Cross. A Royal Navy gallantry award instituted in 1914 for commissioned officers

DSO – Distinguished Service Order. An award instituted in 1886 for acts of gallantry and distinguished leadership

Flak – slang for anti-aircraft fire

HAC – Honourable Artillery Company

LCA – Landing Craft Assault, a small landing craft of the Second World War capable of carrying up to forty troops

Lewis gun – a British light machine gun of the First World War, which also saw limited service in the Second World War

MC – Military Cross. A British Army gallantry medal instituted in 1914 for commissioned officers and Warrant Officers. Today, all ranks are eligible

ME 110 – Messerschmitt Bf 110, a twin-engined German fighter-bomber of the Second World War

Mills bomb – the standard British Army hand grenade, 1915 on

ML – Motor Launch

MM – Military Medal. A British Army gallantry medal instituted in 1916 for NCOs and soldiers. Now discontinued

NCO – Non Commissioned Officer

Nieuport – a French biplane fighter of the First World War

O Group – Orders Group. A group into which personnel are called together to be briefed and issued orders

OC – Officer Commanding

Oerlikon – Swiss-designed 20-millimetre automatic anti-aircraft gun

OTC – Officer Training Corps

PIAT – Projector, Infantry, Anti Tank. A platoon-level British anti-tank weapon during the Second World War

PO – Petty Officer

POGI – Petty Officer Gunnery Instructor

Pom-pom – nickname for the Royal Navy's 2-pounder multi-barrelled anti-aircraft gun during the Second World War

RAF – Royal Air Force

RAMC – Royal Army Medical Corps

RAP – Regimental Aid Post

RE – Royal Engineers

RFC – Royal Flying Corps

RNAS – Royal Naval Air Service

RNR – Royal Naval Reserve

RTO – Railway Transport Officer

SE5 and **SE5a** – a single-seat British biplane fighter of the First World War

Spandau – British nickname for the German MG42 medium machine gun of the Second World War

Stokes mortar – a three-inch British trench mortar of the First World War

Thompson / tommy gun – sub-machine gun of American make

VC – Victoria Cross

Very light – a flare fired from a pistol

Vickers machine gun – a belt-fed British medium machine gun of the First World War, which also saw limited service in the Second World War

X-craft – a British midget submarine of the Second World War

Index of Contributors

Number in brackets denotes IWM Sound Archive catalogue number.
Page numbers in **bold** refer to photographs.

General Index

Entries in **bold** indicate photographs.

FORGOTTEN VOICES

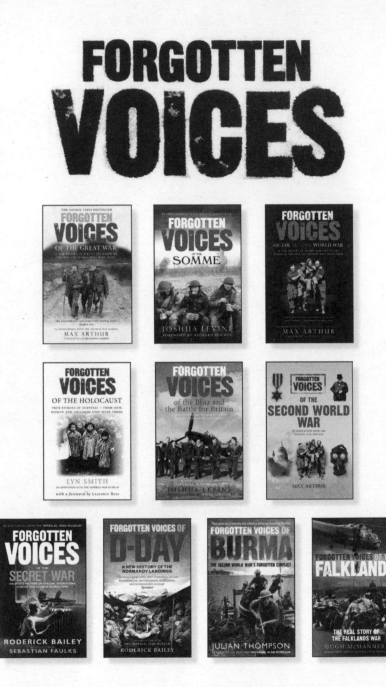

www.forgottenvoices.co.uk